Thomas Adès: *Asyla*

Thomas Adès (b. 1971) is an established international figure, both as composer and performer, with popular and critical acclaim and admiration from around the world. Edward Venn examines in depth one of Adès's most significant works so far, his orchestral *Asyla* (1997). Its blend of virtuosic orchestral writing, allusions to various idioms, including rave music, and a musical rhetoric encompassing both high modernism and lush romanticism is always compelling and utterly representative of Adès's distinctive compositional voice. The reception of *Asyla* since its premiere in 1997 by Sir Simon Rattle and the City of Birmingham Symphony Orchestra (CBSO) has been staggering. Instantly hailed as a classic, *Asyla* won the 1997 Royal Philharmonic Society Award for Large-Scale Composition. An internationally acclaimed recording made of the work was nominated for the 1999 Mercury Music Prize, and in 2000, Adès became the youngest composer (and only the third British composer) to win the Grawemeyer prize, for *Asyla*. *Asyla* is fast becoming a repertory item, rapidly gaining over one hundred performances: a rare distinction for a contemporary work.

Edward Venn is Associate Professor in Music at the University of Leeds and Critical Forum editor for *Music Analysis*. His research focuses on twentieth-century and contemporary music, and his first monograph, *The Music of Hugh Wood*, appeared in 2008. His research on Adès's *Asyla* was supported by a Leverhulme Research Fellowship.

Thomas Adès: *Asyla*

Edward Venn

University of Leeds

LONDON AND NEW YORK

First published 2017
by Routledge
2 Park Square, Milton Park, Abingdon, Oxon OX14 4RN

and by Routledge
711 Third Avenue, New York, NY 10017

Routledge is an imprint of the Taylor & Francis Group, an informa business

© 2017 Edward Venn

The right of Edward Venn to be identified as author of this work has been asserted by him in accordance with sections 77 and 78 of the Copyright, Designs and Patents Act 1988.

All rights reserved. No part of this book may be reprinted or reproduced or utilised in any form or by any electronic, mechanical, or other means, now known or hereafter invented, including photocopying and recording, or in any information storage or retrieval system, without permission in writing from the publishers.

Trademark notice: Product or corporate names may be trademarks or registered trademarks, and are used only for identification and explanation without intent to infringe.

British Library Cataloguing-in-Publication Data
A catalogue record for this book is available from the British Library

Library of Congress Cataloging-in-Publication Data
CIP data has been applied for.

ISBN: 978-1-409-46884-4 (hbk)
ISBN: 978-1-315-45401-6 (ebk)

Bach musicological font developed by © Yo Tomita

For eBook customers, please email AcademiceBooksSupport@informa.com with proof of purchase to obtain access to the supplementary content of any CDs or DVDs for this book. An access code and instructions will be provided.

Typeset in Times New Roman & Bach
by codeMantra

Printed in the United Kingdom
by Henry Ling Limited

To my father, and in memory of my mother

Contents

List of figures and tables	ix
List of music examples	x
General editor's preface	xiii
Preface	xv
Acknowledgements	xvii
List of abbreviations	xxi
1 Thomas Adès in the 1990s	1
2 Towards *Asyla* (1990–97)	16
3 'Trying to find refuge': The symphonic logic of the first movement	43
4 'A safe place to go in times of trouble'	71
5 'Ecstasio': A 'freaky, funky rave'?	98
6 Asylum gained?	116
7 Interpreting *Asyla*	136
Epilogue: After *Asyla*	154
References	165
Index	171
CD details	177

List of figures and tables

Figures

2.1	Instrumentation in *Asyla*.	37
4.1	Successive melodic embellishments, second movement, bars 48 ff.	89
4.2	Embellishment of phrases 1–2 of the theme, second movement, bars 75–86.	93
5.1	Normative rave form (from Rick Snoman, *The Dance Music Manual*).	103

Tables

3.1	Formal overview of *Asyla*, first movement	48
3.2	Formal details of *Asyla*, first movement, bars 14–82	53
4.1	Formal overview of *Asyla*, second movement	79
5.1	Distribution of material in *Asyla*, third movement, bars 1–24	102
5.2	Formal overview of *Asyla*, third movement	103
6.1	Formal overview of *Asyla*, fourth movement	117

List of music examples

2.1 (a) (i) expanded intervallic series; (ii) expanded harmonic progression; (b) 'New Hampshire', *Five Eliot Landscapes* Op. 1/i, bars 17–28.   17

2.2 *Powder Her Face* Op. 14. (a) Act I Scene 1, bars 396–404; (b) Act I Scene 2, bars 285–297.   20

2.3 *Still Sorrowing* Op. 7, bars 1–9.   24

2.4 'Chori', *Traced Overhead* Op. 15/iii, bars 45–50.   26

2.5 Chamber Symphony Op. 2/i, bars 1–14.   27

2.6 *Darknesse Visible*. (a) bars 1–3; (b) bars 8–10; (c) bars 35–38; plus extracts from Dowland, 'In Darknesse Let Mee Dwell' (1610).   32

2.7 *The Fayrfax Carol*, bars 1–5.   34

2.8 *Asyla* Op. 17, motivic material (pitch and rhythm). (a) dyads; (b) drum beats; (c) trochaic rhythms; (d) expanded harmonic progressions; (e) octatonic patterns; (f) whole-tone patterns.   39

3.1 *Asyla* Op. 17/i, melodic details. (a) bars 14–18; (b) bars 27–33; (c) bars 52–57; (d) bars 69–73.   44

3.2 *Asyla* Op. 17/i, introduction. (a) bars 1–3 (detail); (b) harmonic reduction of bars 1–13; (c) bars 10^3–13 (detail).   50

3.3 *Asyla* Op. 17/i, contrasting material. (a) bars 18–20; (b) bars 25–27; (c) bars 33–40; (d) bars 46–49.   55

3.4 *Asyla* Op. 17/i, bars 102–108.   64

3.5 *Asyla* Op. 17/i, bars 140–154.   67

3.6 *Asyla* Op. 17/i, bars 160–165.   68

4.1 *Asyla* Op. 17/ii, bars 1–11 (accompaniment slightly simplified).   72

4.2 (a) *Asyla* Op. 17/ii, bars 11–18; (b) J. S. Bach, *Weinen, Klagen, Sorgen, Zagen* BWV 12, bars 14^3–21; (c) Frank, Symphony in D minor/ii, bars 16^3–26.   74

4.3 *Asyla* Op. 17/ii, bars 19–48.   81

4.4 *Asyla* Op. 17/ii, bars 52–59.   91

4.5 *Asyla* Op. 17/ii, bars 95–114.   94

5.1 *Asyla* Op. 17/iii, selected material from bars 1–24.   101

5.2 *Asyla* Op. 17/iii, melodic material from bars 25–111.   104

5.3 *Asyla* Op. 17/iii, harmonic relationships bars 25–147.   110

List of music examples   xi

5.4   *Asyla* Op. 17/iii, harmonic relationships in bars 157–205.   112
5.5   Wagner, *Parsifal*, end of Act II.   113
6.1   *Asyla* Op. 17/iv, bars 1–12 (reduction, with melodic
     details of bars 1–8).   120
6.2   *Asyla* Op. 17/iv. (a) bars 9–13; (b) bars 20–23; (c) bars 60–63.   122
6.3   *Asyla* Op. 17/iv, reduction of bars 13–19.   126
6.4   *Asyla* Op. 17/iv, reduction of bars 20–28.   127
6.5   *Asyla* Op. 17/iv, reduction of bars 29–60.   130
6.6   *Asyla* Op. 17/iv, reduction of bars 61–74.   133

General editor's preface

Thomas Adès is without doubt one of the most gifted British composers of his day. Not only has he established an international reputation based partly on the originality of his output in the 1990s, he is also in great demand as a performer (piano and percussion), conductor and artistic director (of, for example, the Birmingham Contemporary Music Ensemble and the Aldeburgh Festival). One might well wonder how he still finds time to fulfil the many commissions that come his way; indeed Edward Venn has noted the reduced volume (but *not* quality) of his output since *Asyla* (1997). All things are relative, however, and works such as his opera *The Tempest* (first staged at Covent Garden in 2004) and the orchestral *Tevot* (premiered by Simon Rattle and the Berlin Philharmonic in 2007) attest to the continuing brilliance of his scores and the cultural richness of his inspiration.

Although a substantial critical literature has accumulated around Adès's performances and significant aspects of his works (such as narrativity), this book is, as far as I am aware, the first monograph devoted to a single work by the composer. In accord with the general format of Ashgate's *Landmarks* series, Venn sets *Asyla* within the context of the composer's career development and his output both before and after the selected composition. The comprehensive introductory chapters and the concluding epilogue will prove invaluable reference-points for all students of contemporary music – as will the author's sharpness of perception within the central chapters devoted to *Aslya* itself.

Edward Venn has published on a wide range of contemporary and Modernist composers from Hugh Wood (Ashgate, 2008), Harrison Birtwistle and Michael Tippett to Luciano Berio, David Matthews and Thomas Adès. The sheer breadth of his interests and scholarly writing is impressive and makes him an ideal author to tackle the complexity of Adès's scores. He combines the insight of a practical musician (he is himself a talented conductor) with the objectivity of a distinguished music analyst and critic.

I am delighted to commend this volume as an outstanding contribution to twenty-first-century scholarship and an eminently readable evaluation of Thomas Adès's role in British, European and American musical culture.

Wyndham Thomas
Corsham, 2016

Preface

The music of the composer, performer and music director Thomas Adès (born 1971) has brought him to international attention, provoking interest in both general and musicological circles. The ways in which it raises issues of conflict, paradox and crisis is significant for contemporary classical music as well as broader social and cultural discursive practices, demonstrating the need for considered and careful critical musical analysis.

In this context, Adès's 1997 orchestral work *Asyla* emerges as a work of considerable importance. On the one hand, the ways in which the music alludes to styles, genres and specific works places it within a web of signification in which the music lives out the tension between conflicting musical and ideological positions, at times teasingly, at others with utmost sincerity. On the other hand, the work's title (the plural of asylum) and a well-publicised programme that draws on notions of madness, freedom, drug culture and religion implicates it more explicitly within social and cultural discourses on these and other issues. Its popular and critical success – not just in prizes garnered, but in an almost unprecedented adoption into the repertoire – demands sustained enquiry.

The account of *Asyla* offered in this book is by definition my personal response to a work that I have listened to, studied and enjoyed for nearly two decades. To provide the basis for my interpretative judgements, I offer a close analytical reading of the score, along with theoretical reflection (both musicological and critical) upon this analysis. By carefully laying out the grounds for my argument, I hope to demonstrate (without overloading the text with theoretical jargon) why the music moves me in the way it does, whilst enabling readers to reach their own alternative interpretative conclusions: the semantic richness of *Asyla* makes the notion of a single, definitive reading nonsensical. The CD that accompanies this book (the City of Birmingham Orchestra, conducted by Sir Simon Rattle) is an integral component of what I hope proves to be an open, suggestive text,[1] and I would like to direct readers to – for as long as it remains available – the score of *Asyla*, which Faber Music, Adès's publisher, has placed online.[2]

Throughout the text, I have drawn liberally from the collection of interviews given by Adès in 2011 (and published a year later),[3] as well as upon the various sources that describe *Asyla*'s extramusical programme. When dealing with composer's utterances (either directly or indirectly), there is a continuous danger,

xvi   *Preface*

to cite Charles Wilson, of treating as 'constative – as "fact" or neutral description – statements that are equally performative in nature',[4] as well as to assume that what was true for Adès in 2011 was equally true for him in the mid-1990s. At the same time, to neglect these sources, the latter of which in particular has to date dominated the reception of *Asyla*, is not an option. My approach throughout has been to use them as a springboard for interpretation, rather than as a prescriptive framework: along the way, I critically examine concepts that abound in Adès's writings, such as 'metaphor', 'symphonic logic' and the notion of 'musical problems', as well as 'asylum' itself, and hope to refine them in ways that are meaningful for an understanding of *Asyla* in particular, and Adès's music more broadly.

The first two chapters of the book contextualise Adès and his music. The first chapter is largely biographical, situating Adès within the 1990s, teasing out themes in British cultural and musical life to which his music both responds and contributes. Chapter 2 introduces Adès's compositions prior to 1997, highlighting recurring musical and extramusical ideas that are also significant in *Asyla*. Chapters 3–7 are the core of the book, offering in-depth analytical and interpretative readings of the four movements of *Asyla* in turn before providing in Chapter 7 a critical analysis of the work. The book concludes with a short epilogue that surveys Adès's music post-*Asyla*.

Edward Venn
Caldie, York
January 2016

Notes

1 At the time of writing, two alternative performances are commercially available. The first is by the BBC Symphony Orchestra, conducted by Thomas Adès, in the documentary *Thomas Adès: Music for the 21st Century*, produced and directed by Gerald Fox (LWT 1999). The documentary was first broadcast on 29 December 1999. It is included on the DVD of Adès's *Powder Her Face* (Digital Classicals DC 10002, 2005). The second is by the Berliner Philharmoniker, conducted by Rattle (EMI DVD 7243 4 90325 9 0, 2003).

2 The score of *Asyla* can be found at http://scorelibrary.fabermusic.com/Asyla-23782.aspx [accessed 12 August 2015].

3 Thomas Adès and Tom Service, *Thomas Adès: Full of Noises* (New York: Farrar, Straus and Giroux, 2012), hereafter *TA:FON*.

4 Charles Wilson, 'György Ligeti and the Rhetoric of Autonomy', *Twentieth-Century Music*, 1/i (2004), pp. 5–28, at p. 17.

Acknowledgements

My original intention was to write this book during the academic year 2013–14 whilst on a sabbatical from Lancaster University that would be extended, if possible, by means of external funding. My thanks go to my Lancaster colleagues, Alan Marsden and Deborah Mawer, for their guidance in the autumn of 2012 in finding the right wording for my funding proposal. A couple of weeks after the grant application was signed off and submitted by the university, however, an announcement was made that led to the eventual closure of Music and with it multiple staff redundancies. Then, in April 2013, word came from the Leverhulme Trust that I was the recipient of a Research Fellowship, but that in order to take it up, I required a post at an academic institution. I found myself in the position of seeking refuge. I was beyond fortunate: though I gained eventual asylum at the University of Leeds, I remain deeply grateful to Roderick Watkins for his offer for me to work temporarily in the School of Music and Performing Arts at Canterbury Christ Church University. Throughout this period, the Leverhulme Trust demonstrated exceptional understanding and patience, and my thanks in particular go to Anna Grundy for her kindness and support.

My love and thanks must go to my wife, Lois, who has not only sacrificed her free time to proofread my text, but has done such a wonderful job looking after our boys, Sam and Will, when I've been jetting around the world to conferences or incarcerating myself in my office to type.

Though the writing of the book took place in the two years after my appointment at Leeds, its origins date back to 1997 when I first heard *Asyla*, and more concretely to 2003, when I gave a paper on *Asyla*'s final movement at the Hull University Music Analysis Conference. Since then, I have had the opportunity to present and discuss my ideas at conferences and seminars in Europe and the United States, and have benefitted enormously from the comments and criticisms garnered in return. Two of these trips could not have happened without vital financial assistance from the *Music Analysis* Development Fund and the Leverhulme Trust; my gratitude goes to both. Personal thanks must go to Emma Gallon, Kenneth Gloag, Drew Massey, John Roeder, Philip Rupprecht and Philip Stoecker for their astute observations and their collegiality, to Susan Greenwood, Alexi Vellianitis and Aleksandra Vojcic for sharing their work with me, and to Helen Thomas for her stimulating discussions about musical metaphor. I am grateful, too, to Martin xviii *Acknowledgements*

Iddon and Drew Massey, for their helpful and insightful comments on drafts of the first couple of chapters, and to Thomas Schmidt, who assisted me with a thorny translation at incredibly short notice.

Some of the material in this book revises, either slightly or substantially, work that has been published in the following:

- 'Thomas Adès's "Freaky Funky Rave"', *Music Analysis*, 33/i (2014), pp. 65–98.
- 'BBC Proms 2013: David Matthews and Thomas Adès', *Tempo*, 68 (January 2014), pp. 59–61.
- 'Thomas Adès and the *pianto*', in Nearchos Panos, Vangelis Lympourdis, George Athanasopoulos and Peter Nelson (eds), *Proceedings of the International Conference on Musical Semiotics in Memory of Raymond Monelle* (Edinburgh: ECA – The University of Edinburgh and IPMDS, 2013), pp. 309–17.
- 'Thomas Adès', trans. Agnieszka Kotarba, in *Nowa Muzyka Brytyjska* (Kraków: Ha!Art, 2010), pp. 182–200.
- 'Asylum Gained?: Aspects of Meaning in Thomas Adès's *Asyla*', *Music Analysis*, 25/i–ii (2006), pp. 89–120.
- 'Thomas Adès's Piano Quintet', *Tempo*, 59 (October 2005), pp. 73–4.
- 'London, Royal Opera House: *The Tempest*', *Tempo*, 58 (July 2004), pp. 72–3.

My thanks goes to the editors and anonymous readers who helped shape the content of the above.

Finally, for their assistance throughout the entirety of this project, I'd like to extend my gratitude to Heidi Bishop, Emma Gallon and Beatrice Beaup at Ashgate and Routledge, and to Wyndham Thomas for recommending this volume to Ashgate. At Faber Music, Elaine Gould and Matt Smith have provided copious amounts of support and assistance; my thanks to them.

I acknowledge with gratitude the permission given by publishers for the reproduction of extracts from the following works:

'New Hampshire' (from *Five Eliot Landscapes*). Music by Thomas Adès. Text by T.S. Eliot. Music © 1993 by Faber Music Ltd, London WC1B 3DA. Text © the Estate of T.S. Eliot and reprinted by permission of Faber and Faber Ltd, London WC1B 3DA. Reproduced by permission of the publishers. All Rights Reserved.

Chamber Symphony. Music by Thomas Adès. © 1995 by Faber Music Ltd, London WC1B 3DA. Reproduced by permission of the publishers. All Rights Reserved.

Darknesse Visible. Music by Thomas Adès. © 1998 by Faber Music Ltd, London WC1B 3DA. Reproduced by permission of the publishers. All Rights Reserved.

Still Sorrowing. Music by Thomas Adès. © 1992 by Faber Music Ltd, London WC1B 3DA. Reproduced by permission of the publishers. All Rights Reserved.

Powder Her Face. Music by Thomas Adès. Libretto by Philip Hensher. Music © 1996 by Faber Music Ltd, London WC1B 3DA. Libretto © 1995 by Philip Hensher. Reproduced by permission of the publishers. All Rights Reserved.

Traced Overhead. Music by Thomas Adès. © 1997 by Faber Music Ltd, London WC1B 3DA. Reproduced by permission of the publishers. All Rights Reserved.

The Fayrfax Carol. Music by Thomas Adès. Text by Early Tudor, anon. © 1998 by Faber Music Ltd, London WC1B 3DA. Reproduced by permission of the publishers. All Rights Reserved.

Asyla. Music by Thomas Adès. © 1999 by Faber Music Ltd, London WC1B 3DA. Reproduced by permission of the publishers. All Rights Reserved.

Figure 10.5 from Rick Snoman, *The Dance Music Manual: Tools, Toys and Techniques*, 2nd edn, Chapter 10, 'Music Theory' (Oxford: Taylor and Francis/Focal Press, 2009), p. 225. Reproduced by permission of the publishers. All Rights Reserved.

The Leverhulme Trust

List of abbreviations

TA:FON	Thomas Adès and Tom Service, *Thomas Adès: Full of Noises* (New York: Farrar, Straus and Giroux, 2012)

Abbreviations of instruments and performance techniques

Orch.	orchestra
Str.	strings
D.b.	double bass
Hp	harp
Vla	viola
Vlc.	violoncello
Vln	violin
Wind	woodwind
A.fl.	alto flute
B.cl.	bass clarinet
Bsst.cl.	basset clarinet
B.ob.	bass oboe
Bn	bassoon
Cbn	contrabassoon
Cb.cl	contrabass clarinet
Cl.	clarinet
Cor ang.	cor anglais
Fl.	flute
Ob.	oboe
Picc.	piccolo
Br.	brass
B.tbn.	bass trombone
Hn	horn
Picc.tpt	piccolo trumpet
Tba	tuba
Tbn.	trombone
Tpt	trumpet

xxii   *List of abbreviations*

Perc.	percussion
B.D.	bass drum
Bong.	bongo
Cel.	celesta
Cwb.	cowbells
Cymb.	cymbal
Glsp.	glockenspiel
H.h.	hi-hat
Mar.	marimba
Pno	piano
Rt.	rototom
S.D.	snare drum
Susp.cymb.	suspended cymbals
Timp.	timpani
W.bl.	wood block
S	sopranos
A	altos
T	tenors
B	basses
div.	divisi
l.h.	left hand
r.h.	right hand
gliss.	glissando
pizz.	pizzicato
con sord.	con sordini [with mutes]
trem.	tremolando
sul pont.	sul ponticello [play on the bridge]

Pitch collections

<x y z >	Ordered collection of pitches x y and z
{x y z}	Unordered collection of pitches x y and z
CI octatonic collection	<C♯ D E F G G♯ B♭ B>
CII octatonic collection	<D E♭ F F♯ G♯ A B C>
CIII octatonic collection	<E♭ E F♯ G A B♭ C C♯>
WT0 whole-tone collection	<C D E F♯ G♯ A♯>
WT1 whole-tone collection	<C♯ D♯ F G A B>

The abbreviation 'Fig.' refers to rehearsal figures in scores without bar numbers; a superscript suffix (e.g. Fig. 23^{+2}) refers to the number of bars after the rehearsal figure (or before it, if the number is negative).

1 Thomas Adès in the 1990s

The announcement in late November 1999 that Thomas Adès was to receive the 2000 Grawemeyer Award, the largest prize available to a classical composer, provided confirmation of Adès's increasing international reputation.[1] It marked the end of an extraordinary decade, for Adès's first acknowledged work was completed just ten years earlier.[2] At the time of the award, Adès's star was firmly in the ascendency, for he had recently been a featured composer in the 1999 Musica Nova Festival (Helsinki) and *America: A Prophecy* Op. 19 (1999), his first overseas commission, had just been performed by the New York Philharmonic and Kurt Masur. The Grawemeyer Award, in recognition of an 'outstanding achievement by a living composer in a large musical genre', and judged solely on 'excellence and originality',[3] was awarded for Adès's 1997 orchestral work *Asyla* Op. 17.

Asyla had been commissioned by the John Feeney Charitable Trust for the City of Birmingham Symphony Orchestra (CBSO), who premiered it, with Sir Simon Rattle conducting, on 1 October 1997.[4] Rattle programmed *Asyla* in his final concerts with the CBSO (29–30 August 1998) and by the time he had introduced it to German audiences in his first performance as principal conductor of the Berlin Philharmoniker (7 September 2002), *Asyla* had been taken up by numerous conductors and orchestras worldwide. In an era when new works are too often performed once and never heard again, the fact that *Asyla* received its one-hundredth performance less than a decade after its premiere is astounding.[5] Early reviews tended towards the rapturous;[6] critical plaudits followed with the receipt of the 1997 Royal Philharmonic Prize for large-scale composition and the nomination of the 1999 recording of the work for a Mercury Prize.[7] Even before the Grawemeyer Award announcement, *Asyla* had become a landmark in contemporary music.

Much has been made in *Asyla*'s promotion and reception of its title, which is the plural of 'asylum'. Arnold Whittall cites *Asyla* and *Living Toys* Op. 9 (1993) as examples of Adès's 'use of titles to establish allusions to extramusical factors'.[8] Accordingly, *Asyla*'s music plays on the multiple connotations of 'asylum', drawing together notions of refuge, madness and incarceration. In 'Ecstasio', *Asyla*'s third movement, Adès turned to electronic dance music (EDM), and through it was able to depict – depending on your point of view – a modern-day site of madness or sanctuary. As with *Asyla*, the dual connotations of the movement's title (is it ecstasy or Ecstasy?) invite, rather than constrain, interpretative responses.

2 *Thomas Adès in the 1990s*

The social and political issues hinted at in these titles also tap into concerns that were prominent at the time of *Asyla*'s composition and premiere (see below), but which are perennial topics of national and international debate.

The instant success of *Asyla*, and its ability to command critical attention, reflects something of Adès's own phenomenal rise to prominence. In the following survey of Adès's early musical life, I shall draw attention to those aspects of his music that are of particular significance for *Asyla*, and which I shall develop at greater length in Chapter 2.

Adès was born on 1 March 1971, and grew up in north London. His father, Timothy Adès, is a linguist, translator and writer, and his mother, Dawn Adès, is a noted art historian specialising in Spanish art and Surrealism; he has two younger brothers. Through their extensive record collection, along with that of his grandmother, Adès became acquainted not only with 'all those "classical great things", but also with '"odds and ends of folk music," which he loved for the sounds of the earthy voices and "twiney instruments"'.[9] Indeed, the *sound* of the recordings rather than their meaning was often what captured Adès, as in the case of a tape of the actor Sir Alec Guinness reciting the poetry of T.S. Eliot, as well as their corporeality: '[t]hese pieces all had physical dimensions to me: I didn't feel them as music, I felt them as landscape'.[10] The eclecticism, sensitivity to colour and timbre, and 'visual' qualities of Adès's later compositions almost certainly have their origins in his childhood listening habits.

Although his father 'must have taught [Adès] how to make a piano work', Adès claims he was largely self-taught.[11] Composition began when he was eleven years old, writing what he describes as 'weird, little, sort of peculiar piano pieces that drew from pieces that someone else had already written, and I didn't realise it'.[12] At the age of twelve he joined the Guildhall School of Music (initially in the Junior School), eventually studying with Erika Fox and Robert Saxton (composition) and Michael Blackmore and Paul Berkowitz (piano); he was also a talented percussionist. Adès first came to attention as a performer, winning the 1986 Guildhall Lutine Prize for instrumentalists. He studied piano in chamber music with György Kurtág in Szombthélty, Hungary, between 1988 and 1989, and in 1989 he had a national platform when he reached the semi-final of the biennial BBC Young Musician of the Year competition.[13] Adès read music at King's College, Cambridge University, studying composition with Alexander Goehr and Robin Holloway, and graduated in 1992 with a double-starred first. The assuredness of the works from this period secured him a publishing contract with Faber Music.

Adès's first two acknowledged works are both for voice: *The Lover in Winter* for countertenor and piano (1989), and *Five Eliot Landscapes* for soprano and piano Op. 1 (1990).[14] In the following years he also wrote the two Op. 3 choruses for male voices, *O thou who didst with pitfall and with gin* and *Gefriolsae Me* (1990), and *Fool's Rhymes* Op. 5 (1992) for SATB choir. Adès returned to solo voice for his setting of Tennessee Williams's *Life Story* Op. 8 (1993), initially scored for two bass clarinets with double bass and arranged the following year for voice and piano (Op. 8b). Even at this early stage, the choice of texts is indicative of Adès's eclectic tastes, drawing respectively on medieval Latin texts;

'minor' poems by Eliot; lines from Edward Fitzgerald's translations of Omar Khayyam; Psalm 51, verse 14 (in Middle English); Elizabethan and Medieval sermons and Williams. There is a similar breadth of reference within the music, most notably in the collision of high and low styles that occurs when a melody from 'My Curly Headed Baby' appears in the coda of the first *Eliot Landscape*, and in *Life Story*, where the singer is instructed to adopt 'the late style of Billie Holliday' as a model.

The bulk of Adès's output prior to his first opera, *Powder Her Face* Op. 14 (1995), however, is instrumental. The Chamber Symphony Op. 2 (1990) is a remarkable achievement. Its generic title, along with its four-movement structure, appears to signal a commitment to traditional modes of thought, though the teeming imagination underpinning the musical design toys with such expectations. Adès has claimed that the work came to represent in his mind a 'super basset clarinet' (one of the fifteen instruments in the score), and his fascination with novel timbres can be felt in nearly every bar. Theatricality comes to the fore in *Catch* Op. 4 (1991) for piano trio and clarinet, in which the clarinettist walks on and off the stage twice before eventually joining the ensemble at the end. The playground atmosphere is given music that is by turn ebullient, spiky and even sullen; a lyrical passage midway through highlights Adès's penchant for juxtaposing contrasting emotional states. *Under Hamelin Hill* Op. 6 (1992) for chamber organ employs a similar trick, with two players coming on stage to join the organist for a lively central fugue of Nancarrow-like rhythmic complexity.

The two works for solo piano from this period, *Still Sorrowing* Op. 7 (1991–2) and *Darknesse Visible* (1992), explore (and exploit) the timbral and dynamic extremes of the piano. Adès premiered the former in a Park Lane Group recital (11 January 1993) that brought him to the attention of the national press; its use of adhesive putty to dampen the middle register of the piano and provide contrast to the sonorous bass and glistening treble, highlights again Adès's fecund musical imagination. In *Darknesse Visible*, Adès refracts the individual voices of John Dowland's 'In Darknesse Let Mee Dwell' across the entire range of the piano, mining new and deeply expressive resources from old and familiar material (see Chapter 2).

International recognition came with *Living Toys*, for a chamber ensemble of fourteen players, which received the 1994 Paris Rostrum award for the best work by a composer under the age of thirty. To accompany the vivid musical content, Adès invented a story of a child's dream of angels, matadors, soldiers, death in space and a funeral fit for a hero. The work demands much from the performers: Adès takes technical prowess for granted, for the most part presses it into the service of communication rather than for dramatic effect. Virtuosity is fundamental to the four instrumental scores that follow,[15] all of which also share with *Living Toys* a proclivity for programmatic and musical allusion. ... *but all shall be well* Op. 10 (1993), a 'consolation' for orchestra, takes its name from the close of Eliot's *Four Quartets*; it ends with a reference to the *Romance oubliée* by Liszt, another composer of consolations. The Baroque stylisations of the *Sonata da Caccia* for chamber ensemble Op. 11 (1993) evoke Couperin, to whom (along with Debussy) the work pays homage. The *Origin of the Harp* for ten players

4   Thomas Adès in the 1990s

Op. 13 (1994), composed during Adès's tenure as composer-in-residence with the Hallé orchestra (1993–5), is named after a painting. The seven movements of *Arcadiana* for string quartet Op. 12 (1994) are given titles and musical content that evoke 'an image associated with ideas of the idyll, vanishing, vanished or imaginary'.[16] The work progresses from Venice via Mozart and Schubert to the tango mortale of the central movement, and from there passing first through a *galant* response to Watteau's *The Embarkation from the Island of Cythera* and then Elgarian England to arrive finally at the mystical River Lethe. Adès's accommodation of such a broad range of references in these works – literary, painterly, musical, mythical, historical and stylistic – without sacrificing his own musical voice or resorting to empty pastiche, is astonishing.

In 1995, Adès was rewarded with a composer portrait concert at the Aldeburgh Festival; later that year, his chamber opera, *Powder Her Face*, was premiered at the Cheltenham Festival to equal degrees of acclaim and controversy, critics by turn scandalised and tantalised by its so-called fellatio aria. Adès and his librettist, the novelist Phillip Hensher, based the opera around the fall from grace of the Duchess of Argyll (1912–93), offering a series of eight scenes that shift between key moments in her life and her eventual eviction from the hotel in which she spent her final years. The score is stylistically allusive: the tango of the overture, for instance, connotes sexual drama and opulence, and the scenes set in the 1930s are rewarded with a period-appropriate crooning song. Literary references in the libretto coexist with intertextual musical quotations: Berg's *Lulu* and Stravinsky's *The Rake's Progress* are both prominent during the Duchess's divorce trial, and references to Richard Strauss, Schubert, Mussorgsky and Verdi can also be found. Hensher has suggested that there exists 'a bigger, ampler meaning through these allusions [that] make undercurrents of ancient lust and violence run underneath the obvious subjects of money, marriage and clothes. Once or twice the facade cracks'.[17] Such undercurrents make the Duchess an ideal candidate for operatic portrayal. Although neither Hensher nor Adès flinch in their depiction of her weaknesses, by virtue of words and music that are unceasing in their attention to detail and craftsmanship, that never give over to empty parody, and that catch you unawares with moments of surprising tenderness amidst the spiky fun, the Duchess emerges at the end of the opera with a modicum of dignity.

The two original works that follow *Powder Her Face* both explore space and movement.[18] *Traced Overhead* Op. 15 (1996) for piano was inspired in part by images of angels ascending in shafts of light; lurking in the background and in some of the figuration is the nineteenth-century piano repertoire. *These Premises are Alarmed* Op. 16 for large orchestra (1996) is a wittily virtuosic concert piece in the tradition of Stravinsky's *Fireworks*, but here the outside festivities of the Russian composer are traded in for the internal setting of alarms going off in a concert hall in order to explore and exploit the acoustics of the Hallé orchestra's new home in the Bridgewater Hall.

Asyla followed, in 1997, along with the *Concerto Conciso* Op. 18, a work in which intricate, if not fiendishly complex, Ligeti-like rhythmic mechanisms are set up, only to spiral out of kilter in playful and unpredictable ways. It was during this year, too, that Adès signed to EMI records as both performer and composer. Since then, not only have nearly all of his own compositions been recorded (often by Adès himself as conductor or pianist), but he has also offered interpretations of composers as diverse as Schubert, Busoni, Janáček, Kurtág, Stravinsky and Nancarrow. In 1998 he was appointed the director of the Birmingham Contemporary Music Group (BCMG), providing a further opportunity to explore music he admired. Adès's open-minded approach to programming also characterised his tenure as Music Director of the Aldeburgh Festival (1999–2008). Further critical recognition came with the Elise L. Stoeger Prize for *Arcadiana* (New York, 1998) and the Ernst von Siemens Prize for young composers (Munich, 1999). In 1998 Adès was composer-in-residence at the Minnesota Orchestra's *Sommerfest*, and the following year his music was celebrated at the *Musica Nova* festival in Helsinki.

America, commissioned by the New York Philharmonic as a 'message for the millennium', was the last major work of the decade. Adès sets Mayan texts foretelling the fall of their empire, his initially ebullient music gradually becoming more disjointed. An interjection of jubilant Spanish choral music intensifies the growing desolation; the final movement is a long harrowing lament. The work has gained in its emotional impact as a result of the 2001 attack on the World Trade Centre; even without this added resonance, it is a stark and sombre work. The *January Writ* (1999) for SATB chorus offers a more orthodox millennial celebration; it, together with the earlier *The Fayrfax Carol* (1997) combine Adès's technical preoccupations with traditional choral textures.

The critical reception of Adès's music has frequently been adulatory. British critics, ever keen to laud the next Benjamin Britten, have celebrated both Adès's youth and his success in multiple fields.[19] Richard Taruskin, reviewing *Asyla* (amongst other works), for *The New York Times*, suggested that '[i]n Mr. Adès late modernism has a winner at last, a respectably hard-core talent to whom audiences, trusting their noses, have responded with enthusiasm'.[20] Yet his rapid rise to prominence has brought with it suspicions of hype: the critic Rupert Christiansen, for example, early on described Adès as an 'overrated golden boy'.[21] Early unguarded comments by the composer in interviews led Richard Morrison, in an article entitled 'Prodigy with a Notable Talent for Sounding Off', to wonder whether 'this is genius […] or the biggest piece of arrogance and pretension to hit British culture since Damien Hirst pickled his first fish'.[22]

The casual and dismissive nature of Morrison's comparison of Adès with Hirst (b. 1965) wrongly packages Adès's carelessness with Hirst's knowing courting of the media.[23] Yet it highlights how Adès's rise to prominence coincides with the (seemingly) 'sudden revitalization of British arts and culture' in the 1990s,[24] that benefitted individuals like Adès as well as heterogeneous groupings such as the Young British Artists (of which Hirst was a member)[25] and the 'in-yer-face' theatre playwrights.[26] The increasing importance of the media as a tool for promotion and dissemination of art and artists in the 1990s is just one of the characteristics of this period; others include the nature of political (dis)engagement within the arts and a general lack of optimism that ran kilter to the prevailing atmosphere. The

6   *Thomas Adès in the 1990s*

portrayal and reception of Adès during the 1990s was undoubtedly coloured by the concerns of the era (self-referentially, in the case of Morrison's allusion to the media, for instance), but such concerns also reveal themselves in Adès's thought and work.

In the remainder of this chapter, I shall critically situate Adès's early career in the context of Britain in the 1990s. Though this account draws on interviews with Adès conducted over the last two decades, I do not assume that he has maintained a consistent artistic stance throughout his career. Indeed, Adès often draws a line between his earlier and later music, necessitating a degree of caution when interpreting the former in the light of more recent statements.[27] Nor do I suggest that the extramusical issues to which his music alludes can only be understood with reference to the 1990s (although such issues clearly had immediate contemporary relevance), nor Britain alone (for Adès's outlook was increasingly cosmopolitan as the decade progressed). Nevertheless, Adès's aesthetic concerns overlap with many of the artistic, social and cultural practices embodied by the arts in 1990s Britain.[28] This is unsurprising, for he tended to move in wider artistic circles. Through his mother, the then-thirteen-year-old Adès had met Francis Bacon;[29] in the early 1990s, he formed friendships with novelists such as Hensher and Alan Hollinghurst, and later still entered into a relationship with the video artist Tal Rosner. Such connections, coupled with Adès's frequent reference to non-musical media in his writings and interviews, justifies the broader perspective adopted here.

A cultural snapshot of Britain, 1989–2001

Although '[t]he character of a tendency in art cannot just be read off from the prevailing political and social atmosphere of its time',[30] commentators nevertheless tend to agree on the major political, economic and social changes that informed and shaped British culture in the period, bounded at one end by the fall of the Berlin Wall and collapse of Eastern European Communism (1989–92), and at the other by the attacks on the World Trade Centre in New York (2001).[31] Against this backdrop, the British political landscape shifted considerably. Margaret Thatcher's resignation as Prime Minister in 1990 was followed by seven years of Conservative Government beset by crippling in-fighting over Europe and scandal. British identity came under renewed scrutiny as Britain renegotiated its relationship with the rest of the world in acts such as the Maastricht Treaty (1991), its involvement in the 1991 Gulf War and later the Balkan crisis (a renewed urgency of the issue of refugees emerged in response to the latter), and the ceding of Hong Kong (1997). A political emphasis on heritage at this time,[32] inadvertently channelled by Thatcher's successor, John Major, into visions of cricket and warm beer,[33] might be interpreted as a nostalgic mourning for a past and an identity that was to varying extents both lost and illusory.

The emergence of New Labour under Tony Blair and Gordon Brown climaxed with its comprehensive victory in the 1997 General Election. Immigration remained a cause of national division, with the new Conservative leader of the opposition William Hague 'more ready than Major to take up traditional right-wing attitudes, with the "bogus" status of many asylum seekers becoming a stock taunt against the Government'.[34] Asylum of a different, internal kind was also a matter of debate as a result of the 1990 National Health Service and Community Care Act, not least in the provision of support for mental health services.[35]

It is deceptively easy to identify parallels between the political issues described above and certain extramusical themes in Adès's music. *Asyla* emerged at a time when public discourse on asylum(s) was at a high; *Arcadiana*'s focus on lost idylls is not so distant from the cultural packaging of heritage and concern with identity. We should be careful not to assert uncritically too strong a link between music and politics, however: allusions to Elgar in *Arcadiana*'s penultimate movement, 'O Albion', cannot be considered a direct musical equivalent to John Major's homely vision of rural life.[36] Adès has guarded against the use of philosophical, political or even ethical ideas as musical metaphors,[37] claiming that he is 'incapable' of understanding the idea that art can be political.[38] Nevertheless, Adès's choice of titles certainly have political implications; as with many of Adès's comments, we can detect here 'an artful dodge on Adès's part, saving him from having to come down too strongly on either side of the debate between relevancy and autonomy that has been ongoing in contemporary composition circles for decades'.[39]

Adès's stance is symptomatic of the rejection of the political idealism and visionary 'fervour'[40] of his predecessors found in many of the artists who came to prominence during this 'holiday from history'.[41] Thus in fine art, the politicised use of 'metaphor and allusion in the output of the older generation' was superceded by the 'matter-of-fact' work by emerging artists that was 'free of any such explicit burden'.[42] Noting how '[q]uite often, young writers today refuse to offer solutions', the theatre critic Alex Sierz asks '[i]s that a negation of artistic responsibility? Perhaps. After all, writers such as Mark Ravenhill, who seem to be funky young people, actually have a very traditional leftwing morality […] But he says he doesn't want to use his plays to preach'.[43] There's a parallel to be drawn with the emerging drug culture of the period, fuelled by the growth in underground raves, which 'has an open-access formula: rather than a defined ideology […] It is endlessly malleable, pragmatic to new meaning […] The idea of Ecstasy culture has no politics because it has no manifesto or slogans, it *isn't saying anything* or actively opposing the social order'.[44] This non-commital, semantically slippery quality has much in common with aspects of 'Ecstasio' (see Chapters 5 and 7), and indeed, Adès's music of the 1990s writ large.

The younger generation's wariness towards politics went hand-in-hand with an increasing suspicion towards Modernism, the dominant contemporary artistic ideology in teaching institutions, galleries, theatres, concert halls, and so on. For Adès, High Modernism 'was a disgrace'.[45] Nevertheless, recalling his teenage experiences of listening to Stockhausen, Adès acknowledges some connection between the older composer's artistic choices and his social and political situation:

> [The music] seemed to be driven more by some kind of dilemma that he'd got himself into, whatever it was, some artistic conundrum, which was no

8   *Thomas Adès in the 1990s*

longer present for me as a fifteen-year-old in the mid-Eighties. German post-war guilt, perhaps, or the denial of it, I don't know. So that didn't have much relevance to me, musically or otherwise.[46]

Such comments align Adès with wider contemporary critiques in which the ethical and revelatory content of traditional (and modernist) art were continually challenged in response to postmodern suspicion towards grand narratives and with it the possibility of privileged viewpoints.[47] Adès has accordingly stressed his freedom from schools, dogma and pigeonholing.[48] Noting that at the start of his career, 'something like minimalism was still seen as an attack on other types of contemporary composition', he observed that

that sort of division and anger doesn't seem to matter so much any more and it actually feels very last century. It was so polarised and thank goodness it is over. [...] And looking back the only pieces that really survived from that terrible ideological time are the ones that stepped away from the whole thing.[49]

The political and ideological disengagement amongst the younger generation had the general consequence of a tendency towards individualism rather than movements, in which artists 'tend to distance themselves from any binding allegiance to a single way of working'.[50] Writing of music in the 1990s, although his general point can be extended to the arts in general, Peter O'Hagan noted that the 'bewildering stylistic plurality of the contemporary [...] scene' caused the 'certainties which categorized so much of the [art] of the preceding decades [to be] increasingly challenged'.[51] Such developments encouraged and enabled artists to address in their work

issues of provincialism and globalization, multiculturalism and specific national and regional identities, experimentation and a reengagement with a realist tradition, as well as renewed and reinvigorated interest in a range of differing and overlapping identities: nation, gender, class, ethnicity, sexuality and even the post-human.[52]

To a certain extent this mirrored the questioning of national identity observed in the political sphere, and counterbalanced the avoidance of mainstream political issues with a heighted sense of social awareness: 'underneath [the] eclecticism there has been a strong thread of social awareness, of looking at all kinds of different issues – from care in the community to race and the humiliation of the unemployed, and so on'.[53]

In this instance, Adès draws a line in the sand between his aesthetic concerns and those of many of his contemporaries. Not only does he assert (somewhat disingenuously, perhaps) that 'when people start talking about atonal or tonal or postmodern, or whatever – I'm not being weird, but I really don't know what they are talking about',[54] but he categorically refuses to engage with questions of identity

Thomas Adès in the 1990s 9

(which isn't to say that his music does not address it nevertheless). In a radio interview broadcast in 2010, Adès was asked about the 'Britishness' of his music:

[TOM SERVICE]: OK, do you have a sense of a responsibility to audiences or even the culture here because of your, you know, fame as a young British composer?

[THOMAS ADÈS]: Well, I don't think they're sitting there as individuals saying, 'I'm a Briton who's going to learn about my national identity by listening to Thomas Adès's Violin Concerto'. I mean, you know, who thinks like that?[55]

Service's question highlights the question of the relationship between artist and audience. This relationship was reconfigured in the 1990s, in part due to the impact of the economic recession of 1990–91, and after that as a result of the way that both Conservative and Labour Governments allocated, and sought for accountability of, arts funding. The distribution of (in particular) National Lottery proceeds, overseen by the Arts Council, undoubtedly boosted the arts, but also determined something of the nature of the resulting work, bringing to the fore issues of accessibility as well as the nature of its artistic content. New British Art became increasingly media-friendly (and savvy, as in the work of Young British Artists such as Hirst), headline-grabbing (as with the work of the 'in-yer-face' playwrights), oriented towards artistic prizes and prize culture,[56] and youth-focussed (the Turner Prize for fine art is an excellent instance of these last two points). Adès, of course, ticks nearly all of these boxes,[57] save for the first – the fallout from Morrison's 1995 article led him to treat the press with suspicion,[58] but the feeling was not mutual. Works such as *Powder Her Face*, 'Ecstasio' and *America* generated (and continue to generate) considerable press attention, as much for their topics (respectively, sex, drugs and the downfall of empires) as for their music.

The charge of superficiality is one that is made repeatedly against art of the 1990s; indeed, artists frequently courted this viewpoint.[59] Thus the artist Gary Hume claimed that '[t]he surface is all you get of me';[60] though there exists an ambiguity as to whether this itself is a comment on the media simulacrum or an aesthetic endpoint.[61] Such strategies are part of a wider turn to greater degrees of accessibility: '[i]t allows those without specialist knowledge of art a way into itself by airing material from the mass media that most people cannot help but know about'. This included reference to popular culture – sometimes preventing those *with* specialist knowledge from understanding! – but also irreverent attitudes towards material that, with a knowing wink, 'seemed not to worry about many of the issues that had tied art up in knots'.[62] The reception of Adès's music is coloured by such issues, whether emphasising superficiality over depth (see the discussion of *Powder Her Face*, below), or, more positively, as when Taruskin comments on the 'gentle tease' of *Asyla*'s title, which 'like the music, [is] sportively provocative'.[63]

Taruskin also observes Adès's 'omniverous range of reference', from 'fifteenth-century England to [...] the Chemical Brothers'.[64] Such polystylism

10 Thomas Adès in the 1990s

reflects the way in which, for many artists, 'the past offers neither any principle of continuity between then and now nor any values in relation to which individuals can locate or define themselves'.[65] Unshackled from traditional meanings and values, the signification of material emerges contextually, and this is precisely what critics are referring to when they praise Adès's music for finding new virtues in old material. For Andrew Porter, 'Adès, like Purcell and Britten, without repeating himself, has freshly touched and revitalized mainsprings of living music: the clash or consonance of note against note; the force of an interval leap [...] The old basics are freshly heard and ordered'.[66]

But the past remained a fruitful topic for authors and playwrights, however, as a means for documenting 'alternative, marginalized and unofficial experiences that offered alternative and often competing perspectives on official histories',[67] as well as for the exploration of 'the cultural genealogies and "psychogeographies" that intimately connect our presents/presence with the past'.[68] Perhaps because of its initial *succès de scandale*, the 'competing perspective on official history' offered in *Powder Her Face* is frequently overlooked. In its depiction of a woman who was 'all cladding – powder, scent, painting, furs – nothing inside',[69] the opera left itself open to the same accusation of superficiality (a charge, as noted, made frequently of art in this period). As it established itself in the repertoire, critics began to turn on the perceived lack of sympathetic characters and the almost moralising glee with which the Duchess's life is documented. For David Mermelstein, the 'shallow flash' that is the opera is coloured by a 'pervasive meanspiritedness':[70] others have been far less measured with their criticisms.[71] Underpinning such comments is the lingering desire – whether one calls it late-Romantic or Modernist – for music to express both emotional depth and a unique identity.

Supporters of Adès's music can claim, and indeed have done so, that his music possesses both, and as a result is able to connect with audiences. For Taruskin,

> [w]hat has put *Powder Her Face* [...] in such demand worldwide as to be newsworthy [... is] that having set up its main character, an aging nymphomaniac duchess, as a figure of cruel and predictable fun, it turns around and honors her, and the audience as well, with unsentimental and affecting sympathy at the end.[72]

Indeed, juxtaposed against the hypocrisy of the mocking hotel staff (no less sexually motivated than the Duchess), the lascivious Duke (whose infidelities are *not* made public knowledge), the rubbernecking public (who condemn the Duchess whilst eagerly lapping up her story) and above all the moralising, holier-than-thou attitude of the Judge, the Duchess emerges as the more rounded personality, flaws and all.

For Adès,

> *Powder Her Face* is very much set in London and I think you can hear that atmosphere of the late Nineties. It was a very explosive place at that time, in a way very decadent, the crumbling city and the dissonance between the established London culture, and the new, rougher one.[73]

Such an atmosphere benefitted from what the cultural historian Robert Hewison described as 'the makings of a cultural renaissance [... T]here is a renewed sense of creative vigour and excitement'.[74] The resurgence was felt keenly in popular culture: the confidence and pride encapsulated in the phrase 'Cool Britannia' could be applied to phenomena ranging from Britpop and the Spice Girls through to the fashion designs of Alexander McQueen. By November, *Newsweek* described London as 'the coolest city in the world'.[75] The sense of public optimism failed, however, to mirror such buoyancy: although 'the press was full of the vitality of British art and design', and despite the fact that 'the economy began to recover with an export-led growth in 1995–7, commentators puzzled over the apparent absence of a "feel-good factor". The public mood appeared strangely downbeat'.[76] By 6 July 1998, *Newsweek* carried the headline 'Uncool Britannia', and the Labour Government, who had been quick to embrace the resurgent youth culture, 'slowly dissociated themselves from their early policies that placed "creative industries" at the centre of their political vision'.[77]

Thus, despite the energy, pluralism and media-friendly nature of the arts in this period, there was 'a marked absence of optimism. [... T]he work [...] produced was often dark and intensely sceptical. It was concerned with isolation, fragmentation, dislocation and frustration. [...] Whether overt or implicit, a preoccupation with transience and extinction ran through much'.[78] Here, perhaps, we find some of the richest seams of Adès's art. Death haunts his early music. It is one of the central themes of *Powder Her Face*; it can be found too in *Five Eliot Landscapes*, *Under Hamelin Hill*, *Arcadiana*, *Living Toys* and *Cardiac Arrest*. The protagonists of *Life Story* burn to death, the fate of the baby Jesus is the subject of *The Fayrfax Carol*, and empires turn to dust in *America*. Loss and sorrow are the central topics of *Darknesse Visible* and *Still Sorrowing*.[79]

Such concerns could lead to nihilism,[80] but also moments of great poetry: for all that critics such as Michael Billington question the binary opposition between naturalism (the political) and the metaphysical,[81] an emphasis on *aesthetic* experience rather than moralising or preaching can be traced throughout the art of the period.[82] And this, too, is typical of Adès's music:

> I imagine a miracle that one day might happen, that there will be a glint from this shiny unnecessary thing I've made, a ray that strikes reality in a light that makes visible the thing that supposedly can't be described: the present, perhaps. The gratuitousness of music is one's best chance of this.[83]

Paradoxically, such aesthetic transcendence is often sought through a deliberate undermining of realism,[84] through Adès's deliberate signposting of formal or stylistic conventions (see Chapter 2), or through the dream-like sequences of *Arcadiana* and *Living Toys.* In this way, although Adès is at pains to emphasise the primacy of musical relationships, his music cannot but let the real world in, and pushes consistently, and critically, into the interstices between art, politics and culture.

12   *Thomas Adès in the 1990s*

Notes

1 At the time of writing, Adès remains the youngest composer to have received the award.
2 The manuscript for *Five Eliot Landscapes* Op. 1 is dated 1.1.90–11.1.90. An earlier work, *The Lover in Winter*, has since been published.
3 http://grawemeyer.org/music-composition/ [accessed 12 August 2015].
4 Soon after, the Minnesota Orchestra, conducted by Jeffrey Tate, gave the USA premiere in St. Paul, Minnesota (20 November 1997) and further performances in Minneapolis over the next two evenings. Rattle and the CBSO then performed *Asyla* three times in Austria (27, 29, 30 November 1997).
5 Berlin Philharmoniker, dir. Sir Simon Rattle, Carnegie Hall, 28 January 2006. *Asyla* has remained in the international repertoire; a list of performances is maintained at http://thomasades.com/compositions/asyla [accessed 12 August 2015].
6 See Chapter 7.
7 The recording was a composite of live performances given by Rattle and the CBSO (EMI 5 56818 2).
8 Arnold Whittall, 'Thomas Adès', in Stanley Sadie and John Tyrell (eds), *The New Grove Dictionary of Music and Musicians* (London: Macmillan, 2001), vol. 1, p. 156.
9 Anthony Tommasini, 'Young, but with Enough Experience to Look Back', *New York Times* (31 March 2008). See also *TA:FON*, pp. 134–5.
10 *TA:FON*, p. 134.
11 Nicholas Wroe, 'Adès on Adès', *Guardian* (5 July 2008).
12 Michael Anthony, 'The Astonishing Thomas Adès', *American Record Guide* (March/April 1999), pp. 23–6, at p. 25.
13 Hilary Finch, 'Thomas Adès', *The Times* (19 March 1994). Leon McCawley won the piano heat and took part in the final the following year. Confusion about the nature of the competition can be found in many biographical accounts. Alex Ross, Andy Hamilton and Hélène Cao all erroneously suggest that Adès came second overall; David Patrick Stearn even claims that, at eighteen years, Adès 'was the BBC Young Musician of the Year'. Ross, 'Roll Over, Beethoven: Thomas Adès', *New Yorker* (26 October 1998), pp. 111–41, at p. 126; Andy Hamilton, 'Introduction to the Music of Thomas Adès', in *Thomas Adès: List of Works* (London: Faber Music, 2005), p. 3; Hélène Cao, *Thomas Adès Le Voyageur: Devenir compositeur. Être musician* (Paris: Éditions M.F., 2007), p. 7; and David Patrick Stearn, 'Adès' Unique Sound Bows to Nobody', *USA Today* (24 July 1997).
14 *Audabe*, an unpublished 1990 setting of Philip Larkin for solo soprano, has received occasional performances.
15 A fifth, *Les baricades mistérieuses* (1994), is a transcription of a work by Couperin.
16 Composer's Note to Score of *Arcadiana* Op. 12 (Faber Music, 1995).
17 Philip Hensher, 'How to Write an Opera', *New Statesman & Society*, 8 (6 June 1995), p. 31.
18 The first completed work after the opera was an arrangement of *Cardiac Arrest* by the British pop group Madness (1995).
19 Alex Ross compared the British tendency to award composers' (seemingly) overnight fame, as with Adès in the 1990s, Oliver Knussen in the 1970s and George Benjamin in the 1980s, with the 'energy – and competitiveness – of televised sports'. 'Roll Over, Beethoven', p. 116.
20 Richard Taruskin, 'A Surrealist Composer Comes to the Rescue of Modernism', *New York Times* (5 December 1999), reprinted with a postscript in *The Danger of Music and Other Anti-Utopian Essays* (Berkeley, Los Angeles and London: University of California Press, 2010), pp. 144–52, at p. 145.
21 Cited in Wroe, 'Adès on Adès'.
22 Richard Morrison, 'Prodigy with a Notable Talent for Sounding Off', *The Times* (9 June 1995).
23 Adès was subsequently reluctant to engage with the press, contributing to his so-called 'spoiled brat' public persona. See Taruskin, 'A Surrealist Composer', p. 145. Years

later, he suggested that '[i]f my personality was going to be an obstacle, there was no point putting myself out there'. Tim Teeman, 'Thomas Adès: Why I Have to Compose', *The Times* (16 February 2011).

24 Ken Urban, 'Cruel Britannia', in Rebecca D'Monté and Graham Saunders (eds), *Cool Britannia? British Political Drama in the 1990s* (Basingstoke: Palgrave MacMillan, 2008), pp. 38–55, at p. 39.

25 See Julian Stallabrass, *High Art Lite: British Art in the 1990s* (London: Verson, 1999), pp. 2, 18–32.

26 The term was coined by the critic Aleks Sierz for his *In-Yer-Face Theatre: British Drama Today* (London: Faber and Faber, 2001).

27 Adès doesn't give a clear sense of where he views the boundary between early and late works, though the prominence given to *Asyla* in his interviews suggests that he views this as an important landmark in his output (see also Chapter 2).

28 This observation provides a corrective counterbalance to the assertions of aesthetic autonomy one finds in Adès's writings (see below).

29 Wroe, 'Adès on Adès'.

30 Stallabrass, *High Art Lite*, p. 129.

31 See, for instance, Nick Bentley, 'Introduction: Mapping the Millennium. Themes and Trends in Contemporary British Fiction', in Nick Bentley (ed.), *British Fiction of the 1990s* (London and New York: Routledge, 2005), pp. 1–18, and Mireia Aragay *et al.* (eds), *British Theatre of the 1990s: Interviews with Directors, Playwrights, Critics and Academics* (Basingstoke: Palgrave Macmillan, 2007), pp. x, 160, 164 and 173–4; Eddie Dyja, *Studying British Cinema: The 1990s* (Leighton Buzzard: Auteur, 2010); and Stallabrass, *High Art Lite*.

32 See Peter Clarke, *Hope and Glory: Britain 1900–2000* (London: Penguin, 2004), p. 386 and Kenneth O. Morgan, *Twentieth-Century Britain: A Very Short Introduction* (Oxford and New York: Oxford University Press, 2000), p. 109.

33 Major was frustrated that his actual point – that 'international cooperation did not mean the death of distinct cultures' – was lost amidst the soundbites that followed his speech. Alwyn W. Turner, *A Classless Society: British Culture in the 1990s* (London: Aurum Press, 2013), p. 295.

34 Clarke, *Hope and Glory*, p. 433.

35 See Roger Hadley and Roger Clough, *Care in Chaos: Frustration and Challenge in Community Care* (London: Cassell, 1996).

36 On Elgar and 'O Albion', see Arnold Whittall, 'Dillon, Adès, and the Pleasures of Allusion', in Peter O'Hagan (ed.), *Aspects of British Music of the 1990s* (Aldershot: Ashgate, 2003), pp. 3–27, at 16–21.

37 *TA:FON*, pp. 17–18.

38 Cited in Drew Massey, 'Thomas Adès at 40', *Salmagundi*, 174–5 (2012), pp. 194–202, at p. 201.

39 Massey, Ibid., p. 202.

40 Richard Cork, *Breaking Down the Barriers: Art in the 1990s* (New Haven and London: Yale University Press, 2003), p. 127.

41 Charles Krauthammer, cited in Bentley, 'Introduction', p. 3. The phrase encapsulates the sense in which the collapse of Marxism was said to engender the 'end of history' (Fukuyama), only for a new ideological 'enemy' to emerge in the form of Islam.

42 Stallabrass, *High Art Lite*, p. 3.

43 Aragay *et al.*, *British Theatre of the 1990s*, p. 147.

44 Matthew Collin, *Altered State: The Story of Ecstasy Culture and Acid House* (London: Serpent's Tail, 1997), pp. 4–5. Ravenhill's breakthrough work, *Shopping and Fucking* (1995), has an extended scene in which the principle characters take Ecstasy.

45 *TA:FON*, p. 81.

46 Ibid., p. 136.

47 See, for instance, Stallabrass, *High Art Lite*, p. 59. It should be noted in this respect that the 'gentrification of the avant-garde' – its adoption into mainstream culture as a

14 *Thomas Adès in the 1990s*

commodity like any other – served to neutralise its radical, oppositional potential. See Michael Bracewell, *The Nineties: When Surface Was Depth* (London: Flamingo, 2002), pp. 122–200.

48 Such claims of autonomy are far from unique to artists from the 1990s, of course, though in the context of increased commercial pressures they become an increasingly 'valuable promotional tool'. Wilson, 'György Ligeti and the Rhetoric of Autonomy', p. 6.

49 Wroe, 'Adès on Adès'.

50 Cork, *Breaking Down the Barriers*, p. 127.

51 Peter O'Hagan, 'Introduction', in Peter O'Hagan (ed.), *Aspects of British Music of the 1990s* (Aldershot: Ashgate, 2003), pp. xv–xviii, at p. xv. The editorial elisions and amendments have been made to generalise O'Hagen's music-specific account.

52 Bentley, 'Introduction', p. 1. Although Bentley's focus is on fiction, his point applies across the arts. The relationship between Adès's music and his sexuality will be considered by Drew Massey in his forthcoming book on Adès's music; Adès 'knew he was gay from a young age'. Teeman, 'Why I Have to Compose'.

53 Aragay *et al.*, *British Theatre of the 1990s*, p. 117.

54 Peter Culshaw, 'Don't Call me a Messiah', *Daily Telegraph* (1 March 2007).

55 Interview with Thomas Adès, *Music Matters*, BBC Radio 3 (first broadcast 15 May 2010).

56 Bentley, 'Introduction', p. 1.

57 Many of Adès's commissions at this time came from publicly funded institutions. A list of his works, including commissioning details, can be found at http://thomasades.com/compositions/[accessed 12 August 2015].

58 See Ross, 'Roll Over, Beethoven', pp. 112, 114.

59 On Adès and 'surfaces', see Chapter 2.

60 Cited by Stallabrass, *High Art Lite*, p. 34.

61 Ibid., *High Art Lite*, p. 35.

62 Ibid., pp. 4 and 8.

63 Taruskin, 'A Surrealist Composer', p. 144.

64 Ibid.

65 Andrzej Gąsiorek, writing of J.G. Ballard, in '"Refugees from Time": History, Death and the Flight from Reality in Contemporary Writing', in Nick Bentley (ed.), *British Fiction of the 1990s* (London and New York: Routledge, 2005), pp. 42–56, at p. 43.

66 Andrew Porter, Sleeve notes to Adès, *Living Toys*, EMI CD 72271 (1998).

67 Bentley, 'Introduction', p. 12.

68 Ibid., p. 13.

69 Andrew Porter, Sleeve notes to Adès, *Powder Her Face*, EMI CD 56649 (1998).

70 David Mermelstein, 'The Meanspirited Wunderkind', *New Criterion*, 17/vii (1999), p. 51.

71 For examples of sharp-tongued, and not always measured, criticism of *Powder Her Face*, see Stephen Hicken, Review of Adès, *Living Toys*, EMI CD 72271, *American Record Guide* (March/April 1999), pp. 71–2, at p. 71, and Rupert Christiansen, 'Blissfully Calm after the Storm Opera', *Daily Telegraph* (11 February 2004).

72 Taruskin, 'A Surrealist Composer', p. 145.

73 *TA:FON*, pp. 170–1.

74 Robert Hewison, 'Rebirth of a Nation', *The Times* (19 May 1996).

75 See Urban, 'Cruel Britannia', p. 39.

76 Morgan, *Twentieth-Century Britain*, p. 102.

77 Urban, 'Cruel Britannia', p. 51.

78 Cork, *Breaking Down the Barriers*, p. 8.

79 Laments also feature prominently in the work of Adès's near-contemporaries Mark-Anthony Turnage (b. 1960) and Julian Anderson (b. 1967).

80 See Urban's defence of the nihilist strain in in-yer-face theatre, which he argues has a critical function within 1990s commodity culture. 'Cruel Britannia', pp. 44, 50–1.

81 Aragay *et al.*, *British Theatre of the 1990s*, p. 114.
82 See Mark Ravenhill, 'A Touch of Evil', *Guardian* (22 March 2003), and Aragay *et al.*, *British Theatre of the 1990s*, pp. 161–2.
83 *TA:FON*, p. 66.
84 An equivalent technique can be found in Ravenhill's *Shopping and Fucking*, in which the main characters are named after members of the band Take That. Aragay *et al.*, *British Theatre of the 1990s*, p. 161.

2 Towards *Asyla* (1990–97)

Adès made the decision to prioritise his compositional activities over performing in 1989:

> [The BBC Young Musician of the Year competition] gave me quite a fright. [...] Did I want to go through all this again, play the same things again? I went home and said 'I'm going to become a composer today, and do it properly'. I started at the top note of the piano and went on from there.[1]

The result was 'New Hampshire', the first of the *Five Eliot Landscapes*, which does indeed begin with the piano's top C. The focus on a registral extreme, and its subsequent development, is characteristic of Adès's later music. Descending from the C, successive intervals between pitches increase by one semitone to form an *expanding intervallic series* (schematised in Example 2.1a(i)). An equivalent contracting series begins in the bass shortly afterwards; both series change direction upon reaching their respective limits. Example 2.1b picks up the musical argument from bar 17. Each version of the series (a)–(d) is set to a repeated trochaic (long-short) rhythm that implies the same triple time, but moving at a different speed (a *mensuration canon*). The metrical independence of the series prevents them from realigning with one another, so that each circle aimlessly in musical space. Adès's performance instructions 'Suspended: sempre quasi in sogno' ([always as if in a dream]) and 'lontanissimo' heighten this sense of timeless, introverted fantasy.[2]

With the entry of the soprano in bar 22, the texture stratifies into three discrete *strata* (respectively the piano right hand, soprano and piano left hand), each with its own organisational principle. Though a number of the resulting harmonies are commonplace (such as the A major triad in bar 22), the logic that governs the progression from one to the next is not that of traditional tonality. The motion of each stratum is restricted to a single (non-expanding) *intervallic cycle*;[3] when superimposed, either in strict alignment or staggered so that they move at independent rates, the lines create an *expanded harmonic progression*.[4] Example 2.1 places this information in braces, ordered from the top stratum to the bottom; intervals are represented numerically in semitones, either ascending (+) or descending (–)

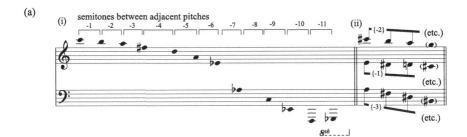
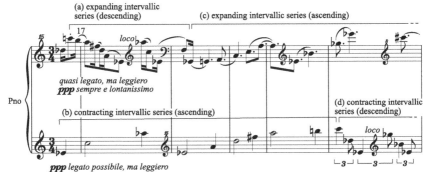

Example 2.1 (a) (i) expanded intervallic series; (ii) expanded harmonic progression; (b) 'New Hampshire', *Five Eliot Landscapes* Op. 1/i, bars 17–28.

18   *Towards* Asyla *(1990–97)*

(e.g. the motion from bar 22 to 23 is represented by $\left\{ \begin{smallmatrix} -2 \\ -1 \\ -3 \end{smallmatrix} \right\}$). Once the vocal phrase has been completed, the expanding intervallic series from bars 1–21 pick up where they left off, as if unperturbed, or even aware, of the intrusion by the chordal passage. Just as the text introduces the memory of 'children's voices in the orchard' (later we learn that this was twenty years ago from the narrator's perspective), the music recalls harmonic materials from a bygone era, but renders them strange in a new, modern context.

Adès's music of the 1990s rarely repeats itself: the vocal works set a heterogeneous range of texts, and the instrumental works differ considerably in instrumentation and genre. Beneath the surface, however, there are consistent threads that weave their way through this output and which offer degrees of unity amidst the diversity. From this perspective, Adès's designation of the *Five Eliot Landscapes* as his 'opus 1' was more than just an announcement of a change of career direction. Retrospectively, the songs can be heard to present particular musical and expressive themes that Adès subsequently developed in his later music; the 'opus 1' (perhaps unwittingly) becomes a prescient statement of aesthetic ambition.[5]

Writing a dozen years later, the critic Bernard Holland suggested that

> Mr. Adès seems to be one of those talents that arrive, almost intact, out of nowhere, somewhat like Chopin or Debussy. If we dig hard, we might find who and what influenced all three, but in essence these are men who arrived with something never heard before.[6]

Adès's influences are often not, in fact, that hard to discern.[7] Many composers throughout the twentieth century have drawn on intervallic cycles to structure individual lines, or, when superimposed, harmonies; given Adès's stated admiration for both Berg and Ives,[8] it is conceivable that he was stimulated by their examples.[9] Adès claims to have 'found', rather than 'invented' the expanded intervallic series;[10] its embrace of all of the possible intervals smaller than an octave in as short a span as possible echoes the concerns of composers such as Berg, Nono and Carter, without replicating their own practice.[11] What matters, however, is less the observation of technical affinities between Adès and other composers, and more the often startlingly novel way in which Adès puts them into musical practice. In this respect, Holland's emphasis on Adès's individual voice rings true.

Nevertheless, one rarely gets the impression when listening to the music of this period that any given piece builds directly upon the last. Whilst this might be attributable in part to Adès's youth (it would be unreasonable to expect a fully formed compositional personality from someone in their early twenties, though many critics did so), the non-linear development might plausibly stem from his compositional practice at the time. In 1995, Morrison observed that Adès's 'method of composition is to start with a sequence of notes or chords and then work out "sheets and sheets of permutations" derived from that sequence'.[12] There is a sense in which this might be extended by analogy to Adès's treatment of all the building blocks at his disposal, musical and otherwise, for each successive work attempts a different combination and exploration of the multitudinous possibilities inherent within them.

In what follows, I build upon my survey of Adès's early music in Chapter 1 to explore the principle building blocks that are pertinent to an understanding of *Asyla*. The account is deliberately non-chronological, in order to avoid suggesting a strictly linear artistic development. The frequency with which such building blocks can be found across Adès's output suggests that they possess limited explanatory function when considered in abstract away from their specific realisations and functions in individual works. Chapters 3–6 offer close readings of each of the movements of *Asyla* in order to address just this point. But there are other ways one might 'read' these elements interpretatively. Moving beyond the syntactical role played by particular musical ideas, this chapter will also consider the function of genre and topic in communicating and shaping musical meaning. From here it is but a short step to consider the metaphorical and critical implications of Adès's music, and in doing so, to reconnect with the ideas and concepts left hanging at the end of the previous chapter.

Pitch

Morrison's early glimpse into Adès's compositional studio demonstrates the important role played by harmony in Adès's thinking. The 'sheets and sheets of permutations' he describes suggests a combinatorial mindset and with it the systematic *musical* exploration of different possibilities. To observe Adès's use of the expanding intervallic series without identifying its specific local (syntactic) function is to miss a vital aspect of the musical argument: Hélène Cao's observation that the expanding intervallic series can allude to various keys (or none at all, as in Example 2.1 above) demonstrates its harmonic potential.[13] *Powder Her Face* offers a masterclass in the way that the same pattern can take on a multitude of musical meanings, depending on – amongst other things – its harmonic, rhythmic and stylistic environment.

Example 2.2a reveals the multilevelled nature of Adès's language. The Duchess, retreating into her memories, appears to be recalling the arrival of her future husband, the Duke of Argyll. The texture consists of three strata (seen most clearly in the analytical reduction beneath the score): three-note chords in the upper and lower registers (each with their own metrical organisation) bounding the voice in the middle. The Duchess sings '(and) here he comes' three times, initially ascending through the first four notes of an expanding intervallic series, and then combining the second and third iterations in a six-note ascent in which the anticipated final note, a G♮, is replaced by a G♯. Pattern disruption frequently assumes a significant role in Adès's music. Here, the deviation from expectation has, amongst other things, a dramatic function. Despite the Duchess's mounting excitement and hopes of a future of unimagined wealth, the G♯ points to the fact that something is wrong. It might even be understood as standing for what we (as the audience) and the Duchess (recalling the event from the perspective of 1990) know is going to happen: her eventual divorce and disgrace.

Example 2.2 *Powder Her Face* Op. 14. (a) Act I Scene 1, bars 396–404; (b) Act I Scene 2, bars 285–297.

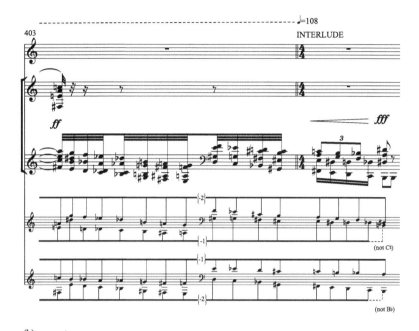

Example 2.2 (Continued)

22   *Towards* Asyla *(1990–97)*

But whilst the G♯ is musically surprising from the perspective of the strict patterning of the vocal line, it is partially assimilated into the broader harmonic language as the vocal stratum continually weaves in and out of the material that bounds it.[14] Thus, in bars 396–397, the <E F G> in the voice combines with the bass stratum to suggest a half-diminished seventh chord on E, whilst at the same time, the vocal B♭ belongs (enharmonically) with the A♯ of the F♯ major chord in the *upper* stratum. Similarly, the climactic (and somewhat deviant) soprano G♯ of bar 401 is simultaneously the bass of the chord above it, the product of a $\left\{ \begin{array}{c} -2 \\ -1 \\ -2 \end{array} \right\}$ expanded harmonic progression. From this moment of high drama, the accompaniment begins to tumble down, constructed from three (later four) intervallic cycles. But whereas two of these cycles conclude as expected on notes of a dominant seventh on B (D♯ and A), the other two cycles have to be altered in order to land on B♮ (rather than the otherwise anticipated C and B♭). Here the pattern disruption is used to signal the start of a new formal section. In this way, deviations on one level (i.e. surface intervallic patterns) are assimilated into another, larger level (that of the form).

The same melodic material is recalled in Example 2.2b. Here, the harmonic language offers a marvellous pastiche of 1930s popular music, full of rich altered seventh chords. Bars 285–290 contain a rising and falling version of the expanding intervallic series as before, now in a D major context; in bars 291–297 the melody is derived from two *interlocking intervallic cycles*, another practice that may well have been learned from Berg or Ives (or both). Whilst the recollection of the expanded intervallic series contributes to a sense of motivic coherence across the opera, its musical affect is radically altered by its context. In abstract, therefore, intervallic patterns such as these are semantically and expressively neutral: they require specific musical realisation in order to come to life.

The capacity for such patterns to allude to different modes of organisation enables Adès to incorporate into his music, without incongruity, functional harmonic progressions such as the root motion by perfect fifths found in Example 2.2b.[15] It is perhaps the perfect fifth's connection with common-practice tonality that gives it, for Adès, such an elemental force; many of his compositions (including *Asyla*) emerge out of it.[16] Thus, in *Arcadiana*, the opening perfect fifth is followed by three further fifths, each a minor sixth below the last, in order to map out a tonal space distinct from traditional diatonic norms;[17] in *The Origin of the Harp*, the opening clarinet line is based on superimposed fifths as part of a depiction of primeval transformation scene.[18] The {G, D} fifth that opens the second movement of *Living Toys* (over a B in the bass) signals a shift from the heavenly angels of the first movement to the earthly Aurochs of the second.[19]

As can be observed in Example 2.2, Adès's choice of pitch material is frequently determined by the demands (or disruption) of underlying intervallic structures. But his music reveals other tendencies, too. One is to derive material from a limited collection of pitches and to explore the melodic and harmonic potential contained within them. Thus, for instance, the close of the first movement of *The Origin of the Harp* is based entirely on permutations and combinations of the notes {B♭, E♭, A♭, D♭}.[20] The restriction of material creates a balance between cyclic and directional tendencies, suspending it in poised equilibrium. By way of contrast, Adès attempts elsewhere to employ all (or nearly all) the chromatic pitches at his disposal. The bass line from Figure A in the Chamber Symphony gradually accumulates chromatic pitches that serve to shift its tonal moorings from B towards F♯. The final movement of *Arcadiana* combines both of these approaches, repeating an eleven-note melody first played by the cello a further four times in various settings in the manner of a varied ostinato.[21]

Many of these features can be observed in *Still Sorrowing*. The placement of adhesive putty across the strings of the middle register of the piano to create percussive tones that contrast with the sonorous bass and glistening treble is just one means of differentiating the various registers of the piano. Another is to restrict its pitch material: as shown in Example 2.3, the upper two strata (the top two staves) at the outset of the work are restricted to a particular four-note collection of pitches (sometimes with chromatic alterations). The lower stratum, choked by the adhesive putty, slowly spells out a chromatically descending bass from C♭, embellished with flurries of rising fifths (the use of florid ornamentation can be found in all of the strata, and is a common device in Adès's music). The obsessive circling around of the same pitches (and later, a propensity to descend into lower registers) is eminently suitable for this character study in frozen grief.

The various techniques surveyed so far have predominantly been small-scale. However, Adès frequently combines or extends them in order to generate larger structures or even the premise behind entire movements. The use of cycles lends itself well to chaconnes and passacaglia sections and movements. Prominent examples include the second section of *Still Sorrowing* (from bar 37), the judge's verdict on the Duchess in *Powder Her Face* (Act II, Scene 6, from bar 181) and 'Et … (tango mortale)', the central movement of *Arcadiana*. Functioning in a similar vein, entire sections are generated through the establishment of an intervallic process that is left to run its course, as in … *but all shall be well* and the opening of *These Premises are Alarmed*. An extreme example of this can be found in 'Arietta', the final movement of *Under Hamelin Hill*, in which the opening material sinks lower and lower (with minor surface variations for variety) until it reaches the very bottom of the instrument's register.

The title 'Arietta' suggests a song-like character; at the very least, it draws attention to the unfolding melodic line. And it is a sense of line, a connecting thread, which forms another important aspect of Adès's formal thinking. In 1999, Adès suggested that his music exhibits 'a very, very strong line – not literally like a melody but everything has to go from one section to another very logically'.[22] Sometimes such lines have a clearly audible basis as projected motion (as in the descending chromatic bass heard in the opening of

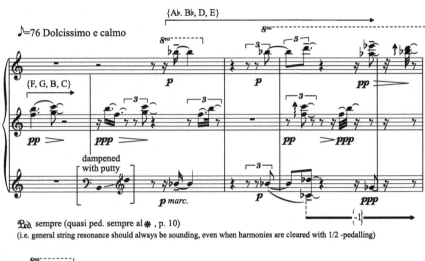
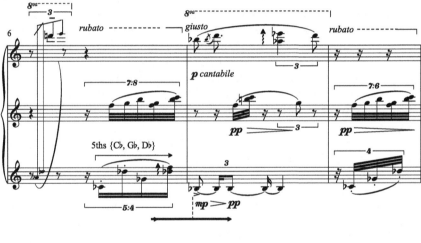

Example 2.3 Still Sorrowing Op. 7, bars 1–9.

Still Sorrowing); at other times, it is more abstract, fluid in concept, relating to quasi-traditional developmental and organicist procedures, motivic working and symphonism.

Rhythm

Many of the rhythmic devices employed by Adès in his early music parallels or complements those used for pitch (and vice versa; there is no necessary priority here). The individual metric organisation of the various strata in Examples 2.1–2.3 is typical, and from *Traced Overhead* onwards, there is an increasing tendency for Adès to differentiate strata in this way. Taruskin, writing of the 'striking' quality of Adès's rhythms, observes how 'fast ostinatos, often of a tricky, ear-beguiling complexity, coexist at varying speeds in contrasting colours and registers, evoking not linear distance but gyres and vortexes: sound in motion but not going anywhere'.[23] Given Adès's admiration for Ives and Nancarrow, it is likely that the complex layerings found in their music, and in particular Nancarrow's use of polymetre and rhythmic canons, shaped Adès's own approach.[24]

The passage reproduced in Example 2.4 is characteristic of much of Adès's music.[25] The complexity of its rhythmic organisation does not, however, lend itself to the experience of hearing multiple metres and tempi; rather, it gives the impression of time suspended.[26] An early instance of this occurs in the fugue from *Under Hamelin Hill* Op. 6/ii (1992), in which the entry of each voice is in an independent tempo: only after a caesura do the voices proceed together. In such cases, the moments in which the various unsynchronised strata come together suggest structurally significant points of arrival, marking the beginning of a new stretch of time (which itself may have dissipated momentum).

Related to this is the use of rhythmic cycles in one or more parts that coincide only occasionally with the material around them. Such cycles can be found in the percussion at the outset of the Chamber Symphony (Example 2.5),[27] *Fool's Rhymes* and *Living Toys*,[28] though variations to the cycles occur relatively quickly. Typically, the intricate rhythmic patterns within the cycles occur *around* rather than *on* the beat; coupled with unusual phrase lengths and deviations from patterns, one frequently encounters an absence of defined pulse. Thus, Adès's use of percussion often provides noise, agitation and the anticipation of an established pulse that may or may not come, rather than an automatic sense of direction and purpose, or a clear framework within which other events happen. Huw Belling notes how the opening rhythmic pattern of the Chamber Symphony distorts a 'drumming cliché' (and how a similar pattern in the second movement of *Living Toys* does the same to 'some other cultural archetype' – that of Spanish castanets and the matador).[29] This, perhaps, suggest a critical as well as musical function: although Adès often uses the metaphor of a mechanism to describe such cycles (especially in the 'winding up' of the opening of the Chamber Symphony),[30] it is noteworthy that these passages are nearly always corrupted, flawed – which is to say, human.

Example 2.4 'Chori', *Traced Overhead* Op. 15/iii, bars 45–50.

Example 2.5 Chamber Symphony Op. 2/i, bars 1–14.

28 *Towards* Asyla *(1990–97)*

The fluidity of Adès's rhythms owes much to the use of both irrational and additive rhythms. In his early music, Adès frequently inserts irrational bars based on incomplete triplet rhythms (an example can be found in Chapter 4, Example 4.2). The practice can be traced back to Henry Cowell; Adès may have absorbed it via his interest in Nancarrow, though irrational rhythms were also employed in the music of composers such as Brian Ferneyhough. Additive rhythms, in which the organisation is based upon irregular groupings of an underlying pulse (see, for instance, Chapter 3, Example 3.4), can be used to create rhythmic buoyancy and energy. Aligned with this technique is the expansion and contraction of rhythmic ideas (as found, for instance, in the music of Stravinsky and Messiaen; see Chapter 3, Example 3.1a). Depending on context, both irrational and additive rhythms can give the impression of rubato, uncertainty, spontaneity, and so on; they can also undermine metre and contribute greatly to the floating quality of Adès's music identified by Taruskin.

Sonority

Adès's description of Ligeti and Kurtág as 'inventors of genius, inventors of colours and instruments – not in the sense of actual instruments, but an "instrument" being a complex of timbre and interval and harmony and rhythm' highlights the intimate relationship between such parameters in his own thinking.[31] Given the important role played by sonority in Adès's early encounters with music (see Chapter 1), the significant role it plays in his own compositions is unsurprising. For instance, the hazy aural halo that arises from Adès's imprecise doubling of material forms a sonic parallel to the blurring of the edges (and audibility) of musical processes generated by the superimposition of conflicting harmonic and metric strata. This technique has a number of functions: it can be used to recreate a particular acoustic (or characteristic sound of a period),[32] create a woozy, distorted texture, or simulate the rich overtones of a pedalled piano (in this context, see the pedalling instructions in Examples 2.1, 2.3 and 2.4). Just as characteristic a device can be found with the opening melody of the Chamber Symphony, given to the alto flute but doubled to varying degrees of exactitude by various instruments, colouring both its motivic content and also – by virtue of anticipations, glissandi and sustaining of certain notes in the strings – surrounding it with echoes and refractions of itself (Example 2.5). Paradoxically, the deliberate imprecision of the soundworld arises from an exacting approach to notation, in which players are given highly detailed instructions, both graphically and verbally.

Adès's performers frequently double on unusual instruments: in the Chamber Symphony, the trumpeter and pianist play a wine bottle and accordion respectively (certain pitches on the piano are prepared with erasers and screws in advance; the performance notes give incredibly detailed instructions for this); in *Living Toys*, amongst other doublings, the oboist plays a sopranino recorder, the hornist has a whip, the trumpeter has a virtuosic part to play on piccolo trumpet with a plunger, and the percussionist a talking drum. Indeed, Adès's percussion parts vary considerably from work to work, requiring multiple players and instruments; what connects them is their virtuosic and imaginative colouristic demands. Normal sounds are distorted through playing techniques, mutes, covers and preparations, all in the service of conjuring up specific timbres for specific moments and sections.

Except for glissandi (which are quite frequent in his music), Adès tends to restrict his pitches to the equally tempered twelve notes of the chromatic scale; the use of natural harmonics in *Catch* and *Living Toys* are colouristic, evocative and perhaps symbolic (as in Britten's *Serenade for Tenor, Horn and Strings*) rather than a determined exploration of quarter tones as a compositional resource. Though Adès 'love[s] the mad acidic colours of the natural horns in Ligeti', he claims not to have 'seen yet how quarter-tones could be a way forward at a structural level'.[33] Nevertheless, quarter tones are prominent in *Asyla*, and in this light, it is feasible that Adès was influenced by Kurtág's *Eletút* for two bassett horns and two pianos tuned a quarter-tone apart, which Adès included, and performed, in a portrait concert at the Aldeburgh Festival in 1995.[34]

The frequent avoidance of timbral norms extends to their deployment in 'space', too. Adès's music often exploits extremities of pitch, with material presented in the grumbling bass or glittering treble (see Examples 2.1, 2.2a, 2.4 and 2.6). Although material might be presented within the 'normative' middle registers, it might have limited or no connection to that which surrounds it, or the middle might be left entirely vacant. As with so much of Adès's music, this approach defamiliarises his material, subverts expectations and opens up new possibilities. For instance, in *Still Sorrowing*, the use of adhesive putty chokes off the register that typically carries thematic material (and with it, the register most associated with the human singing voice and subjectivity). Although the putty is gradually peeled back to give almost unrestricted voice to this register, for much of the work the capacity of the musical subject to 'speak' is stifled. The piece thus opens with an instance of literal loss (of voice) to parallel the (presumed) loss conveyed by the title.

Genre

Adès conforms neither to modernism's aversion towards existing genres and material, nor to an uncritical romantic or postmodern adoption of them. Instead, his invocation of traditional genres, forms and procedures in works such as the Chamber Symphony and movements such as the Fughetta in *Under Hamelin Hill*,[35] or the very act of composing an opera, is part of a communicative process. So too is the act of scoring for familiar ensembles, as in the string quartet of *Arcadiana* or the symphony orchestra of *These Premises are Alarmed*. But what is being communicated as part of this process? On the one hand, genre (and form, and so on) provides a framework for the listener – a cluster of expectations, based on past precedent. In the case of a composer working in the late twentieth century, the notion of genre carries with it not only its traditional (in this context, pre-twentieth century) associations, but also the traces of twentieth-century experiments with (or discarding of) generic models. As Jeffrey Kallberg has argued, genre therefore operates not so much as a system of classification, but rather as a rhetorical device: deviations from expectations can carry a powerful charge, throwing attention onto the specifics of the musical and expressive argument.[36]

30   *Towards* Asyla *(1990–97)*

The deliberate undercutting of climaxes in works such as the Chamber Symphony and ... *but all shall be well*, offering reflections and new perspectives on material rather than resolutions and closure, is one such example of how Adès plays with generic expectations (in this case, symphonic).

As with many of his contemporaries, Adès tends to avoid the use of generic, abstract titles; traditional (generic) expectations are often instead aroused through the use of programme notes and interviews. As Whittall has observed,[37] Adès's titles typically suggest multiple meanings. Thus, even before a note has been played, Adès extends an invitation (or even a demand!) for listeners to engage creatively with the material that they hear. This engagement is intensified when semantically rich titles are combined with evocative programme notes: the scenario Adès invented for *Living Toys* is an extreme example, providing an extra-musical narrative that frames the musical argument and 'explains' the order of clearly defined expressive sections. This narrative isn't strictly necessary, for the musical argument works in and of itself. But it does highlight the way in which Adès's material readily (and prolifically) enables a dialogue between external and internal sources (respectively, the narrative and the musical logic).

External references

Another such way is through Adès's use of intertextual reference. *Living Toys* contains a near-quotation of James Brown's 'I feel good' (bar 336; this is rather ironic, in that it is used in the violent 'Militiamen' movement). The title of the following movement, 'H.A.L.'s Death', is a reference to Stanley Kubrick's *2001: A Space Odyssey*, and Adès apes the climax of that film by having 'Daisy, Daisy' intoned slowly in the bass register (from bar 353). In pieces such as *Powder Her Face*, quotations arise thick and fast, typically when Adès gives substance to reminiscences of other works that emerge out of his own musical processes.[38] Cao notes how quotations are embedded into the opera's musical fabric,[39] but she also ascribes a critical function to them that enables a 'dialogue' between past and present.[40] Quotations can work 'sideways' too, providing links between 'high' and 'popular' culture,[41] or play with theory (the cover of Chamber Symphony has a Schenkerian analytical graph, and the horn call that permeates the work in various traditional and distorted forms makes play with cadential expectations). In short, Adès's use of quotation cannot be reduced to a simple formula. In some cases it is used to highlight mood and scene; in others, it provides a commentary on the context; in others still the invocation (and juxtaposition) of different styles, musical periods and contexts opens out an interpretative space that can be discursive, critical or ironic.

Adès recognises that the multiple quotations and stylistic allusions in his music leaves it open to charges of eclecticism. His defence is that they are a means of making 'what's under the surface clearer, by making it honestly unignorable that the surface is just that – transparent, evanescent – and moving through the available material in such a way that the real form becomes clearer'.[42] But such surface gestures are not *just* transparent, for styles can function *topically* in order to suggest extramusical content. The jazz influences in a work such as *Life Story*, and the use of rhythm and timbre to depict a matador in *Living Toys*, evoke particular

Towards Asyla *(1990–97)*   31

environments (urban and 'exotic' respectively) that colour listeners' responses to the underlying logic. Such associations are not therefore interchangeable, but rather a fundamental part of the musical experience.[43]

Expressive topics: the lament

The playful treatment of stylistic topics is one means by which Adès's music encourages an active, interpretative response from its listeners. Another is through the invocation of *expressive* topics. As noted in the previous chapter, Adès frequently draws on the lament and associated emotional states; it is a vital component of *Asyla*'s expressive world too. Perhaps the most important compositional resource at Adès's disposal in the portrayal of sorrow is the *pianto*, the falling semitone figure that traditionally connotes crying or weeping.[44] On the one hand, the *pianto* is a conventional musical gesture that, in its representation of a bodily action, requires no further explanation, save to note that once the figure is recognised as a symbol of crying, it no longer functions as 'purely' musical (that is, it has a meaning in addition to its role in the musical argument). It should be noted that not all semitones need be expressive of sadness: additional factors, such as rhythm, tempo, harmony and articulation can all have a bearing on their interpretation. Thus, the semitonal motion of the soprano's line in Example 2.1b (bars 22–28) takes on something of the *pianto*'s mournful quality by virtue of the slow speed and austere texture, tingeing the recollection of children's voices with sadness. By way of contrast, the jazzy drumming and double bass pizzicati of Example 2.5 steer the alto flute's melody into entirely different topical waters.

A clearer connection to traditional musical gestures can be found in the chromatically descending bass of Example 2.3. Here, the reference is that of the musical lament and the *passus duriusculus*, the chromatic descent from tonic to dominant typically located in the bass, as in the ground that underpins Dido's Lament in Purcell's *Dido and Aeneas*.[45]

Recent musicological writings have illustrated the continued presence of both the *pianto* and the lament in the music of the twentieth century. Significantly, their usage points to wider cultural changes, for the stylised weeping connotations of the late Renaissance *pianto* have been replaced by those of particular lamenting and grieving practices in the modern era.[46] Adès's use of the *pianto* also has cultural associations, one of which takes the form of a typically English melancholy.

Adès describes *Darknesse Visible* as an 'explosion of John Dowland's lute song "In Darknesse Let Mee Dwell"', in which he fragments the material of one of British music's most celebrated evocations of the melancholy, in order to discover and explore 'patterns latent in the original'.[47] Thus the opening <E F E> of Dowland's melody (bars 4–5, with the falling *pianto* nuancing the emotional resonances of the word 'darknesse') is given a tremulous reworking by Adès at the outset of his own piece (bars 1–3, and again in the bass, bars 8–10; see motif *n* in Examples 2.6a and b). This gesture unlocks the potential of the falling minor second to be expressive of sadness, as well as providing a more specific reference to Elizabethan melancholic traditions. On the other hand, Adès radically reworks

Example 2.6 Darknesse Visible. (a) bars 1–3; (b) bars 8–10; (c) bars 35–38; plus extracts from Dowland, 'In Darknesse Let Mee Dwell' (1610).

a decorated version of the *pianto* motif in bars 18–19 of Dowland's original (motif *p*), inverting the rising steps of Dowland's melody into racking, falling sevenths (bars 35–36; Example 2.6c), the embodied weeping of the embellished *pianto* intensified by a plunge into the depths of more recent expressionistic styles.

However, this angular treatment of the decorated *pianto* points as much to more recent British musical and cultural traditions as it does European modernism. The *locus classicus* for its falling sevenths is the ninth variation ('Nimrod') from Elgar's *Enigma Variations* Op. 36 (1899). Adès characteristically inverts these sevenths in 'O Albion', his ambivalent homage in *Arcadiana* to 'Nimrod'. Nevertheless, the allusion enables Adès to co-opt the cultural idea of late Edwardian British nostalgia into his evocation of idylls 'vanishing, vanished or imaginary'. Here the *pianto* is implied rather than stated, its presence felt in tender rising and falling seconds passed imitatively – and sequentially – around the ensemble. Whereas the reworked *pianto* motifs in *Darknesse Visible* aligned Renaissance representations of weeping and melancholy with more recent expressionistic musical styles, those in 'O Albion' posit connections between early twentieth-century nostalgia and the 'sighing' associations of the eighteenth-century *pianto*.[48]

The use of sequences in 'O Albion' points towards Adès's characteristically systematic treatment of the *pianto*. More typically, as in *The Fayrfax Carol*, the *pianto* (and the *passus duriusculus*, for that matter) emerges out of particular realisations of intervallic cycles. As with *Darknesse Visible*, the carol turns to the Renaissance, setting a poem that describes both the birth of Christ and Mary's premonition of his crucifixion. The opening bars embellish an expanded $\begin{Bmatrix} -1 \\ -2 \\ -2 \end{Bmatrix}$ harmonic progression (Example 2.7). The irregular rate of descent in each of the superimposed intervallic cycles (see the annotations to the analytical reduction) helps contribute to the highly expressive musical surface that evokes the *pianto* and implies a static tonal background of E♭ minor. The overall effect is akin to that of a single *pianto* gesture – a tear, a sigh – extended over some ten to fifteen seconds of time: a perpetual present, a frozen pose expressive of sadness. Despite the Renaissance text, the frigid emotional world afforded by the musical structures is redolent of late twentieth-century characterisations of immobilised grief.[49]

Through such means, Adès's highly allusive music invokes (though frequently with degrees of critical distance) a variety of historically situated cultural representations of sadness; it also refers to traditional musical techniques and contexts that are expressive of this emotion. One particularly relevant consequence of such invocations is that Adès's harmonic language, so often generated systematically rather than through tonal processes, retains a sense of consonance and dissonance, of tension and release. Thus the falling semitones that permeate the above examples share the expressive and syntactical qualities of appoggiaturas (the soprano G♭ of Example 2.7, bar 3, can be felt to resolve to the subsequent F). Similarly, the expanding intervals of his descending leaps gain from evocations of both the exaggerated rhetoric of expressionism as well as an English tone of voice. Finally, the propensity for system enables a refraction – or in Adès's terms, an explosion – of more traditional melodic–harmonic patterns. All this enables the

34 *Towards* Asyla *(1990–97)*

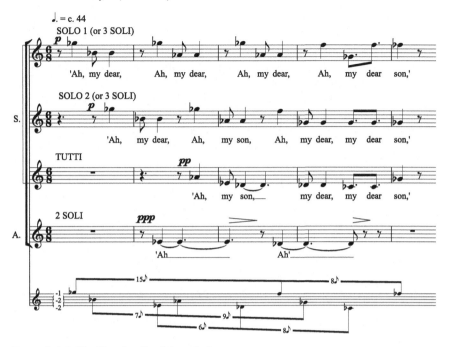

Example 2.7 *The Fayrfax Carol*, bars 1–5.

play of cultural and expressive codes that combines the *pianto*'s cultural significations with other musical and historical associations – and this is where listeners must make an interpretative leap – in order to modify the basic emotional state of which the *pianto* is expressive. In the cases considered above, 'sadness' has been nuanced by cultural practices of melancholy, nostalgia and grief.

Metaphor

The play of musical, historical and cultural codes provides one means by which Adès's musical structures connect with the external world. Another is through metaphor. For Adès, 'all music is metaphorical, always', and his descriptions of his music frequently result in the deployment of multiple networks of metaphor, often mixed.[50]

Many of Adès's metaphors recall those of traditional musical discourse. The notion of 'organic' music is a typical Romantic conceit: '[i]t doesn't matter what the idea [behind the work] was – the important thing is that realisation that the thing is alive [...] When you have that feeling, you're very lucky because you are suddenly inside a living organism'.[51] Adès suggests that he stands independently from such processes but also, as composer, that he is able to harness and guide them:

> the moment a note is written down, for me, it immediately starts to move, it starts to slide down the page or up the page or move around. The extent

Towards Asyla *(1990–97)* 35

to which you bully it and push it towards stability – that's what creates the energy in the piece and defines its position relative to reality.[52]

Although Adès's metaphors frequently suggest life on the molecular level, he also invests in the music a sense of humanity: Cao notes the large number of performance instructions designed at replicating vocality,[53] and much of Adès's music, vocal and instrumental, has an overtly theatrical element. This is played out on-stage in *Catch* and *Under Hamelin Hill*, in which performers walk on and (in the case of *Catch*) off the stage. Adès did not return to this device in his later music, perhaps because it reinforces visually what is happening already in the music. Rather, drama and theatricality finds other outlets in his music, as in *Living Toys*. Here, and elsewhere in Adès's output, specific instruments take on clear roles within the unfolding musical narrative, but it should also be emphasised that instruments and musical ideas can take on *multiple* roles: meaning emerges out of the context; it is not fixed.

Another recurrent metaphor is that of landscape, announced in the subject matter and titles of *The Lover in Winter* and *Five Eliot Landscapes*, and prominent in *Arcadiana*. If these works emphasise exterior environments, then others, such as *These Premises are Alarmed* and *Life Story* highlight interiors (a concert hall and motel room respectively; *Powder Her Face*, too, takes place in contained rooms, most notably a hotel room). More abstractly, musical arguments can be described in terms of the passage through environments (a traditional way of conceptualising both form and musical time). Adès is fond in this respect of describing music as a 'vehicle' to carry us through (musical) space, or of music as a building through which we pass.[54] In the former case in particular, metaphors that suggest a cinematographic representation of landscape are common, and in particular the sense of shifting perspective: 'One way I tried of ending things – I did this as early as in my Chamber Symphony – is suddenly to have an aerial view of the whole thing. *In Seven Days* also pulls the camera out at the end. *Tevot* does that, *Asyla* does that.'[55] Cao has observed the translation of cinematic techniques into musical and dramatic processes in *Powder Her Face*,[56] and the cinematic references in *Living Toys* have already been noted. One consequence of all of this is that the musical landscapes in Adès's music are presented at a remove – the filmic metaphor suggests that we are experiencing a mediated, mediatised representation of a landscape, a simulacrum rather than the landscape 'itself'.

Adès typically employs metaphors conventionally, to explain the unfamiliar and allusive (the musical content) by using something familiar and concrete (such as visual imagery). But there is another sense in which one might understand 'music as metaphor, always'. Michael Spitzer, drawing on Ricoeur, notes that the quasi-corporeality of musical material that emerges when we appreciate such material 'in itself', as an acoustic phenomena, rather than in 'grasping it functionally as part of an internal compositional logic', can itself be considered as metaphor.[57] Our apprehension of such *figural* metaphors occurs on the one hand as an infringement of grammaticality; this infringement, in turn, creates a new meaning at a higher level whilst retaining the older meaning 'as a source of productive resistance'.[58] Returning to Example 2.2a, the soprano's G♯ is a disruption to the grammatical norm

36   *Towards* Asyla *(1990–97)*

provided by the expanding interval series in the voice. Following Spitzer's argument, we can say that the G♯ has the potential to become quasi-corporeal, drawing attention to itself as a discrete event. But in its wider context, taking into account the interaction between the vocal line with other strata, its function within the general harmonic language can be understood (that is, at a higher level it is assimilated). Yet even though the G♯ can be 'explained' by this context – we can give it meaning – it retains something of the original sense of (figural) strain and shock.

The accumulation of figural metaphors such as this G♯ across a work results in a situation in which figures 'can no longer be assimilated into an overarching interpretational context, as was the case with grammar. With this path blocked, the listener's only resort is to relate to the music in a mode that is open, dynamic, and self-critical' – in short, an active rather than passive interpretative stance.[59] By encouraging listeners to engage critically, drawing on whatever interpretative framework they have to hand, musical metaphors have the capacity to enable us to 'perceive reality in different ways'.[60] This, perhaps, is one of the means by which we might understand Adès's claim that 'I think what happens [when composing] is that you try to create *a simulacrum of the real world*, a reflection. The piece is *a way of trying to make the real world real again*, in a sense'.[61]

Writing of British fiction in the 1990s, Nick Bentley has observed that '[t]he uncertain relationship between the real and the unreal, and the past, present and future that challenged a teleological and rational model of historical progress resulted in many narratives that engaged in self-reflection, and the transparency (or opacity) of writing'.[62] Adès's self-reflective use of figural metaphors, the transparency of his stylistic references and musical procedures, and his historical breadth of reference aligns him with such authors. But Adès's emphasis on his musical logic, reflected in the structuring of this chapter, should guard us against the notion that his music is simply communicating something to us that can be readily verbalised: 'When you're making a work – any artist will have a little bit of this – you're trying to deal with the problem of being and consciousness in some way, really. And in the musical work particularly, you can end up with something that deals with that in a way that you couldn't through just speaking about it'.[63]

Asyla

Asyla marks a watershed moment in Adès's artistic development: a synthesis and development of the trends surveyed in this chapter. For the composer, '[i]t's been a turning-point, I'd realised how small-scale some of my music had been. It's an event in my life'.[64] In some ways *Asyla* was more than just an event in Adès's life, for its composition documents Adès's burgeoning international success:

> The first time I wrote any music in America would have been in 1996, when I first went to Los Angeles. And I was halfway through writing *Asyla*. I'd already written the first two movements in a form that was fairly close to that of the finished piece. I was aware that the third movement needed to be a kind of dance movement [...] And then I sat down in Los Angeles, in a windowless room in the Dorothy Chandler Pavilion [...] And in two or

three sittings I had the whole thing sketched in Los Angeles. I don't know whether that would have happened here at home in London. I did much of the detail in London, but I was definitely conscious of an opening up of a new landscape over there.[65]

Consequently, '*Asyla* is [...] beginning to move away from London. It's more about turning away. It's nothing very mysterious, but I just happen to like it, those different lights and spaces. So there is some relation between the place and the music, but it's not absolute'.[66]

There is perhaps something tangible of both London and Los Angeles in *Asyla*, for Adès 'wrote the score so that it would contain that sound that we live with all the time now: that electrical hum or hiss, that sheen on the texture of life, especially in a city, where it is inescapable but takes on so many different, iridescent colours'.[67] Thus, for instance, the opening of the first movement of *Asyla* uses string harmonics to blur the edges of harmonies; elsewhere, high pedal points and a barrage of percussion create a continuous background noise. But perhaps most important in the presentation of the shifting colours of city life is the use of an expanded orchestra (see Figure 2.1). The timbral range is extended still further by means of frequent requests for instrumental doublings, unusual playing techniques (such as striking the outside of the timpani) and altering sonority by means of mutes and muffles. The expanded percussion section is predominantly metallic in timbre, including water gongs, cutlery and paint tins. The result is a kaleidoscopic

3 flutes (2nd doubling piccolo; 3rd doubling piccolo and bass flute)
3 oboes (2nd doubling cor anglais; 3rd doubling bass oboe and cor anglais *ad lib.*)
3 clarinets (2nd doubling bass clarinet; 3rd doubling contrabass clarinet)
3 bassoons (3rd doubling contrabassoon)

4 horns
3 trumpets (3rd doubling piccolo trumpet)
3 trombones (2 tenor, 1 bass)
Tuba
Percussion (6 players): 5 or 6 timpani; 3 or 4 rototoms (tunable); 5 very small tuned finger drums or bongos; 2 bell plates; tuned cowbells; 4 tubular bells; Chinese cymbal; 2 hi-hat cymbals; 3 large tins (e.g. paint tins); geo-phone; tam-tam; 2 water gongs; large ratchet; washboard; 2 bass drums; kit bass drum (flat); 4 tuned gongs; 4 suspended cymbals; very small choke cymbal; side drum; sandpaper blocks; bag full of metal knives and forks; glockenspiel; clash cymbals; small ratchet; sizzle cymbal; large gong; 6 other gongs; crotales;
Grand piano (doubling upright piano with practice pedal and normal tuning)
Upright piano (with practice pedal, tuned ¼ tone lower than orchestral pitch; doubling celesta and grand piano [as second player])
Harp

Strings

Figure 2.1 Instrumentation in *Asyla*.

38 *Towards* Asyla *(1990–97)*

tumult of sound and effect, of 'shrieks, wails, moans, bangs, mis-tunings, pain, sadness, alienation and the extremes of noise and quiet'.[68]

The disorienting effect of the sound is intentional. For all of the virtuosic writing and tantalising effects of Adès's two previous works for full orchestra, ... *but all shall be well* and *These Premises are Alarmed, Asyla* represents a significant advance in defamiliarising the sound of the symphony orchestra. As Adès notes, over the course of the twentieth century, 'composers have evolved, whereas the orchestra has been frozen in a pre-First World War state'.[69] Adès attempts to rethink the orchestra from within, not just though the battery of percussion, but through the ways in which the traditional instruments are used on their own and in relation to each other.

It is perhaps for this reason, and not just due to his ambivalence towards generic titles, that Adès avoids describing *Asyla* as a symphony, despite being in four movements and employing an orchestra. For Mathias Tarnopolsky, 'if we try too hard to relate *Asyla* to the shape of the Romantic and Classical symphony then we are missing the point'.[70] Tarnopolsky doesn't state what the point *is*, however, and to judge the reception of *Asyla*, his warning was not heeded by critics. Thus, Andrew Clark describes *Asyla* as a 'symphony in all but name',[71] and Paul Driver concludes that it is an 'old-fashioned cyclic symphony'.[72] It seems more likely that Tarnopolsky was suggesting that *Asyla*'s should be considered less as a formal mould (a 'shape') and more as a communicative act – a set of expectations that a composer might toy with – offers a fruitful vantage point for understanding *Asyla* and the ways it brings the genre in and out of focus.

Accordingly, Andrew Clements's description of *Asyla*'s 'marvellously clear shape and *logic*' highlights the important role that symphonic thought ('logic') plays in the work,[73] and how it marries together – or holds in opposition – its constituent elements as part of a musical and expressive discourse. In this respect, *Asyla* represents a significant advance for Adès, for he explores the implications of his material on a far grander canvas than he had hitherto attempted. Although a full inventory of these building blocks is beyond even a book-length study, Example 2.8 presents some of the principal motivic material that is developed throughout the work.[74] This example should be viewed with caution: although a good deal of emphasis is placed on pitch and rhythmic material in the coming chapters, to assume that *Asyla*'s symphonism resides solely in these domains would indeed be to miss the point. To this provisional list we might thus add textural motifs, such as in the deployment of extreme registers, or the contrast between sharply defined textures and those suffused in the glow of string harmonics or tuned percussion. Equally, the use of specific timbres, such as the horn, is as much a part of the musical design as expanded harmonic progressions. There is also the 'symphonic' development of metaphor, both musical (in the presentation of and playing with generic norms) and extramusical.

The early publicity for *Asyla* made much of the fact that the strained relationship between the work and the symphony as genre (and symphony orchestra as vehicle) enables an exploration of the 'pull between the safety of tradition and

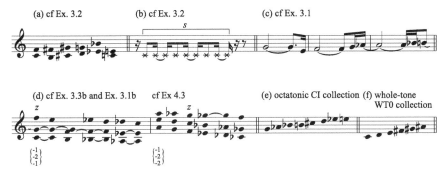

Example 2.8 Asyla Op. 17, motivic material (pitch and rhythm). (a) dyads; (b) drum beats; (c) trochaic rhythms; (d) expanded harmonic progressions; (e) octatonic patterns; (f) whole-tone patterns.

daunting freedom'.[75] In this sense, *Asyla* can be considered a large-scale metaphor of asylum (elsewhere, Adès summed up his artistic position at the time as 'whether to be safe, or mad');[76] specific details within the argument as it unfolds explores other facets of the metaphor. But here there is a signal difference in modes of presentation: whereas the musical argument of *Asyla* unfolds continuously, the metaphorical content (at least, as it relates to the work's title) does not – and indeed, *cannot* – offer a continuous (verbal) discourse on the nature of asylum and our attitudes towards it. Rather, the idea of asylum is presented in a series of snapshots that dynamically examine through the medium of music different facets of how we as a culture understand, or might come to understand, it and which in turn provides a framework through which listeners grapple with the interpretative challenges posed by the musical design.

Notes

1. Ross, 'Roll Over, Beethoven', p. 126.
2. The use of non-aligned patterns recalls the similarly non-directed first movement of Messiaen's *Quatuor pour la fin du temps* (1941).
3. I am distinguishing between *series* in which the intervals between pitches change, and *cycles* where they do not.
4. Adès talks of 'expanded harmonies': see *TA:FON*, p. 152. Staggered expanded harmonic progressions, in which the cycles move at different speeds, can be found in Examples 2.7 and 2.8d.
5. Many of these themes can however be heard in nascent form in *The Lover in Winter*.
6. Bernard Holland, 'Burying the Hatchet, Sounding Fine', *New York Times* (23 November 2002).
7. In the introduction to *TA:FON*, Tom Service cites (in no particular order, and with no attempt to be comprehensive) Couperin, Ligeti, Beethoven, Kurtág, Berlioz, Sibelius, Janáček and Gerald Barry as positive influences, and Mahler, Brahms, Britten and Wagner as more problematic forebears (pp. viii–ix); to this list we might immediately add Bach, Schubert, Nancarrow, Ives, Stravinsky and Berg, along with many others.
8. For Adès on Berg, see *TA:FON*, pp. 120, 123, 128 and 129. On Ives (and Nancarrow), see Ross, 'Roll Over, Beethoven', p. 116.

40 *Towards* Asyla *(1990–97)*

9 Critics most often cite Berg as an influence: one of the earliest comparisons can be found in Andrew Clements's review of *Powder Her Face*: 'There's a good deal of Berg in some of the harmonic working [... but] the sound world [...] is totally fresh'. 'Crocodile Tears Before Bedtime', *Guardian* (3 July 1995). For a technical introduction to both Berg and Adès's use of interval cycles, see Philip Stoecker, 'Aligned Cycles in Thomas Adès's Piano Quintet', *Music Analysis*, 33/i (2014), pp. 32–64. On Ives's use of interval cycles, see Philip Lambert, 'Interval Cycles as Compositional Resources in the Music of Charles Ives', *Music Theory Spectrum*, 12/i (1990), pp. 43–82.

10 'Adès declare avoir "trouvé" et non "inventé" cette échelle'. Cao, *Thomas Adès Le Voyageur*, p. 38.

11 Both Berg and Nono employed 'all-interval series' (see, for instance, the *Lyric Suite* and *Il canto sospeso*); Carter made frequent use of an 'all-interval tetrachord'.

12 Morrison, 'Prodigy with a Notable Talent'. Morrison notes that the approach the 'doesn't sound all that different from the mathematical aridity of 1950s serialism'.

13 Cao, *Thomas Adès Le Voyageur*, p. 39.

14 The complete expanding intervallic series can be reordered as an *octatonic scale* of alternating semitones and tones. From this perspective, the soprano's G♯ belongs to the octatonic collection <C♯ D E F G G♯ B♭ B> that is implied by the opening notes of the vocal line. There are three discrete transpositions of the octatonic collection. Set CI is the octatonic collection beginning on C♯, as here; CII begins on D <D E♭ F F♯ etc.>; CIII begins on E♭ <E♭ E F♯ G etc.>. The use of angle brackets < > indicates an *ordered* collection of pitches, whether melodic (indicating pitch succession) or harmonic (reading from the bass upwards).

15 Ross notes that it is a trait of twentieth-century British music to combine aspects of twentieth-century modernism with common chords without the need for 'violent stylistic lurches'. He cites Alexander Goehr and Oliver Knussen, but the list could be extended much further, to include various near-contemporaries of Adès such as George Benjamin, Julian Anderson and Mark-Anthony Turnage ('Roll Over, Beethoven', p. 124). Adès was also struck by Ligeti's incorporation of traditional chords in his Horn Trio (1982), which seemed to him to be 'a genuine discovery' (*TA:FON*, pp. 140–1).

16 *TA:FON*, pp. 32–3. It should be noted that Adès treats fourth and fifths as equivalent: 'I hear the fourth as an inverted fifth; the top note is the bass' (*TA:FON*, p. 32). There is a parallel with the treatment of these intervals in much atonal music (and set theory); I, too, shall be treating them as more-or-less interchangeable. See also Dominic Wells, 'Plural Styles, Personal Style: The Music of Thomas Adès', *Tempo*, 66 (April 2012), pp. 2–14.

17 See John Roeder, 'Co-operating Continuities in the Music of Thomas Adès', *Music Analysis*, 25/i–ii (2006), pp. 121–54, at p. 128, and 'A Transformational Space Structuring the Counterpoint in Adès's "Auf dem Wasser zu singen"', *Music Theory Online*,15/i (March 2009) www.mtosmt.org/issues/mto.09.15.1/mto.09.15.1.roeder_space.html. Wells notes the similarity between the openings of *Arcadiana* and Ligeti's Violin Concerto. 'Plural Styles', pp. 7–8.

18 See Jaqueline Susan Greenwood, 'Selected Vocal and Chamber Music of Thomas Adès: Stylistic and Contextual Issues' (PhD diss., Kingston University, 2013), p. 382.

19 The use of curly braces in this context indicates a collection of pitches (in this case, a *dyad* [i.e. a pair of notes]) in which register and order are not important.

20 See Greenwood, 'Selected Vocal and Chamber Music', p. 385.

21 Roeder, 'Co-operating Continuities', pp. 145–8. Many composers have employed twelve-note melodies in non-serial contexts, such as the theme of Britten's *The Turn of the Screw*. Adès's dislike of this work (see *TA:FON*, pp. 122–3 and 174) draws attention to the distance he perceives between Britten's practice and his own.

22 Anon., 'Not Yet 30, Britain's Leading New Composer Goes From Strength to Strength', *Economist* (12 June 1999).

23 Taruskin, 'A Surrealist Composer', pp. 147–8.

24 For a comparison of Adès and Nancarrow's approaches to rhythm, see Andrew McManus, 'Nancarrow's Rhythmic Structures in Thomas Adès's *Asyla*' (MA diss., Eastman School of Music, 2009).

25 Where there is an underlying 'pulse' to a stratum, a duration has been given above the curly braces in Example 2.4. Thus each chord in the stratum beginning in the second stave of bar 45 is four quavers long; coming in in the next bar, the chords of the stratum in the upper stave are each nineteen semiquavers long. For further discussion of this passage, see Roeder, 'Co-operating Continuities', pp. 135–6, and Emma Gallon, 'Narrativities in the Music of Thomas Adès' (PhD diss., Lancaster University, 2011), pp. 118–20.

26 For an extended analysis of the second movement of *Traced Overhead*, see Aleksandra Vojcic, 'Rhythm as Form: Rhythmic Hierarchy in Later Twentieth-Century Piano Music' (PhD diss., City University of New York, 2007), pp. 341–51.

27 See Greenwood, 'Selected Vocal and Chamber Music of Thomas Adès', pp. 240–1.

28 See Roeder, 'Co-operating Continuities', pp. 123–4.

29 Huw Belling, 'Thinking Irrational, Thomas Adès and New Rhythms' (MA diss., Royal College of Music, 2010), pp. 9, 11.

30 Composer's Note to Score of Chamber Symphony Op. 2 (Faber Music, 1995). There is a similarity here with Ligeti's injection of irregularities into otherwise mechanistic rhythmic patterns.

31 *TA:FON*, p. 138.

32 '[I]n *Powder Her Face*, I wrote the sounds of the eras into each scene – so that the pre-war scene would have a Palm Court acoustic […] and the Fifties scene the acoustic of a Paul Anka pop record' *TA:FON*, p. 114.

33 *TA:FON*, pp. 142–3.

34 Also on the programme was Adès's *The Origin of the Harp* and (featuring Adès as pianist) Schubert's piano duet *Lebenstürme* and Nancarrow's *Two Canons for Ursula*. Writing of *Eletút* (*Lebenslauf*), but it could almost be of the opening of *Asyla*, Zoltán Farkas has noted that '[t]he result of the quarter tone mistuning and the strict canonic motion of the parts in consecutive seconds is that the lines of the polyphonic texture do not seem to be thinly engraved lines but rather thick stripes drawn in crayon. And these thick lines glow, pulsate, vibrate disquietingly. […] Because of the lower second piano the whole sound gravitates downwards as if attracted by some power towards the abyss. The final result of the mistuning is paradoxical: clarity and powerful lines, at the same time blurred obscurity; the synchrony of harshness and softness'. 'The Path of a Hölderlin Topos: Wandering Ideas in Kurtág's Compositions', *Studia Musicologica Academiae Scientiarum Hungaricae*, T. 43, Fasc. 3/4 (2002), pp. 289–310, at. p. 300.

35 Cao notes that the Fughetta was written to fulfil Cambridge University requirements (*Thomas Adès Le Voyageur*, p. 12).

36 Jeffrey Kallberg, 'The Rhetoric of Genre: Chopin's Nocturne in G Minor', *19th-Century Music*, 11/iii (1988), pp. 238–61, at p. 243.

37 Whittall, 'Thomas Adès', p. 156.

38 See *TA:FON*, pp. 27, 76 and 152–3.

39 See Cao, *Thomas Adès Le Voyageur*, pp. 69–84, and especially her discussion of Adès's use of the *Tristan* chord (p. 82).

40 Ibid., p. 29.

41 Adès has praised both Poulenc and Berg for their ability to incorporate popular music into their own (*TA:FON*, pp. 22–3).

42 Ibid., p. 80.

43 Massey has noted how Adès's use of quotation draws 'listeners deeper in, rather than leaving them glancing off a shimmering surface of reference and allusion'. 'Thomas Adès at 40', p. 197.

44 On the history of the *pianto* up to the music of Wagner, see Raymond Monelle, *The Sense of Music: Semiotic Essays* (Princeton: Princeton University Press, 2000), pp. 66–73.

42 *Towards* Asyla *(1990–97)*

On the use of the *pianto* as part of a broader discussion of lament in the twentieth century, see David Metzer, *Musical Modernism at the Turn of the Twenty-First Century* (Cambridge: Cambridge University Press, 2009), pp. 144–74.

45 Monelle, *The Sense of Music*, pp. 73–9.

46 See, for instance Amy Bauer, *Ligeti's Laments: Nostalgia, Exoticism, and the Absolute* (Aldershot: Ashgate, 2011); Jonathan Cross, *Harrison Birtwistle: The Mask of Orpheus* (Aldershot: Ashgate, 2009); and Arnold Whittall, *Exploring Twentieth-Century Music: Tradition and Innovation* (Cambridge: Cambridge University Press, 2003).

47 Composer's Note to Score of *Darknesse Visible* (Faber Music, 1998).

48 On the use of both major and minor seconds in eighteenth-century musical sighs, see Monelle, *The Sense of Music*, p. 70.

49 See Elizabet Kübler-Ross, *On Death and Dying* (New York: Macmillan, 1969).

50 *TA:FON*, p. 5.

51 Ibid., p. 40.

52 Ibid., p. 54. On 'reality', see below.

53 *Thomas Adès Le Voyageur*, p. 101.

54 *TA:FON*, pp. 41, 39.

55 Ibid., p. 44.

56 *Thomas Adès Le Voyageur*, p. 72.

57 Michael Spitzer, *Metaphor and Musical Thought* (Chicago and London: University of Chicago Press, 2004), p. 105.

58 Ibid., pp. 95, 97. Thus, in the sentence 'no man is an island', the word 'island' draws attention to itself because 'men' and 'islands' are two distinct concepts that normally do not belong together. At the level of the sentence, however, we assimilate 'island' by interpreting the new meaning that arises from the bringing together of these concepts, even though traces of the original disruption remain.

59 Ibid., p. 111.

60 Ibid., p. 101.

61 *TA:FON*, p. 54 (emphasis added). See Chapter 7 for more on this point.

62 Bentley, 'Introduction', p. 7.

63 *TA:FON*, p. 52.

64 Anon., 'Not Yet 30'.

65 *TA:FON*, pp. 166–7. Adès was participating in a concert with the Los Angeles Philharmonic.

66 Ibid., p. 171.

67 Ibid., p. 114.

68 Alan Rusbridger, 'Rattle's Glorious Berlin Debut', *Guardian* (9 September 2002).

69 Cited in Mathias Tarnopolsky, Programme Note to Thomas Adès, *Asyla* (1997).

70 Tarnopolsky, Ibid.

71 Andrew Clark, 'Adès Delights the Ear', *Financial Times* (31 October 1997).

72 Paul Driver, 'A New Spin on the Cycle', *Sunday Times* (12 October 1997).

73 Andrew Clements, 'Thomas Adès Takes over the Asylum', *BBC Music Magazine* (December 1997).

74 There are two distinct whole-tone collections: WT0, as in Example 2.8f, and WT1 {C♯, D♯, F, G, A, B}. All other transpositions are enharmonically equivalent to one or other of these sets.

75 Tarnopolsky, Programme Note to *Asyla*.

76 Anon., 'Not Yet 30'.

3 'Trying to find refuge'

The symphonic logic of the first movement

The first movement of *Asyla* emerges from a musical 'problem':

> I began that piece, *Asyla*, by writing the melody, in fact, where the horns enter. And […] I found that I had to start to compose the harmonisation at the same time in order to understand how the melody was moving. And then the accompaniment, the harmonisation, began to take on a life of its own.[1]

The opening of the melody, a lyrical but expansive line based on the CI octatonic scale, scored for three unison horns, is given in Example 3.1a.[2] The trochaic rhythm of the first bar is modified in subsequent bars so that the longer notes begin to anticipate, rather than coincide with, the notated downbeat. The fourth pair of pitches are in turn elongated so that the close of the melody falls on the 'expected' downbeat. But the conclusion is unexpected: the fall of a perfect fifth to an F♯, rather than the (anticipated) rise to a D creates a kink in the tail, establishing a musical tension, a pattern of inclusion and exclusion, for the F♯ does not belong to the underlying octatonic set of the rest of the melody. By disrupting the octatonic 'grammaticality' established by the opening of the melody, the F♯ draws attention to itself, becomes *figural*: it requires an interpretative response.[3]

Perhaps Adès felt impelled to 'compose the harmonisation' in order to create a higher-level context within which this F♯ might be assimilated. However, although the long notes of the melody belong to the resulting chords (for instance, the opening G is harmonised by combined G and D major triads, and the A♭ by successive E and A♭ major triads), the harmony is neither octatonic and nor does it provide a higher-level 'explanation' for the melody. Rather, the harmonic material appears to be slightly out of kilter with the melody (and vice versa), like opposing faces of a Rubik's cube in which one has been turned by 45°.

One way to understand the first movement, therefore, is in terms of the 'symphonic logic' arising from the interaction between a long, unfolding melody and the semi-independent harmonic environments through which it passes. For Adès, symphonic thought is not unique to the symphony as a genre, but relates instead to

Example 3.1 *Asyla* Op. 17/i, melodic details. (a) bars 14–18; (b) bars 27–33; (c) bars 52–57; (d) bars 69–73.

Example 3.1 (Continued)

46 'Trying to find refuge'

the manner of thinking through musical problems: 'Chopin's pieces [...] are very definitely symphonic because there's a logic from the first note to the last, you just may not be able to parse exactly what the logic is.'[4] Conversely

> Wagner is not interested in releasing the inherent, organic power – what I would mean by genuinely 'symphonic' power – of his (often magnificent) cells. It's just a pose. Good symphonies are often in some ways an unfolding sequence of miniatures. They have to go through miniature forms as they go along, and what bothers me with Wagner's music is that there's a pretence of some kind of symphonic thought where there actually isn't any.[5]

These miniatures, or entire movements (as in the case of Chopin's pieces), might have distinctive generic or topical associations that interact with the abstract musical logic:

> [t]he topos might be a cantilena, or a recitative and aria, or it might be pastoral, or it might be a tempest scene, or it might be any number of things in one movement. [...] often the symphonic dialogue is a struggle between that topos, or genre, and some logic in the material.[6]

And it is via such means that 'with Sibelius, the function of symphonic completeness passed from the "abstract" into the "metaphorical", and I think it has stayed there. I think he was the first to break, painfully, the mistaken idea that a symphonic argument had to have a sort of structural order to it'.[7]

Adès's understanding of symphonism thus enables conceptual motion from abstract musical procedures via genre and topic to metaphor (and back). Accordingly, no incongruity exists between his account of the genesis of the horn melody and the extramusical imagery that he attached to it. During the procession of composition, Adès

> had the idea of images of huge crowds of people moving across that space, a space that was unpopulated, fleeing to safety, trying to find their own refuge, and of course there's political implications to that – it's an image you see all the time, from the Hungarian refugees in the '50s through to very much the present day.[8]

Adès's comments are consistent with the idea that the music came first and the extramusical image second. Nevertheless, the idea of refugees provides a vivid metaphor for the types of musical process found in Example 3.1a: the sense of a forced quest ('trying to find [...] refuge') for a place where melody and harmony can be in equilibrium maps on neatly to the images Adès describes. Although the visual metaphor thus provides a way into interpreting the movement, the prior existence of the latter suggests that the quest for safety is not what the music is 'about'.

But on the other hand, it becomes *precisely* what the music is about. Once the association between music and image is established, in programme notes as well as in the title of the work, the range of interpretative options is narrowed, channelling listeners' attention towards those musical features that can be made interpretatively to 'fit' the image, and inhibiting the apprehension or understanding of those features that do not. It is therefore significant that Adès draws attention to the *political* implications of his chosen, publicised image, not least given the contemporary discourse that surrounded asylum (see Chapter 7).

To interpret the music in this light is not to point to the depiction of any specific group of refugees, but rather to examine the ways in which musical procedures can be considered analogous to the general experience of seeking asylum. Instead of asking who is fleeing, from whom, via what route, and why (and so on), one might ask how the music can be understood as evocative of flight, danger and particular environments. The answers to such questions give some insight into how music might begin to represent metaphorically such a subject. In the case of the first movement, the symphonic logic manifested by the interaction between melody and harmony, considered alongside the topical worlds in which they are presented, provides a compelling metaphor for the turmoil, physical and emotional, experienced by refugees in flight.[9]

Formal overview

Even though the movement lasts for less than six minutes, its grand sweep, as characterised by the expansive horn melody, suggests something considerably more substantial. An impression of inexorable momentum is gained in part through the proportional halving of section lengths. On the accompanying CD to this book, the contrasting middle section (B) lasts roughly half the time of the combined introduction and main thematic area (A) (1'31" and 3'02" respectively, discounting the ten-second silence at the outset. See Table 3.1). The reprise of the thematic material (Section A') and coda result in another halving of length (0'48"), in a dramatic compression and acceleration of the material presented earlier in the movement. The sensation of flight is thus built into the formal design.

The formal clarity assists with the presentation and identification of generic and topical conventions. The introduction evokes, as well as departs from, symphonic precedents through its use of harmony, timbre and texture. Section A stages conflicts between melody and harmony, between pastoral and popular stylistic topics, and between harmonic flux and stability. In comparison to the extended lines of Section A, Section B offers a fragmentary discourse riven by conflict. There is a shift from the outer world to the inner world in which extremes of violence are juxtaposed with laments. An emphatic reprise of the main melody is one of a number of formal expectations fulfilled in both the recapitulation (Section A') and the ensuing coda, but their intensification of the symphonic argument ensures that any sense of closure they grant is at best provisional, if not illusory.

48 *'Trying to find refuge'*

Table 3.1 Formal overview of *Asyla*, first movement

Section	Bars/Track Timing (CD #1)	Comments	Duration (seconds)
Intro.	1–13 [0:09]	Harmonic focus; tuned percussion prominent	35
A	14–27 [0:44]	First of four strophes; horns have melody	38
	28–51 [1:22]	Second strophe; melody in strings (then strings and horn)	34
	52–68 [1:56]	Third strophe; melody given to solo cello (then upper strings and trumpets)	31
	69–78 [2:27]	Final strophe; flutes, clarinets and violas have melody	29
	79–82 [2:56]	Closing section: tuned percussion prominent again	15
B	83–101 [3:11]	Two varied statements based around violent trumpet outbursts	34
	102–114 [3:45]	Contrasting section: homophonic material in the wind over melodic idea in bass	20
	115–139 [4:05]	Superimposition and development of ideas from bars 83–114	37
A'	140–154 [4:42]	Compressed recapitulation of A	35
Coda	155–165 [5:17]	Varied reprise of bars 1–13	13

Timings taken from CD accompanying this book.

Introduction (bars 1–13)

The movement emerges out of silence with a peal of cowbells; string harmonics and continual decoration from an upright piano tuned a quarter-tone flat impart a ghostly aura to the sound (see Example 3.2a). Other spectres haunt the music, for the material evokes the Brucknerian habit of opening symphonic works with a tremolando.[10] Suggestions of flight are withheld at this stage; instead, a 'struggle between [...] topos, or genre, and some logic in the material' emerges as evocations of the symphonic genre come in to conflict with the unfolding musical procedures.

The most famous precursor to such an introduction, that of Beethoven's Ninth Symphony, begins with a tremolando on A that is retrospectively revealed to be a dominant to the tonic D minor. The canonic importance of this symphony in turn establishes certain expectations when encountering later works, so that one familiar with the symphonic repertoire might initially (and incorrectly) hear Bruckner's opening tremolandi as dominants rather than tonics. The expressive charge of Beethoven's opening comes from the surprising accumulation of dominant tension where a tonic is expected, and Bruckner's from the grand unfolding of the tonic (where perhaps a dominant was implied). Common to both, however, is that the function of the tremolando pitch only becomes clear in retrospect.

Asyla plays against such expectations. Adès steers a fine line between the establishment of a system (thereby offering harmonic bearings) and the undermining of it. Rather than the bare perfect fifth of Beethoven's Ninth Symphony, Adès begins with the dyad of a fourth {C, F}, and infuses life into it via non-tonal procedures:

> if you progress that logically and stack fourth upon fourth upon fourth, you wind up with total entropy, with all twelve notes of the chromatic scale as a sort of block. So to make the thing quiver and spring to life, I would want to move the upper one upwards by a semitone, so a fourth and one step above: C, F and then F sharp. In *Asyla* in fact it quivers by a quarter-tone either side and expands.[11]

Common to all parts of the introduction is the way that the arpeggiation of the harmonies in both the cowbells and timpani progresses upwards in waves; a reduction of the harmonic progression of bars 1–13 is given in Example 3.2b. Bars 1–6 establish an intervallic pattern and its disruption; this is repeated, with an elision, in bars 8–10. There are two principles at work here: first, dyads tend to be linked by semitonal voice-leading motion (thus, {C, F} opens out to {B, F♯}), and second, when viewed as fifths rather than fourths, the lower and upper notes belong respectively to the WT1 and WT0 whole-tone cycles. Yet as soon as the pattern is established, it breaks down: were Adès to follow the sequential pattern strictly, the fifth and sixth pairs would be {A, E} and {E♭, B♭}. Instead, the anticipated {A, E} is omitted and a 'foreign' interval, the major third {C, E} brought in. Both John Roeder and Aaron Travers hear cadential allusions in this conclusion; for Roeder, there is an implied imperfect cadence in F; for Travers, 'an almost quasi-tonal cadence' in C major.[12]

The D♭ major chord that follows (bar 7; CD#1 0:27), scored for timpani, harp and water gong, provides timbral and registral contrast. The annotations to Example 3.2b demonstrate its enharmonic relationship with the opening intervallic pattern ({C♯, G♯} and {D♭, A♭}) and how it connects to the underlying whole-tone cycles and semitonal voice-leading.[13] Nevertheless, the chord remains only partially assimilated into the unfolding musical discourse. It returns again after the varied restatement of the opening chord progression as part of a cryptic concluding statement that leaves unanswered whether the section as a whole is in F major or not (Example 3.2c). The scoring of the passage, rich in unusual timbres, conceals the strict intervallic relationships in the voice-leading (each of the three notional voices is respectively based upon a semitone, whole-tone and expanding interval series). Certain features – notably the descending semitone line <C B B♭> (an extension, perhaps, of the semitone pairs in the opening bars), the emphasis on the pitch B at the end of the extract, and the softly insistent quavers in the bass drum (marked *s*) – pre-empt ideas that are developed in the main body of the movement and beyond.

The introduction thus frames a 'struggle' between the symphony as genre and the logic of the musical material. On the one hand, the determinism bound up in the underlying intervallic structures, and the repetition of the harmonic material (as in a chaconne) imparts a certain static grandeur that is comparable to nineteenth-century precedents. But at the same time, deviations from the patterns and the timbral contrast between materials suggests an internal musical logic that is alien to openings of this ilk.

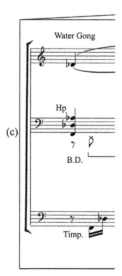

Example 3.2 *Asyla* Op. 17/i, introduction. (a) bars 1–3 (detail); (b) harmonic reduction of bars 1–13; (c) bars 10^3–13 (detail).

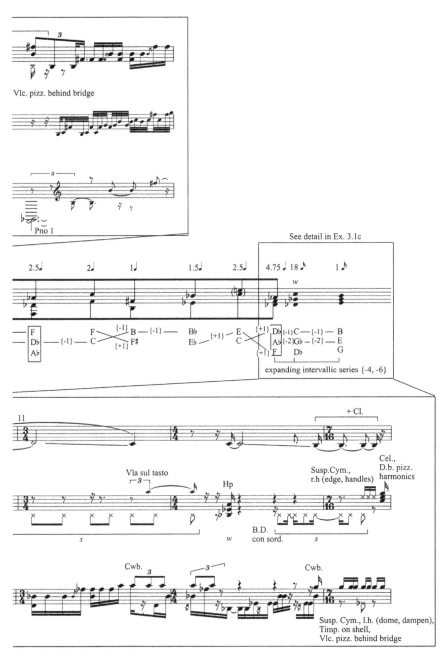

Example 3.2 (Continued)

52   *'Trying to find refuge'*

Section A (bars 14–82)

Section A is characterised by a tensile relationship between melody and harmony that lends itself readily to the metaphor of flight, the sense of a journey to an unspecified and always distant point of repose. Individual dyads from the introduction surface at key moments of the argument in Section A in order to provide points of harmonic focus (see Table 3.2). Particular emphasis is given to {F, C} and, increasingly, {B, F#}. Against this background, the horn melody is spun out, constructed from different modes but returning primarily to the octatonic and whole-tone collections. As in Example 3.1a, no matter how the melody contorts itself, it remains unable to align comfortably with the harmonic 'goal'. Broadly speaking, the most prominent of the referential dyads belong to the CII octatonic collection, but the melodic material identifies mostly with the CI and CIII collections.

Running in parallel with this 'purely musical' argument is a conflict between topical references. Though there is an increased emphasis towards the pastoral topic, it is interspersed with material that hints at more urban, modern environs, with allusions to military and popular styles. Though the pastoral concludes Section A, it is a precarious, questionable victory over the urban, if at all, for the lament begins to intrude in the closing stages. Whatever – or wherever – the pastoral represents, the arrival there is unable to bring joy.

The evolving topical content takes place across, and partially defines, five juxtaposed 'miniatures': four subsections followed by a closing passage that evokes the introduction (see Table 3.2). The first four miniatures are defined melodically: each begins with a version of the horn melody discussed above (phrases a_1–a_4; Examples 3.1a–d) that is paired with a second, related phrase (b_1–b_4), as if in an antecedent–consequent relationship. Contrasting material (c_1–c_5) is at first interspersed between these phrases; increasingly, it overlaps and combines with them. Although each of the phrases a_1–a_4 begins with the same four pitches, their continuations differ. Each statement of the melody can thus be viewed as a repetition, a mythic retelling of the same events over and over from different perspectives in which certain details change (the continuation) but the basic plot remains the same. These repetitions encourage an interpretation of the entire section less as a series of miniatures, and rather as four varied strophes of the same wordless song.

Section A can also be construed as a single extended melodic line. True, it sometimes circles back to revisit certain points, but in common with much twentieth-century music, the concern here is with taking a line for a walk. Reinforcing this impression is the way in which the harmonic and topical environments evolve, evoking a fraught journey through – or towards – an unspecified landscape that, perhaps, recalls the lost and idealised idylls that typified *Arcadiana*.

Strophe 1

The horn melody introduced in bar 14 provides a focal point for the evocation of flight. It belongs to a long symphonic tradition in which the horn is afforded qualities of the heroic, of the masculine, of the hunt:[14] its ascending, yearning motion

Table 3.2 Formal details of *Asyla*, first movement, bars 14–82

Subsection	Bars	Phrase	Governing Set(s)	Concluding Dyad	Comments
Strophe 1	14–18^1	a_1	CI octatonic	{B, F♯} – from CII	Horns 1–3 have melody, harmonised by upper wind and string harmonics.
	18^2–20^2	c_1			Texture separates into distinct strata; fragment of riff-like figure in bass.
	20^3–25	b_1	CIII octatonic	{F, C} – from CII	Horns 1–4 continue melody; more active harmonic rate of change.
	25–27	c_2			One-bar overlap between b_1 and c_2. Riff-like material in bass extended.
Strophe 2	28–33^1	a_2	CI octatonic/ WT0 whole-tone	{A, E} – from CIII	Phrase in strings enters bar 27^2. Material from c_2 continues in accompaniment, moving up into upper wind. Percussion enters in bar 31^2 to prepare for c_3.
	33^2–43	c_3			Tonal centre A in upper stratum, B in middle stratum, with brief bass riff in bars 39–41. Wind chorale begins in bar 41 (extending to bar 48).
	44–48^2	b_2	CIII octatonic	{B, F♯} – from CII	Horns and viola have melody; material from c_3 continues in accompaniment. Bass riff material overlaps end of phrase.
	48^2–51	c_4			Rapid figuration of c_{1-3} now in upper wind, beginning to resemble stylised birdsong.
Strophe 3	52–59	a_3/c_4	CI octatonic/ white note	unstable (chromatic slides)	Solo cello has melody, accompanied by extension of c_4.
	60–68	b_3/c_4	CIII octatonic	unstable (chromatic slides)	Upper strings and trumpets take melody (bars 60–3); oboes and cor anglais extend closing figure in three-part counterpoint (bars 64–7).
Strophe 4	69–72	a_4/c_5	CI octatonic/ WT0 whole-tone	{A, E} – from CIII	Flutes, clarinets and violas have the melody; countermelody in horns, decoration in upper strings. Pedal C♯ in bass, bars 71–2 (c_5).
	73–78	b_4/c_5	CI octatonic	{B, F♯} – from CII	Violas continue with melody without break; upper wind double the line as well as echo it. c_5 continues in bass; tuned percussion recalls figuration of introduction.
Closing section	79–82				Four strata: strings/wind with sustained harmony; tuned percussion; upright piano, celesta and harp.

54 *'Trying to find refuge'*

indicates a quest of some nature, perhaps mythic.[15] However, its stepwise motion lacks the strident quality of the heroic horn call, and its soft dynamic (*p dolcissimo molto cantabile*) evokes instead a singing voice, or of voices in unison.[16] The allusions to the symphonic genre initiated in bars 1–13 encourages listeners familiar with the symphonic repertoire to identify with this melody, to imbue it with agency, but it is presented as a quietly spoken, non-assertive subject, or one that is surveyed from a great distance.

The retention from the introduction of string harmonics and the use of upwards arpeggiation to outline the harmonies create subtle threads of continuity; for the most part, however, Section A represents a shift of musical perspective. This is cued most strikingly in the way that the predominantly harmonic argument of the introduction yields to a clearly defined melodic statement, reinforced by changes in timbre (with upper wind instruments replacing tuned percussion) and tessitura (shifting from bass and tenor registers to higher regions).

Considered alongside its harmonisation, the melody takes on a slightly different identity, for it functions as the bass of the treble-dominated texture. The voicing of the opening chord recalls closely the spacing to be found in the overtone series; the harmonies are also rich in dyads from the introduction (see the square brackets in Example 3.1a). This sonorous manner of scoring combines with the outdoor associations of the horns to give a 'natural' meaning to the music. Yet at the same time, the actual timbre of the harmonisation (at times sounding like a whistling, wheezing pipe organ), the way in which notes are sustained to create an indeterminate halo rather than clearly defined chords and the lack of a real bass contributes to a rather *unnatural* sheen to the music, as if the traditional associations of the horns are being distorted or questioned. Perhaps whatever – or whoever – is travelling through this environment ought not to be there; perhaps they have been displaced.

The texture of the contrasting phrase c_1 separates into three distinct strata (bars 18^2–20^2; Example 3.3a). The upper and middle strata give emphasis respectively to the first and second referential dyads of the introduction, as part of a continuous shuffling of this material. In the middle, in the same register as the horn melody, the melodic F♯ is followed closely by the introduction of a B a perfect fifth below; its continuation is based on a nervous figure in demisemiquavers that pairs the B with its chromatic neighbour A♯. In the stratum above, wind and string harmonics build a chord in fifths around a central {F, C} dyad. The upper reaches of this chord, labelled z <F C G>, becomes increasingly important in later movements; the B♭ beneath it is linked enharmonically with the A♯ in the middle stratum. Finally, in bar 19, a true bass emerges in the lower stratum: the even quavers of motif s returns in the bass drum, to be joined by a riff-like figure, based on an ascending chromatic line in compound perfect fifths that concludes with a descending leap. In contrast to the natural associations of phrase a_1, the topical reference here is to urban EDM, or perhaps (with the brass and percussion) the military. Nevertheless, at this point it is held at a remove: muted and at a low dynamic level, the material lurks in the background.

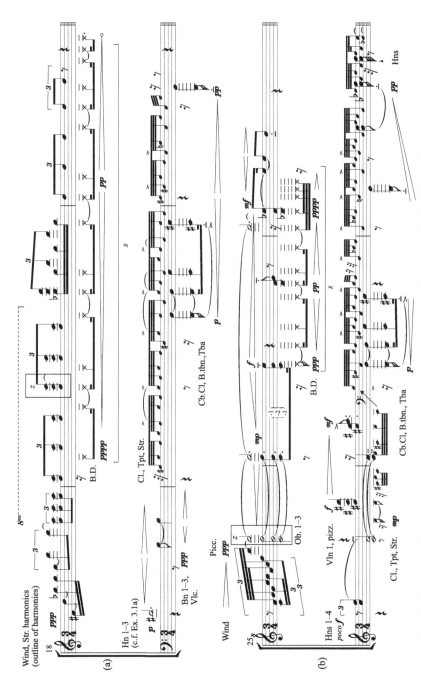

Example 3.3 *Asyla* Op. 17/i, contrasting material. (a) bars 18–20; (b) bars 25–27; (c) bars 33–40; (d) bars 46–49.

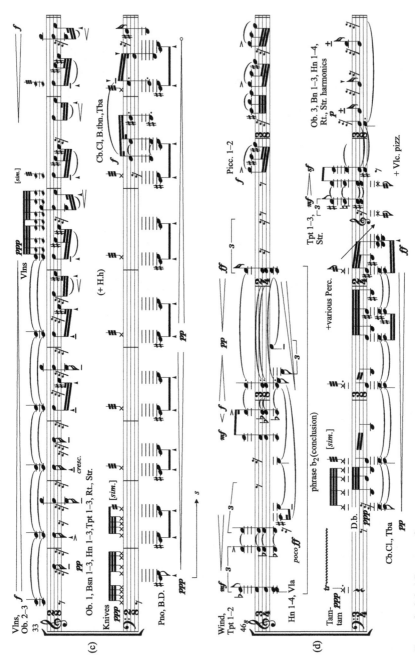

Example 3.3 (Continued)

'Trying to find refuge' 57

The harmony of the consequent (phrase b_1; bars 20^3–23^5) is less stable than in the antecedent, changing at a quicker pace. However, there exists a more clearly defined relationship between melody and accompaniment, for both the melody and roots of the chords draw extensively from the CIII octatonic collection. All four horns now present the melody, dividing into pairs in order to thicken the texture. The predominantly stepwise motion of a_1 is transformed into ever-wider leaps: at the climax of b_1, the horns present the dyad {F, C}, repeating it dramatically an octave lower (bar 25; see Example 3.3b). As with the equivalent close of a_1, this climax emerges out of a harmonic interruption – here, neither the F (nor the B and D that precede it) belongs to the CIII collection; the cadences onto {B, F#} and {F, C} for the antecedent and consequent respectively suggest, in the light of the apparent tonal centre of bars 1–13, an analogy with dominant and tonic closes in traditional period structures.

The conclusion of the melody results in another stratified texture in which *four* distinct strata can be identified (phrase c_2; Example 3.3b). The riff-like figure in the lowest stratum begins as before, but an extension propels the harmonic centre of gravity towards {A♭, E♭}. The nervous middle stratum also untethers itself from its tonal moorings on B. In the highest stratum, the wind announce an expanded $\begin{Bmatrix} -1 \\ -2 \\ -1 \end{Bmatrix}$ harmonic progression, beginning with chord z; by staggering the rate of change in the descending cycles, the impression is given of a series of 4–3 suspensions (see also Example 2.8d). The fourth stratum, suspended between the upper and mid-register strata and played by pizzicato violins, implies a I–V^7 progression in F# major, albeit out of any sort of tonal context (though the A#, combined with chord z, recalls the harmony of bars 18–19; the progression also looks ahead to the harmonic centre of Section B). The increased dislocation between strata provide an unstable close to the strophe, thereby motivating a further attempt in Strophe 2 at resolving the 'musical problem'.

Strophe 2

The second strophe intensifies the sensation of flight by means of an evolving topical argument, a harmonic motion towards B rather than F, and an increased nervous energy. The latter derives in part from the continued presence (save for a couple of beats prior to the entrance of phrase b_2) of the demisemiquaver figuration from the previous strophe, providing surface agitation that by turns animates the harmonic content or adds a percussive sheen. In comparison to the first strophe, the scoring of the second is relatively high and thin.

Phrase a_2 creeps in gradually with the first violins in bar 27, increasing in warmth as it flowers into a melody upon the conclusion of the bass riff of c_2. Aside from the timbre and register, phrases a_1 and a_2 differ primarily in pitch content (rhythmically, both have a similar pattern of contraction and expansion in their trochees). Phrase a_2 retains the first five pitches of a_1, but upon reaching A♭ in bar 30, it continues upwards using pitches drawn from the WT0 collection,

58 'Trying to find refuge'

as if seeking a different outcome to that in the first strophe. Nor is there a melodic fall at the end of the phrase: it keeps rising in order to reach its goal. Yet the goal remains unclear, for the harmonic environment remains at odds with the melody. Thus whilst the melody of bars 27–30 ascends through the CI octatonic collection, a reworking in the upper stratum of the expanded $\begin{Bmatrix} -1 \\ -2 \\ -2 \end{Bmatrix}$ progression from bars 25–27 sounds a descending WT0 line in its lower voice. The WT0 and CI collections overlap on the A♭ in bar 30 (at which point the upper cycle of the progression drops by a tone rather than a semitone; compare Examples 2.8d and 3.1b), whereupon the melody reverses the direction of the lower voice, ascending through the same WT0 collection (bars 31–2). Against this, a $\begin{Bmatrix} -1 \\ -2 \\ -1 \end{Bmatrix}$ progression generates the chords of D major and F minor, which also belong to the CII octatonic collection. Thus when the melody is octatonic, the harmony is built on whole-tone roots; when the melody is whole-tone, it is pitted against octatonic harmonies. All of this is made possible by the fact that the A♭ of bar 30 belongs to all three collections (WT0, CI, CII); these bars 'reveal' a latent potential of this pitch that was untapped in phrase a_1, but also the extent to which the harmonic sands underneath the melody are liable to shift.

The quintal harmony in the mid-to-upper registers that concludes the phrase (this time, <B A E>, Example 3.3c) represents a further shift, for it does not fully belong to any of the governing pitch collections of phrase a_2. Adès's spacing of the chord sets the upper two pitches into relief. Unlike the previous perfect fifths that punctuated the argument to provide formal articulation, {A, E} did not occur in the introduction, though it would have done so had the opening intervallic pattern continued without deviations. It is as if this version of the melody is presented in the subjunctive: an illusory, imagined, hoped-for state rather than anything 'real'.

The {A, E} dyad is sustained throughout the contrasting c_3 phrase, offering a counterbalance to the equally strong harmonic pole offered by the B beneath it, around which wind and muted brass obsessively reprise the {F♯, A♯, B} figuration. Rattling demisemiquavers played first by striking a bag full of knives and forks, then with added hi-hat, along with pulsing bass drum quavers (an extension of motif s), continue the agitation of the previous phrase. In the lowest stratum, the bass drum is accompanied by terse semitone clashes of a B and A♯, played by the piano at the very bottom of its register.[17] There is a truncated reprise of the bass riff in bars 39–41; the chromatic ascent underpinning it is gapped, so that the {A, E} in bar 40 leads (via the descending leap) to a {B, F♯} rather than {B♭, F}. The air suddenly clears: using the <B A E> chord as a point of departure, the wind present a brief chorale-like idea that reverses the horn melody's trochees into short–long iambs (bar 41; CD #1, 1:36). The harmonic progression begins with an expanded $\begin{Bmatrix} -1 \\ -2 \\ -1 \end{Bmatrix}$ progression (and thus can be heard as an extension of the progression in bars 25–27); later phrases are more freely treated (the final three bars can be seen in Example 3.3d).[18]

The wind chorale continues alongside phrase b_2, which, like b_1 before it, is assigned to four horns, albeit with added viola (string timbres become increasingly associated with the melody). In keeping with the higher intensity of the second strophe, the melody grows to a *fortissimo*, the horns registering the strain by adopting what Adès describes in the score as a 'slightly brassed' tone (bar 46). The phrase remains rooted in the CIII octatonic collection; there is a deviation only with the climactic leap from E to D in bar 47 (CD#1, 1:47). This D connects with the upper voice of the wind chorale, so that the closing stepwise descent of the chorale and phrase b_2 combine to end on a {B, F♯} dyad. In the bass stratum, the 'gapped' version of the riff from bars 39–40 returns, now without the descending leap, the final {B, F♯} supplied in a higher register by pizzicato cellos (Example 3.3d).

The coming together of the various strata imbue the return of B as a pitch centre with greater significance; simultaneously, it cues a shift in mood. Although many of the characteristic gestures of phrases c_{1-3} are present in c_4, the relocation of the demisemiquaver figuration of {F♯, A♯, B} to the piccolos resembles stylised birdsong; the more insistent pulsing of the same pitches in the middle stratum is perhaps too brief to accumulate the same level of tension as in phrase c_3. Most significantly, the bass riff is absent, having been dislocated to the previous phrase, as if the urban environments encountered within the first two strophes were finally being left behind.

Strophe 3

Although the pastoral topical allusions of Strophe 3 are more stable than in previous strophes, they occur in the context of a more fluid, unstable harmonic argument that prevents repose. The strophe begins gently; the material of phrase c_4 continues throughout, smoothing over the transition from one section to another. There is a generally thin texture beneath the chirruping piccolos; the soft dynamics suggest again that we are hearing it as if from a distance. But there is darkness amidst the light: phrase a_3, scored for solo cello, high in its register, is marked *quasi senza vibrato*, creating a paler, thinner sound than one might expect. A similar strain is felt in phrase b_3, for second violins playing over the fingerboard (creating a more veiled sound), doubled by trumpets with bucket mutes. The effect is one of dislocation, a restlessness located within the choice of timbre itself.

Such restlessness is matched by the harmonic development (see Example 3.3d, bars 52–56). Phrase a_3 begins as if reasserting the octatonic CI, G-centred point of departure of a_1, though its attempt at closure by drawing on the white-note scale elicits no success. Beneath it, double basses pluck ominous G and D quavers (reinforced by motif *s* in the bass drum, though retaining few of the dance-like associations it had in previous strophes). The piccolo arabesques around {F♯, A♯, B} in the upper stratum sink in a sinuously chromatic descent; similarly, the low D in the bass drops down via a C♯ to B for phrase b_3 (this phrase, as in earlier strophes, is largely based around CIII). The middle stratum, too, falls in Escher-like spirals:

60   *'Trying to find refuge'*

{B, F♯} is briefly regained in bar 64 but the harmonic ground soon slides away once again. In bars 64–68, two oboes and a cor anglais offer a heterophonic extension of the horn melody (CD#1, 2:16), the texture loosely anticipating bars 9–12 of the final movement. Each individual line is constructed from clearly defined pitch collections: oboe 1 is based upon interlocking {-1} and {-2, WT0} cycles; oboe 2 a {-1} cycle and CIII collection; and the cor anglais the CI collection and {-2, WT0} cycle. The heterogeneity of these collections contribute to the lack of harmonic focus of the section; again, CII is avoided.

The harmonic slippage of Strophe 3 thus prevents the melodic material from gaining a fixed tonal identity. This stands in contrast to the increasing solidity of topical reference: the thinner texture, slower rate of harmonic change and birdsong-like material of the strophe all strengthen the movement's pastoral associations. Aligned with this is the reworking of the contrasting material to strip away the dance-like associations, reducing it increasingly to disconnected fragments that lurk on the periphery of the musical argument, distant pulsations that combine with the tonal uncertainty to cast shadows over the would-be pastoral idyll.

Strophe 4

Strophe 4 offers at best a rhetorical rather than definitive point of articulation; a momentary hiatus on a potentially endless journey. It achieves this in part through the slowing down of the harmonic rhythm, which would seem to signal some sort of imminent closure or arrival (compare with the comparable broadening of rhythms at the ends of phrases a_{1-4} and in the introduction, Examples 3.1 and 3.2). This broadening allows greater space in which the decorative figuration, first in solo violins and then piccolos, can expand. Against this, phrase a_4 in the middle strata repeats the pitches of a_2, as if reattempting to force closure with the WT0 collection. The attempt is doomed to fail: the harmonic centre of gravity revolves around the WT1 collection, landing first on B and then a C♯/D♭ (the 'roots' of the second and third pairs of dyads from the introduction).

Although the harmonic rhythm, thin texture and swirling arabesques combine to suggest the pastoral, it is one shrouded in sorrow. The decisive shift in expressive tone begins with the return of the cowbell figuration from the introduction (bar 72; CD #1, 2:37), acting as a harbinger of change. There is a simultaneous bifurcation of the melody in which phrase b_4, the ascending continuation of a_4, is counterbalanced by falling semitones – *pianti* – in the strings (and, in embellished form, in the piccolo arabesques in bars 73–78). Over a repeated C♯ tolling in the bass, phrase b_4 begins to dissipate, to be taken up by different instruments at different paces, and diffusing the prior impression of a single, unitary thematic agent. These refractions differ from previous b-phrases in their use of the CI rather than CIII octatonic collection, as if in response to the B and C♯ harmonic foci of the previous phrase (both these, and the B♭ that follows [bar 77] also belong to CI). Yet the section ends not in CI, but with a reiteration of the {B, F♯} dyad as part of a B major chord (from CII), a temporary port of call, but sufficient to curtail musical development.

Closing section

Just as the transition from the introduction to Section A seemed to offer a shift in perspective, so too does the motion from Strophe 4 to the closing section. There are three clear strata here, in which the first two dyads of the introduction are again prominent. Spread out over many octaves, much of the orchestra contributes to a progression from B major (with added A♯ and D chromatic neighbour notes) to a harmony based upon F and C (eventually thinning out to F and G in the extreme bass and treble registers respectively in order to lead into Section B). By presenting the referential dyads in the reverse order to that of bars 1–3, the progression serves as a closing gesture. This sensation is reinforced by the percussion, which spells out a series of chords derived from inexact intervallic cycles, providing a reflection upon the closing bars of the introduction.[19] Thus, rather than conclude the musical argument of Section A, bars 79–83 return the focus to harmonic rather than melodic content; it is as if a narrator has intruded upon the scene in order to clear the way for the next section. The quest embodied by the melodic material has been placed on hold.

* * *

The musical flight presented in Section A arises from the continued and developing friction between melody and harmony, set against a background that moves from conflict between the pastoral and dance-like urban topics to a pastoral landscape. If the introduction and Strophe 1 assert F as a tonal centre, then by the end of Section A we have moved to its counterpole, B. The strain and strangeness of the journey is composed into the timbres and textures, sometimes naggingly beautiful, sometimes grotesquely so, casting long shadows over the repeated efforts to find a musical refuge for the melody, infusing it with a sense of profound unnaturalness, disorder and dislocation.

Section B (bars 83–139)

Ostensibly, Section B provides timbral, emotional and harmonic contrast to the preceding material. Whereas the lyrical material of Section A aspired increasingly towards some sort of unachievable pastoral idyll, the second opens with baying, fragmentary shrieks from the trumpets and hints of a grim, desperate dance. Certain points of contact exist between the two sections, not least in the retention of intervallic cycles. The trumpet shrieks, performed *fff squillando*, are in essence elaborate embellishments of descending semitone glissandi in the strings; the material for the wind has its ancestry in the expanded harmonic progressions (and their permutations) of the chorale in bars 41–48; the bass riffs of Section A are extended and elaborated, and their percussive support magnified. Increasingly marginalised as Section A progressed, this material returns with a vengeance in Section B, whilst the string timbres which had hitherto dominated the presentation of material recede into the background.

62 *'Trying to find refuge'*

The formal design of Section B is straightforward: two contrasting musical paragraphs (bars 83–101 and 102–114), each of which a statement plus varied restatement, are followed by a third which combines and holds intensified versions of both in a state of heightened tension. There is little attempt either at the level of Section B as a whole or within individual phrases to resolve the topical and harmonic oppositions within the material: the very irreducibility of such tensions can be considered the subject matter of the section. Yet despite this, there are repeated attempts to assert a dominant seventh on F♯ as a harmonic goal. Given the emphasis on B as a tonic in Sections A and A', this is a surprising nod towards traditional tonic-dominant relationships.

Bars 83–101

The first paragraph juxtaposes expressive extremes (threat versus lament) with that of opposing musical tendencies (harmonic immobility versus rapid motion); the result becomes increasingly volatile. The music is based around two extended statements of the trumpet 'shrieks'. In the first of these statements (bars 83–91) there are three such outbursts, each followed by distorted echoes in the orchestra as if from afar. Gaps in the texture enable the slowly descending chromatic line in the strings, the underlying lament behind the threatening trumpet gestures, to be heard. All of these devices combine to create the effect of a cavernous environment, marked out by a sustained G played by a violin harmonic, and a murky bass provided by the double basses with support from the harp and piano, which slowly descends in whole-tone steps from C♯ to A. The fast surface motion provided by the trumpets contrasts with the much slower harmonic background.

The varied second statement (bars 92^3–97) is even more unstable: the three outbursts by the first trumpet are answered immediately by the second and third trumpets in distorted, extended peals of pain. Underneath, reinforced by the cellos plucking behind the bridge, the percussion provides short bursts of regular rhythms that prove unable to establish a constant pulse. The harmonic support begins to move, at first suggesting an expanded $\begin{Bmatrix} -2 \\ -1 \\ -2 \end{Bmatrix}$ harmonic progression (the lower voice reiterating the previous statement's <C♯ B A> bass motion in the manner of a passacaglia), before coalescing again onto a D major chord (bar 98; CD #1, 3:49).

Alternating with these slow, frieze-like depictions of turmoil and sorrow are short, intense eruptions of activity from the wind and brass that propel the music forward (bars 91–92^2 and 98–101). It achieves this both rhythmically (with a predominantly semiquaver surface rate and fast harmonic rhythm) and tonally. In the first burst, there is a motion from an implied D major chord to an implied dominant seventh on F♯, passing through a diminished triad on C♯; in the second burst, this progression appears three times in various voicings, with slight variations to the content of the middle chord. A final trumpet shriek in bar 100 combines with the return of bass riff figure in the lowest stratum that touches briefly on E major, in an upbeat to the second paragraph. Despite this fleeting glimpse of E, it is F♯ that is established as a significant point of arrival: on the level of the movement,

'Trying to find refuge' 63

this creates a tonal tension (with the F/B centres of Section A) that mirrors the local melodic tension of the F♯ in bar 18 of the horn melody.

Bars 102–114

The second paragraph superimposes two dances: the first, a reworking of the chorale-like idea from bars 41–48 into the guise of a shrill dance of death,[20] over an extended version of the bass riff from the c-phrases of Section A. Its first statement (bars 102–108) is shown in Example 3.4. Three oboes announce the dance; above them, a piccolo adds a distorted descant. The content of each line of the 'chorale' consists of scale fragments in semitone or whole-tone steps, sometimes permuted; though the first oboe line is treated sequentially, the specific details appear to be freely composed. Growling in the bass stratum, low wind and brass present an extended version of the bass riff from the c-phrases of Section A, based at first on recurring additive rhythms of 3+2+3 demisemiquavers (cutting across the regular groups of four in the hi-hat), and then contracting towards the end of the phrase (which is marked by a brief recall of the trumpet shriek). The pitch material of the riff is treated in the manner of a loose ostinato that is independent of the rhythmic pattern: extensions are made to both the start and end of the ostinato, interjections are made in the bass and gaps introduced, all in the service of injecting unpredicta-bility into the otherwise regular process. The various strata (chorale, bass, percus-sion, trumpet) are only slightly coordinated: in combination with the irregularities within them, the music has the sense of a teetering on the brink of disaster.

This sensation is reinforced by the second statement (bars 109–114). Every part of the texture is subject to variation. In the upper stratum, the wind chorale accrues additional notes in the upbeat to the first two phrases; the third phrase is extended to close on B; the harmonisation supplied by the other oboes and pic-colo is altered too. The extensions to the ostinato-like bass riff fan out in order to widen its melodic range. The various strata are misaligned in comparison to the first statement: the bass enters sooner than expected, and the trumpet shriek is delayed until the opening of the next paragraph in order to form part of the dialogue there. There is a sense of grim desperation as the various dancers spin towards collapse.

Bars 115–139

The final paragraph begins with an intensification of the variation process of the preceding section, over which is superimposed an increasingly urgent series of trumpet shrieks. The lamenting tone is all but lost amidst the sound and fury. The paragraph falls into three broad groups. In the first, the shrieks are initiated by the wind and followed by the trumpets (bars 115–120); the bass riff is in triads rather than dyads, and the lines of the wind's dance of death contorts into increasingly chromatic forms. The second group (bars 121–129) is marked by an increase in activity in all parts and a thickening of the texture. Though there are certain har-monic points of arrival (a prominent F♯ chord in bar 125 for instance) the music reaches less a climax and more a point of no return. From this, the material in

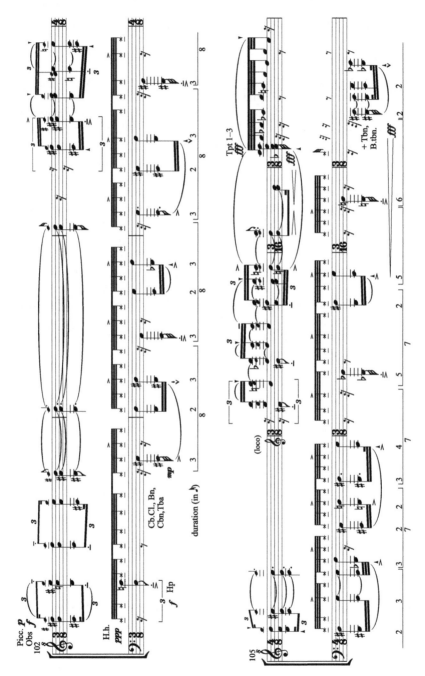

Example 3.4 *Asyla* Op. 17/i, bars 102–108.

the upper registers, now freed from the bass, spirals up (bars 130–139), passing through another F♯ chord (bar 138) and into the recapitulation.

* * *

Musically, Section B as a whole can be read as a steady accumulation of material. Each of its three paragraphs consists of a phrase followed by a varied repetition, in which manipulations of harmonic motion, rhythmic activity and textural density serve to propel the music forward. The final ten bars (130–139) are heard as an extended upbeat into the recapitulation: a panting attempt to inhale before the climax. Expectations for tonal contrast are met through the emphasis on F♯, which has the dual role of acting as the (traditional) dominant of B as well as the figural role of contesting the prevailing syntactical norms. In this sense, Section B can be understood as magnifying the melodic tensions inherent in the F♯ of bar 18 to the level of an entire section, creating a larger-scale dissonance that requires resolution.

But such an account leaves much unanswered. The musical shrieks and laments that pervade the section beg the question: who is screaming? And why? In the presentation of this movement in the documentary *Thomas Adès: Music for the 21st Century*, the visual material for Section B intersperses excerpts from a concert performance amongst archive footage of refugees, including numerous (deliberately and convincingly emotive) shots of men, women and children in tears. In contrast to the depiction of flight in Section A, Section B thus takes a turn inwards to explore the emotional distress of those making the journey. The fragmentation of material and the military connotations of the dominant orchestration of the section complement the instability of the lives of the refugees depicted in the film. Whilst these emotional and stylistic topics are in keeping with the notion of flight, the references to popular music are less easy to incorporate into an interpretation. There is certainly something of the figural about them, awaiting some sort of explanation in 'Ecstasio'. But it is noteworthy that Adès has used allusions to popular music in threatening contexts before, in the 'Militiamen' movement of *Living Toys*. In this earlier instance the purpose was in part a contribution to a surreal welter of musical imagery suitable for the dream-like state being depicted. In *Asyla*, the connotations are less clear, standing perhaps for industrialised Western society (the 'goal' of the refugees) or – as explored later on in the work – as a representation of a different form of asylum.

Section A' and coda (bars 140–165)

A magnificent presentation of the horn melody in bar 140, scored for three horns, trombones and tuba, announces the ostensible reprise of Section A (Example 3.5). Yet the accompaniment in the upper strings and woodwind, a slow, grinding reworking of the dance of death (the top voices of which reinstate the {B, F♯}–{F, C} dyads), makes it abundantly clear that there is no triumph in this thematic return. For all the rhetorical fulfilment of certain traditional formal devices, any concomitant resolution of tonal and expressive tensions that might

66 'Trying to find refuge'

accompany such a gesture is thwarted. There is a recapitulation insofar as the main harmonic material of the movement is reworked, but as in Section A, the focus on B as a centre of gravity ensures that it never coalesces into a harmonic environment in which the melody can belong. This eventual harmonic conclusion is something of a surprise, given the tonal leanings of the introduction and Strophe 1: the emergence of {B, F#} as a 'tonic' rather than a 'dominant' necessitates a large-scale retrospective re-evaluation of tonal function, as if rewriting the introduction to Beethoven's Ninth Symphony on the level of a movement.

The epic quality attending the entrance of the horn melody swiftly dissipates: over a pedal in the bass, the upper strata continue the upward spiral of the dance of death from the conclusion of Section B to evaporate at the top of the orchestral texture. The brevity of this final section – a quicksilver distillation of all that has gone before – is a typical formal trick of Adès, another change of perspective, but the musical flight goes on.

Section A'

The heaving chords at the start of Section A' combine the first two referential dyads with a brief statement of an ascending $\begin{bmatrix} +1 \\ +1 \\ +2 \end{bmatrix}$ harmonic progression. In the bass stratum, a rising gesture links the bass G to the D a perfect fifth above it. The chords in the following bar give emphasis to {A, E} (the 'missing' dyad from the introduction), {C, E} and finally {E♭, B♭}; all told, the outer strata of Section A' provide a concealed and compressed reprise of the harmonic content of the introduction with the exception of {C#, G#}. Just above the bass, a chromatic descent (perhaps an echo of the lamentations from Section B) drags the harmonic centre of gravity from G to B (bar 142), where it remains for a further seventeen bars.

The horn melody returns over this harmonic background. The WT0 continuation of the horn melody again refuses to 'agree' with its harmonic environment, triggering a sequential repetition of the melody on A (bar 143) and then, in stretto, three clarinet entries of the melody on G (beginning with CI octatonic, bar 146), B♭ and E (both CIII octatonic; bars 150 and 153). The proliferation of references to the horn melody develops and extends the process begun in bars 73–78; the individual melodic subject of Strophes 1–3 has increasingly become plural. Above these, the upper wind combine echoes of the horn melody with chromatic versions the dance of death that also recall the stylised birdsong of bars 48–78. Increasingly, parallel fourths and fifths appear between the upper voices, and figuration around {F#, A#, B} emerges in the middle register; together, these provide fleeting reminiscences of the c-phrases from Section A.

If the general texture and scoring of these bars recalls the latter stages of Section A, the mood does not: where Section A suggested a broadening out of the material, an attempt to rest in pastoral environs, bars 140–154 are restless, the upper voices unable or unwilling to accept the B in the bass as a point of repose, and bringing with them the shadow of death. There is no resolution here, but merely the continuation of an endless flight, a continuous accelerando to oblivion.

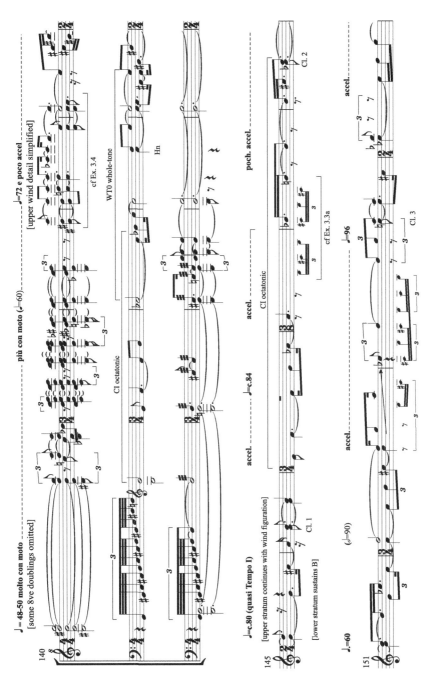

Example 3.5 *Asyla* Op. 17/i, bars 140–154.

68 *'Trying to find refuge'*

Coda

Framed on the one hand by piccolos spiralling to the upper limits of audibility, and on the other by the continued pedal B, the middle stratum announces a compressed reprise of the first six dyads of the movement (from bar 155; CD#1, 5:16). Although the pitch content of these dyads is unchanged, their presentation in this new context highlights the considerable distance travelled in just a few minutes. The most characteristic sonority of the introduction – cowbell and detuned piano tintinnabulations – has been jettisoned for wind alone. Concurrently, the harmonic rhythm has been altered, most notably in the first pair; supported by the underlying pedal, the {B, F♯} dyad is the undoubted harmonic focal point.

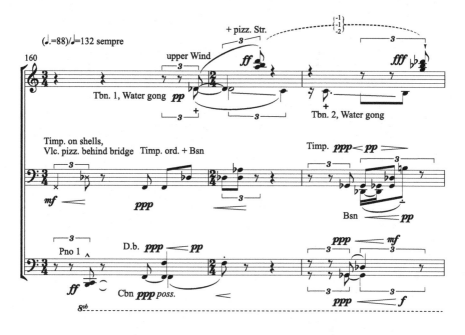

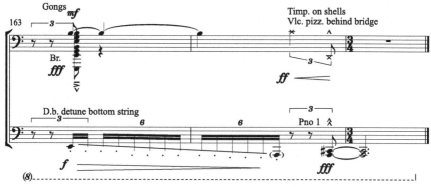

Example 3.6 *Asyla* Op. 17/i, bars 160–165.

'Trying to find refuge' 69

There is a sudden change of timbre and texture in the final bars for a restless, speeded-up recollection of bars 10–13 (Example 3.6; compare CD#1, 0:36 with 5:23). The {C♯, G♯} dyad absent from the start of Section A′ returns as part of a D♭ major chord; as in the introduction it interrupts the logical harmonic progression of the dyads with a more irrational, figural and gestural language. Where it differs is in the addition of two crisply scored chords for wind and pizzicato strings in the upper stratum. These are almost identical in pitch content to the first two chords for piano, celesta and harp in bars 79–80, save for a B instead of a C in the initial chord.[21] This small change allows for an exact $\begin{Bmatrix} -1 \\ -1 \\ -2 \end{Bmatrix}$ expanded harmonic progression between the two chords.

Brief as they are, these closing bars are invested with significance. The recall of the introductory material of bars 1–13 serves to frame the movement; the sense of closure is intensified by the addition of material from the closing section of Section A. Whilst in some respects this can be understood as a rhetorical formal gesture, I shall argue in Chapter 7 that the high degree of contrast between these framing sections and the internal ABA′ form contributes to *discursive shifts* that has narrative and critical implications.

* * *

The concision of the final twenty-five bars intensifies the sensation of flight whilst also drawing attention to traditional symphonic formal gestures. The conventionality of such gestures, as noted in Chapter 2, is designed to be heard, so that 'the real form becomes clearer'.[22] The relationship between unfolding musical logic and governing musical metaphor thus becomes even more tightly intertwined here than elsewhere in the movement, for the overt, if not exaggerated portrayal of formal closure serves to heighten the lack of melodic and harmonic resolution. The problems thrown up by the musical material require more extensive examination before definitive closure can be reached.

Notes

1 *TA:FON*, p. 8.
2 Ross notes a similarity with the subject of Bach's Passacaglia and Fugue in C minor BWV 582. 'Roll Over, Beethoven', p. 128. In 1995, Adès expressed an admiration for Bach. Morrison, 'Prodigy with a Notable Talent'.
3 Elsewhere Adès has described the F♯ as 'an instability which needs to be resolved'; the melody 'has a kind of twist in it and that creates the conditions […] for the rest of the piece'. *Music Matters* (15 May 2010).
4 *TA:FON*, p. 17. Though *TA:FON* post-dates *Asyla* by some fifteen years, there exists a remarkable continuity of (symphonic) thought between the two.
5 Ibid., p. 16.
6 Ibid., p. 78.
7 Ibid., p. 173.
8 *Music for the 21st Century*. The narration begins at 15:08.

70 'Trying to find refuge'

9 For an alternative examination of *Asyla* in the light of symphonic conventions and narrative theory, see Gallon, 'Narrativities', pp. 168–205.

10 On the associations of the cowbells and quarter-tones, see Chapter 7.

11 *TA:FON*, p. 33.

12 Roeder, 'Co-operating Continuities', p. 151. Aaron Travers, 'Interval Cycles, Their Permutations and Generative Properties in Thomas Adès's *Asyla*' (PhD diss., University of Rochester, 2004). 'Interval Cycles', p. 7.

13 Adès has written compellingly on the role of enharmonicism as a determinant in tonal structure in '"Nothing but Pranks and Puns": Janáček's Solo Piano Music', in Paul Wingfield (ed.), *Janáček Studies* (Cambridge: Cambridge University Press, 1999), pp. 18–35.

14 See Raymond Monelle, *The Musical Topic: Hunt, Military and Pastoral* (Bloomington: Indiana University Press, 2006).

15 See Eero Tarasti, *Myth and Music: A Semiotic Approach to the Aesthetics of Myth in Music, especially that of Wagner, Sibelius and Stravinsky* (The Hague, Paris and New York: Mouton Publishers, 1979).

16 Recall that Adès's first example of a topos that might be encountered in a symphonic context is that of a cantilena.

17 This foreshadows the prominent role of these pitches in the second movement.

18 Travers notes that the second and third phrase contains an allusion to phrase a1. 'Interval Cycles', pp. 21–2.

19 See Ibid., p. 32.

20 Compare this dance with the textures and sonority of bars 21–76 of Adès's *Totentanz* (2013). See also the Epilogue to this book.

21 Travers, 'Interval Cycles', pp. 32–3.

22 *TA:FON*, p. 80.

4 'A safe place to go in times of trouble'

The second movement opens with F major and G♯ minor triads, scored arrestingly for muted trumpets (played *fortissimo*), doubled an octave higher by flutes and reinforced on the second chord by pizzicato strings and timpani (see box *u* in Example 4.1). The chords have a forced, strained quality that carries the promise of a new emotional and metaphorical focus. Whereas the first movement suggested masses fleeing across a landscape, the second shifts its attention to a specific locale in which one might take refuge. It is thus an exploration of an interior that offers the promise of asylum, rather than the depiction of external motion:

> I had an idea which was sort of big descending figures and seemed to create a large space [...] And I wanted a sense that you were inside, a human is inside this huge space which I built through details on the score, in the way that a cathedral is made up of tiny details which somebody has worked on [without which] the place wouldn't have the sense of scale and the size that it does when you walk in. I think also the title of the piece, *Asyla*, in that sense [...] you could look to a space as being a sort of safe [...] refuge – a cathedral is always thought of as a safe place to go in times of trouble.[1]

Though the original title for the movement, 'Vatican', was later removed,[2] intertextual allusions in the music align with the spatial details identified by Adès to convey the notion of a sacred, if denominationally non-specific, location.

The opening chords belong to a network of ideas that are transformed, with profound musical and expressive consequences, from one movement to the next. Thus, the two chords conclude the $\begin{Bmatrix} -1 \\ -2 \\ -1 \end{Bmatrix}$ harmonic progression initiated in the final bars of the preceding movement, though the radical change in sonority highlights the emotional distance that has been traversed during the second-long pause between movements. Both movements share the same formal structure, but progress through it at different rates. The dyads that dominate the harmony of the first movement are reworked as melodic intervals in the second, situated within drooping, descending patterns that are themselves free inversions of the predominantly ascending, striving horn melody. In conjunction with the slower tempo (for the second movement functions as the Adagio of *Asyla*-as-symphony) the downward

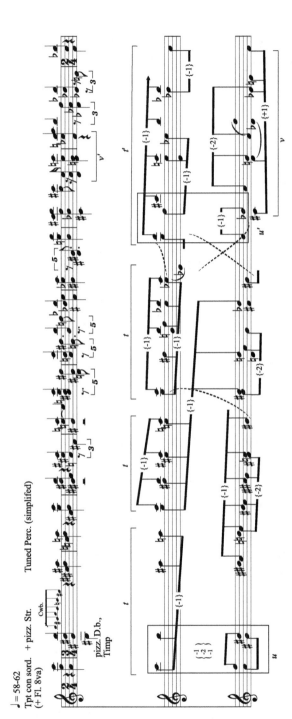

Example 4.1 *Asyla* Op. 17/ii, bars 1–11 (accompaniment slightly simplified).

melodic motion inflects the sacred atmosphere with a lamenting, human voice, giving rise to the movement's characteristic expressive state and questioning what manner of security is provided in this new refuge.

Lament

The intertwining of the human and sacred within the second movement is encapsulated by a reference to the opening of *The Fayrfax Carol* (Example 2.7) in bars 44–47 (CD#2, 2:32; see Example 4.3). Critics have interpreted this moment as human agency within an otherwise impersonal space[3] and have drawn links between the carol's liturgical function and the suppressed title 'Vatican'.[4] Another intertext arises when Taruskin finds himself reminded of Bach's cantatas and Passions.[5] There are, indeed, remarkable correspondences between the main bass oboe melody of the movement and the opening sections of Bach's *Weinen, Klagen, Sorgen, Zagen* BWV 12 (compare Examples 4.2a and b). Specifically, Bach's opening Sinfonia, with obbligato oboe, leads to a chorus of lamentation on the suffering of Christians; each vocal entry begins with a sighing figure. The intervals between the pitches of voices outline two interlocked expanding intervallic series over a *passus duriusculus* in the bass. In *Asyla*, the melody alternates semitones with an expanding interval, and the characteristic chromatic descent of Bach's bass is distributed throughout the texture (compare with Example 2.6c), creating a general background of sorrow.

Nineteenth-century intertexts can be found too, as in Rattle's comparison of the movement with *Parsifal*, [6] another blend of the human and sacred. Joining in the game, Adès has made explicit a connection with the second movement of Franck's Symphony in D minor:

> I remember writing my melody down as a pattern, and noticing that it would fit only on the bass oboe. Then I thought of the texture with the cor anglais and pizzicato in the Franck, and I turned it into the bass oboe with cowbells. Only this morning I realised by complete coincidence that those first three intervals [of the melody] are the same.[7]

The capacity to evoke Bach, Wagner and Franck in the space of a few bars demonstrates the semantic richness of Adès's music. Such evocations act as 'meeting points' in which the collision of meanings give rise to new and unexpected interpretations.[8]

This can be demonstrated by the ways in which these 'meeting points' colour our response to other aspects of the music. Thus, the initial presentation of the oboe melody mirrors closely the musical attributes that Patrik Juslin suggests are expressive of sadness:[9] it is slow, legato, unvaried in articulation, has a low sound level, and so on. This maps on well to a sense of (human) interiority. Yet as the movement progresses, the material begins to proliferate: the twisted, introverted nature of the melody is given multiple echoes and refractions across the orchestra in different registers, timbres, tempi and inversions (see Example 4.3; CD#2, 1:01–2:32), saturating the texture with grief. The increased negative emotional

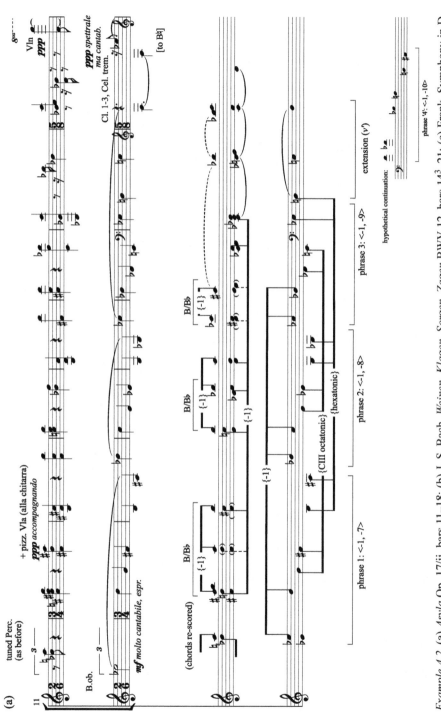

Example 4.2 (a) *Asyla* Op. 17/ii, bars 11–18; (b) J. S. Bach, *Weinen, Klagen, Sorgen, Zagen* BWV 12, bars 14^3–21; (c) Frank, Symphony in D minor/ii, bars 16^3–26.

Example 4.2 (Continued)

76 'A safe place to go in times of trouble'

quality stems too from the increasingly variable instrumental colours, timings and articulations: together with a general increase in musical activity, we might argue that sadness is turning to fear.[10] The suffocating, claustrophobic atmosphere that results is thus far removed from the dignified suffering of BWV 12 or the sensuous spirituality of *Parsifal*, and a considerable expressive charge is generated from the growing distance between the resonances of the works that are evoked and Adès's actual musical surface.

Specifically, Adès transforms the healthy lamenting practices traditionally associated with the *pianto* into something obsessional, all-consuming. Instead of trading on conventional cultural representations of grief, the dysphoric reworking of the falling semitone in this movement creates a compound of sadness and fear.[11] Though the *pianto* is historically not immune from such negative states,[12] Adès conjures up a pathological world of feeling that can only be a product of the post-Freudian world: the emotions that emerge are the province of contemporary psychoanalysis and thus mark the latest development in the *pianto*'s evolving cultural history.

The *Fayrfax Carol* reference is to be heard in this context. Its arrival extends a consolatory voice that momentarily stills the emotional tumult, taking up the lament in an attempt to alleviate it. Listening to this passage with the text of the carol in mind is illuminating. Mary's lullaby to the infant Jesus, 'a my dere, a, my dere Son', offers (human) empathy and love, but it provides neither a solution for, nor an escape from, the suffering that will result from the Passion of Christ. Both musically and intertextually we have a fleeting glimpse of sanctuary (emotional and physical), but it is short-lived.

A series of variations incrementally disturb the spell cast by this allusion, culminating in a turbulent, highly charged passage (bars 68–75, beginning at CD#2, 3:44). Adès commentary over these bars in *Music for the 21st Century* points to another change of listening orientation:

> In the middle of the movement there's a point where I want it to be as though the camera had suddenly flipped round the point of view from the person on the ground to one of these details very high up, and you're looking down, as though it is what it would be like to be the building watching one of the individuals inside it, so you have this kind of turning over perspective.[13]

The narration concludes with a musical clearing of the air: tintinnabulations in the wind and percussion lines shimmer over an extended $\begin{Bmatrix} -1 \\ -2 \\ -2 \end{Bmatrix}$ progression in the bass (bars 76–87; CD#2, 4:09). For all of the beauty of this passage (and for all that it continues to explore material introduced earlier in movement), it is distinctive both registrally and timbrally; it draws attention to itself as a sonic event. Possessing little of the consolatory tone of *The Fayrfax Carol*, the passage reconsiders the lament as if from afar.

The experience is short-lived, but it has ramifications for the close of the movement (bars 88–114; CD#2 from 4:39). The recapitulation elides the introduction with a varied restatement of the oboe melody; the closing section that follows tends, as in bars 33–42, towards thematic saturation (see Example 4.5). Yet here there is less sense of claustrophobia, for the detached tone afforded by bars 76–87 remains dominant to the end. The sense of distance is engendered through a variety of means, most significantly through devices that limit our subjective identification with the material. Thus, the most salient presentation of the melody occurs in inversion, scored for solo violin. Unlike the tessitura of the original bass oboe presentation, which occupies 'human' vocal registers, the violin swiftly moves up into stratospheric heights. A nagging quasi-ostinato in the bass, confined to subhuman depths, prevents the violin line from escaping its earth-bound roots. These lines offer, therefore, fairly dispassionate, distant observations of the trauma of bars 33–42. It is as if, having experienced the building's enduring vantage point, the trials of human existence and the need for refuge are rendered fleeting and irrelevant. It is not the building that provides asylum, but rather the people who, as represented by *The Fayrfax Carol*, administer it.

Fetish pitches and symphonic logic

The lamenting tone that hovered in the background of the first movement, colouring, but not dictating, its emotional trajectory, is significantly expanded to become the governing, if not overwhelming, expressive topic of the second. Similarly, there is a demonstrable relationship between the musical material of the two movements. Most notable is the treatment of the dyads that open the work. For Adès,

> You must imagine that the fourth is an object, like a single note. It's an atom that is quivering, and it wants to split. And depending on the way that it done, something is generated. It can become a melody if played by a bass oboe with an accompaniment, as I do in the slow movement of *Asyla* […]. There are infinite ways it can go.[14]

The shift of emphasis from a harmonic to a melodic treatment of the perfect fourth in the second movement has textural consequences: instead of the melody-plus-accompaniment arrangement that dominates the first movement, the second is primarily contrapuntal. This creates its own musical 'problem', for the spectre of Bach looming over the melody summons the expectation of a *harmonic* counterpoint that parallels the sense of tension, release and direction one would find in tonal music. Adès's solution is elegant. The musical logic of the movement is almost exclusively that of the descending line, which regulates and determines the character of the 'organic power' that is unleashed.[15]

The bass oboe melody in bars 11–18 exemplifies the nature of the interaction between foreground ideas and background intervallic cycles.[16] It consists of descending semitones that alternate with larger intervals; in the first phrase the fall is of a fifth (that is to say, the inversion of the fourth from the first movement), in the second a minor sixth, and the third a major sixth (Example 4.2a). Taking the semitone pairs that emerge in each register, the upper line forms an intervallic

78   *'A safe place to go in times of trouble'*

cycle of descending semitones between E♭ and B♭ (a literal fourth, in this case, a *passus duriusculus*). The middle line is part of a CIII octatonic scale between G and C, and the lower line a complete hexatonic collection from B to D.[17] Nestled within the melody are numerous references to the referential dyads of the first movement (in turn, {G, D}, {B, F♯}, {C, E} and, enharmonically, {G♭, C♭}); many can be found in the accompaniment too.

For Adès, 'certain specific pitches become fetish objects, which are returned to and rubbed by the composer all the time. [...] Whole symphonies are built around this: it's the grit in the oyster'.[18] With some judicious re-spacing of chords in order to highlight implicit patterns (Example 4.2a), it can be seen (as well as heard) how B and B♭/A♯ recur in the accompaniment of all three phrases, and within the melody in the first and third phrases, as 'fetish notes'.

Yet there is also something absent from the music. If the melody were to continue by the same logic to a hypothetical fourth phrase, the pitches would be <A A♭ B♭ A B B♭> (see Example 4.2a).[19] Whilst this notional phrase would reinforce the fetish notes of B and B♭, it would introduce the two pitches – A and A♭ – that have hitherto not appeared in the melody. As with the disruption of the CI octatonic collection in the horn melody of the first movement, Adès breaks the underlying intervallic pattern by changing the contour of the melody (the extension marked v' in Example 4.2a). Doing so disrupts the grammatical 'norms' of the passage, and with it suggests the possibility of the kink in the tail of the melody functioning as a figural metaphor. It also enables the melody to end with an F to a B, providing a backwards glance at two of the centres of gravity of the previous movement.

There are semantic as well as syntactical disturbances within the passage, with the abundance of fifths and sixths evoking a range of possible harmonies; there are in particular strong hints of E♭ minor, with the descending chromatic fourth in the upper register of the melody suggesting a progression between tonic and dominant. By drawing attention to themselves in this way, tonal allusions of this nature are sources of 'productive resistance' to the logic of the unfolding intervals of the underlying voice-leading patterns. As figural metaphors, these allusions contribute to the irreducible tension between functional and 'irrationally functional' logics that give Adès's music its characteristic quality of duality.[20]

Overview of movement

The second movement replicates the ternary design of the first, as well as many of the internal formal details (see Table 4.1). The most significant difference lies in its proportions. Unlike the progressive halving of section length in the first movement, the A and B sections here are of similar duration, and are subdivided into more-or-less equal subsections (those of Section B approximately half the length of those in Section A). The movement generates its momentum through harmonic and rhythmic means as well as through manipulation of instrumental colour and textural density. There is also a moment of functional ambiguity: the close of Section B can be understood as simultaneously the beginning of the melodic recapitulation of Section A, for reasons to be discussed below.

'A safe place to go in times of trouble' 79

Table 4.1 Formal overview of *Asyla*, second movement

Section	Bars/Track Timing (CD #2)	Comments	Duration (seconds)
Intro.	1–10 [0:00]	Begins with completion of expanded harmonic progression; scored for tuned percussion	33
A	11–18 [0:33]	Melody in bass oboe	28
	19–25 [1:01]	Two-part counterpoint	24
	26–32 [1:25]	Three-part counterpoint	29
	33–43 [1:54]	Multiple strata; textural density	38
B	44–47 [2:32]	'Theme' [*Fayrfax Carol* reference]	16
	48–51 [2:48]	Var. 1: melodic line introduced	16
	52–59 [3:04]	Var. 2: canonic treatment	23
	60–67 [3:27]	Var. 3: embellished version of melody	17
	68–71 [3:44]	Var. 4: heightened textural density	14
	72–75 [3:58]	Extension of Var. 4	11
	76–87 [4:09]	Closing section of (B): superimposition of material; beginning of melodic recapitulation	30
A'	88–94 [4:39]	Compressed recapitulation of bars 1–18	25
Coda	95–114 [5:04]	Accel. to close	49

Timings taken from CD accompanying this book.

Introduction (bars 1–10)

Following the two dramatic opening chords, tuned percussion (cowbells, upright pianos, celesta and harp) take up the descending motion of the upper voice.[21] Adès notates the rhythms of these instruments precisely in order to generate calculated *imprecision* by means of staggered attacks and ornamental flourishes. Expressively, such devices give a halting, uncertain quality to the otherwise straightforward triple-time rhythms, enhancing its other-worldly effect (compare with the Franck model in Example 4.2c). There are obvious parallels to be made with the introduction and bars 79–83 of the first movement, though the nature of the material differs significantly. The introduction to *Asyla* suggests some sort of weak harmonic direction, but in the second movement, a short chromatic descent in the upper voice (labelled *t* in the voice-leading reduction), treated as an ostinato, offers little sense of motion. Notwithstanding the subtle differences in the intervallic cycles beneath the repetitions of *t* (along with a fifth, transposed version of both *t* and *u*, so as to *end* with B and B♭ in the upper voice), there is an expressive as well as harmonic immobility redolent of the opening of *Still Sorrowing* (see Example 2.3).

The inner voices can also be heard as continuations of descending lines that emanate from the opening chords (with occasional shifts in register, indicated by dotted lines in Example 4.1). To hear it in this way makes greater demands on the listener, for the 'lines' pass unpredictably between instruments, but the analytical reduction serves the dual function of explaining the harmonic content (as each line wends its own way down, at its own speed) as well as identifying factors

80 *'A safe place to go in times of trouble'*

contributing to the general lamenting atmosphere. As the lines can in principle extend downwards indefinitely, the bass of the final repetition (marked *v*) ascends to indicate formal closure.

Section A (bars 11–43)

Embedded within *v* at the close of the introduction is an anticipation of the extension to the bass oboe melody (<D E F>; *v'*) to be found in bars 17–18.[22] More overt connections between the introduction and the material that follows include the lilting triple-time rhythms in the accompaniment (a recollection of the trochaic rhythms of the horn melody from the first movement) and in the continuation of the intervallic cycles. Thus, the relationship between the first two sections in the second movement is stronger than the equivalent in the first (with consequences for the recapitulation).

The oboe melody is followed by three progressively elaborate variations that ultimately collapse under their own textural weight to bring the section to a close. But there is also an increasing *figural* density that accumulates across the section: as the contrapuntal lines proliferate, they begin to create ruptures in the background intervallic cycles, challenging the underlying grammaticality. The result is that the surface of the music, its acoustic and sonoristic qualities, begin to jostle with the forward motion of the descending lines, threatening to overwhelm it entirely.

Bars 19–25

The A and A♭ (now a G♯) withheld from the bass oboe melody arrive almost immediately, initiating a slowly moving chromatic descent for strings that, by virtue of octave displacement, spans multiple octaves (Example 4.3). Here is the lament in its most direct form so far; an achingly beautiful, yet (by virtue of its register) distant *passus duriusculus* in the upper stratum between A and E that offers the potential for musical and expressive release. In the bass, often (but not always) coinciding with changes of pitches in the falling lament, a funereal B is tolled. The {A♭, E♭} dyad in the bass stratum of bar 24 is less a motion away from the pedal B and more a reinforcement of this dyad in the middle stratum (see the boxed pitches in Example 4.3).

In between these extremes, the melody (now in clarinets, doubled delicately with tremolando celesta) is imitated canonically, with the flutes, muted trumpets and tremolando piano taking up the line beginning on the D a semitone lower (with octave doubling). Yet the third phrase of this canonic imitation, marked by a change of tone colour, enters not on a B♭, as a strict adherence to the canon would demand, but on an A (bar 23).[23] The logic behind this is clear from the voice-leading diagram: the pitches in the various registers of the canonic entries link up to form near-complete chromatic lines that serve as a background to the foregrounded melody. The A that is introduced thus continues the chromatic line initiated by the clarinet's opening E♭ to D; the subsequent <C♭ B♭> (those two pitches again!) also dovetails into the middle line. (The 'missing' bass E in bar 23 arrives in bar 25 as part of *v'*). In short, despite the greater apparent freedom on the musical surface – the various interlocking canonic lines, the lament in

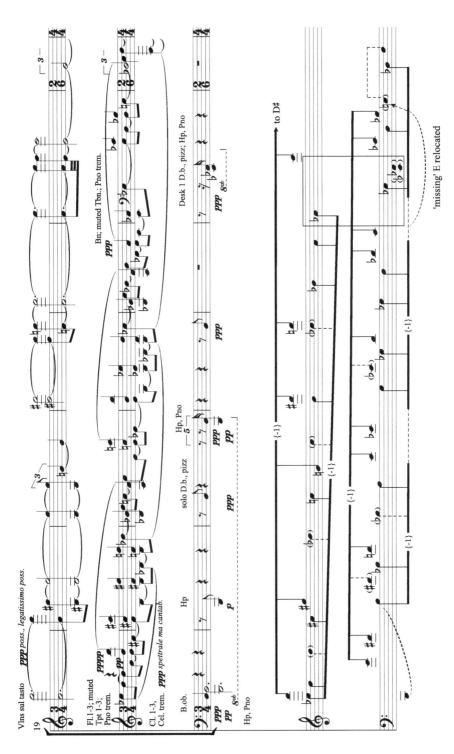

Example 4.3 *Asyla* Op. 17/ii, bars 19–48.

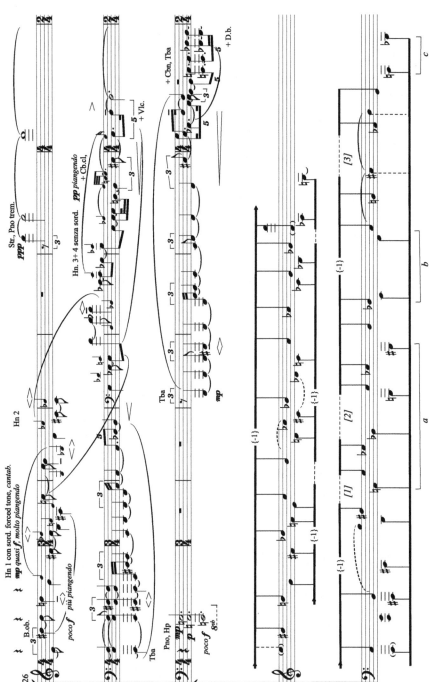

Example 4.3 (Continued)

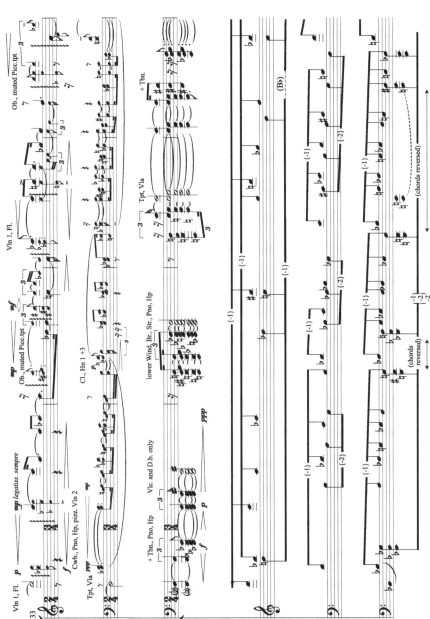

Example 4.3 (Continued)

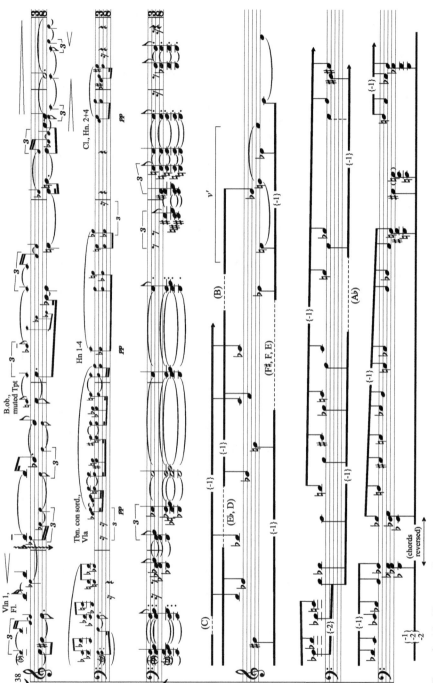

Example 4.3 (Continued)

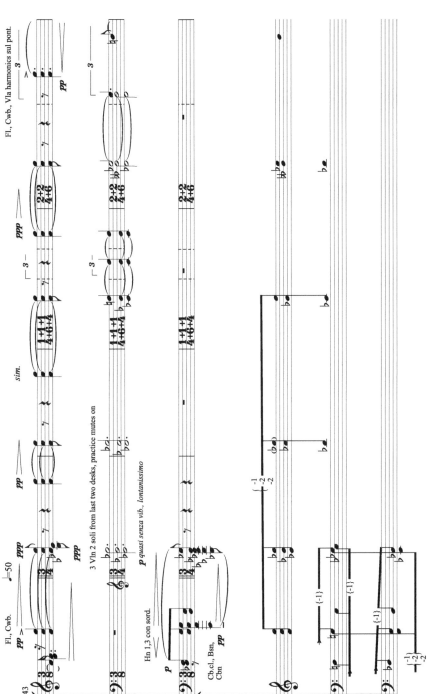

Example 4.3 (Continued)

86 *'A safe place to go in times of trouble'*

the strings and the softly pounding bass – the logic underpinning it is even more exacting, if not choking, than before.

Bars 26–32

For Spitzer, the reflection on, and return of, thematic material contributes to both textural and hermeneutic density.[24] In bars 19–25 the thickening is primarily textural, with strict canonic writing yielding to a more rigid musical logic. But from bar 26, the accumulation of contrapuntal layers begins to fracture the underlying grammaticality. This is most clearly audible in the ascending motion that is taken up by the tuba as part of an inversion of the melody, now in three-part counterpoint with the bass oboe and muted horn. The tuba's line is unable to be accommodated within the descending chromatic lines, and these, too, are starting to splinter, with more frequent omission or relocation of pitches. Thus, in the third stratum (at *[1]*) A and A♭ flat go 'missing' once again at the point where the first phrase in the bass oboe melody ends; these pitches emerge in the bass stratum as part of the group marked *a*. Similar devices connect *[2]* with *b* and *[3]* with *c*. There is a palpable tension between the 'stuff' of the melodic lines and the demands of the intervallic structure; the dramatic transposition of the F that concludes the upper stratum (bar 31, CD #2, 1:46) injects the final bars of the passage with an additional sense of urgency.

Just as significantly, the sonority of this passage revels in its strangeness. The movement up to this point has made use of a variety of unusual timbres, from the tuned percussion of bars 1–10 via the bass oboe for the melody and the discreet tremolandi of bars 19–25. The counterpoint here between the *sounds* of the bass oboe, the strained, forced tone of the muted horn, and the richness of the tuba, irrespective of the pitches they employ, is an intensification of the play of colour heard so far. The effect is strangely disquieting, with the placement of individual lines carving out hollow spaces within the texture, intensified by the emergence of the high strings and tremolando piano in the closing bars.

Bars 33–43

The contrapuntal, intervallic and colouristic trajectories of Section A come together in the remarkable passage beginning at bar 33. The analytical reduction in Example 4.3 highlights the continued presence of the descending intervallic cycles, but increasingly they are fragmented, cut short or gapped, as if yielding to the pressure brought to bear by the figural quality of the melodic ideas and their startling timbres. The sonority is rich and strange, with heaving chords in the bass, groaning glissandi in the trombones and cellos and delicate figuration of the cowbells. In the middle of the texture, interlocking intervallic cycles create a new, seemingly independent layer of detail. The main melody, now followed imitatively with a slightly faster version of itself, continues to float above it all, as if indifferent to the turmoil beneath it. Despite the clear metric, intervallic and timbral contrasts between each of the layers in this passage, there remain certain points of contact between them (metric alignment, shared pitch content) that facilitate its 'post-tonal simulacrum of harmonic counterpoint'.[25]

The reference point for this harmonic counterpoint is a permuted version of an expanded $\begin{Bmatrix} -1 \\ -2 \\ -2 \end{Bmatrix}$ harmonic progression in the bass stratum, in which the lower two voices outline the referential dyads of the first movement's introduction (with the addition of the implied, but not stated {A, E} dyad), as the annotations to Example 4.3 show.[26] It is as if the overwhelming figurality of the material from bar 33 has precipitated a structural crisis, requiring an external hand to stabilise and reorient proceedings. Indeed, the fissures and fractures in the upper strata might be the result of the expanded progression exerting a tonal pull on the descending intervallic cycles, causing them to break under pressure. Whatever the cause, as the emotional tone of the music begins to cool, the permutations in the bass stratum iron themselves out so that roots descend by whole-tones. Unlike previous statements of the melody, the extension v' does not culminate in a descending cadential leap, but remains frozen on F, as all but one of the strata congeal onto chord z, <F C G>. The upper voices stubbornly hold onto this chord whilst the bass stratum closes on the E♭ minor chord with which the passage began. Bars 33–43 are thus striking in their harmonic immobility, their extremes of emotional turmoil masking a significant psychological blockage.

Section B

Cao's suggestion that the middle section is a series of variations over a ground bass provides a useful starting point for an analysis.[27] However, the distance between traditional ground bass procedures and Adès's actual development of bars 44–47 points to a more flexible approach to symphonic form than Cao implies.

The sequence of variations traces a similar path to that found in Section A. Just as bars 1–10 provide a harmonic background to which a melody is added in bars 11–18, bars 48–51 provide a melodic embellishment to the harmonic content of bars 44–47. Similarly, the canonic treatment of the bass oboe melody in bars 19–25 finds a parallel in bars 52–59. The third and fourth variations beginning in bar 60 follow the precedents in Section A less closely, though they share the drive towards textural and figural density.

'Theme' (bars 44–47)

Bars 44–47 function as the still centre of the movement: the harmonic rhythm is dramatically slowed down, and its delicate soundworld offers maximum contrast to the tensions around bar 33. Repeated <F C G> chords intoned softly by wind and cowbells recall Stravinsky at his most neo-classically Apollonian. These provide a calm ritualistic background to the slowly unfolding foreground,

88 *'A safe place to go in times of trouble'*

in which three players from the back desks of the second violins, all but inaudible through the use of practice mutes, continue the $\begin{Bmatrix} -1 \\ -2 \\ -2 \end{Bmatrix}$ expanded harmonic progression from the previous section. The bass line of the first three chords, <E♭ D♭ C♭> traces out the first pitches of each of the phrases in the bass oboe melody of bars 11–18, and the almost-regular alternation between wind and string chords mirrors the rhythms of the melody's accompaniment. Unlike the opening of *The Fayrfax Carol*, there is a fourth chord in the progression: although this contains the next whole-tone step expected in the bass (a B♭♭), it is buried in an inner voice. The actual sounding bass, a D♭, reverses the contour of the bass line in order, once again, to symbolise closure. All told, these bars do not offer a fully fledged musical statement ripe for variation; rather, they might best be considered a proto-theme out of which selected ideas are chosen for exploration.

The radical transformation of the $\begin{Bmatrix} -1 \\ -2 \\ -2 \end{Bmatrix}$ progression from cavernous bass chords (bars 33–43) to a distant hymn (bars 44–46) identify these bars as a possible site for the 'turning over perspective' intended by Adès. The comparable techniques of textural thickening between Sections A and B strengthen the latter being a sense of some external agent (the 'building') contemplating the human drama that had unfolded within it. Such a reading has much to commend it, although the mounting passion and emotional engagement across successive variations is at odds with the detachment that Adès implies. For this reason, I locate the change of perspective with the decisive shift in expressive tone in bars 76–87 that brings Section B to a close.

Variation 1 (bars 48–51)

The first variation continues the mood of the 'theme', transferring the $\begin{Bmatrix} -1 \\ -2 \\ -2 \end{Bmatrix}$ progression to the flutes, with the repeated <F C G> chords given to violas and cowbells. This marks the first point in the movement in which the underlying intervallic thread from one section to the next is sutured, for the material is a varied *repetition* of the preceding, rather than a continuation of its tumbling lines. There is nevertheless a subtle stirring, as if to waken the music from its ritualistic slumber, by means of an embellishment of the inner voice of the expanded progression. Specifically, an additional, interlocked semitone intervallic cycle is added to the whole-tone line, giving rise to a melodic version of the two-note chords in the middle of the texture in bars 33–42. Combined with somewhat lopsided rhythms, what emerges is a new, gently meandering line, the derivation of which can be seen in Figure 4.1 (note the presence of the fetish pitches B♭/C♭ at the outset).

Figure 4.1 Successive melodic embellishments, second movement, bars 48 ff.

The subtle increase in momentum resulting from these embellishments serves as a model for subsequent variations. Concurrent with this generation of energy, however, is an opposing shift of the emphasis of the music from the underlying grammatical sense and direction of Variation 1 towards increasingly figural, gestural ideas. It is useful to examine this before turning in detail to successive variations. Thus, the first four pitches of Variation 2 are an exact transposition (by a minor third) of the equivalent in Variation 1. If it were to continue exactly, the fourth pitch, a C♯, would be followed by a fall of a major third to A. Instead, a chromatic neighbour D is added to the C♯; after this, the remainder of the melody continues almost exactly as in Variation 1, so that the major third descent now travels between D and A♯ rather than C♯ and A (the effective transposition of the latter half of the melody is indicated in Figure 4.1 by italics). A further embellishment comes with a *lower* chromatic neighbour to the C♮ at the end of the Figure, after which there is a free development of the line.

Variation 3 transposes the melody of Variation 2 up another minor third; there is a parallel with the successive transpositions of the horn melody in the recapitulation of the first movement. Once again, there are chromatic insertions, but here the decorations are subject to their own variation: the E♭ added between the second and third pitches results in a complete chromatic subset <E F E♭ D> which the melody cycles through freely prior to the arrival of a C♯ (see Figure 4.1). The original descending chromatic line of the lower voice of Variation 1 remains in the background (and indeed, is extended considerably beyond the confines of Figure 4.1), though the melodic eddies that arise through the proliferation of pitches somewhat mask it (compare with the treatment of Example 2.3). Indeed, such is the profusion of material that the original sense of the Variation 1 melody is all but lost: the melody becomes increasingly figural.

The proliferations of Variation 4 are such that they cannot be accommodated easily into Figure 4.1. The line begins with an agitated figure circling around the first two pitches of Variation 1 <B♭ A C♭ A C♭ A B♭>, in an expanded exploration of the chromatic neighbours of previous variations; it then transfers its attention to A♭ and its neighbours (and so on). Impassioned transpositions of chromatic intervals into minor ninths (or even minor sixteenths; compare with Example 2.5c), characterised by dramatic *portamenti* on the stringed instruments, mark the highpoint in the process of transforming the melody of Variation 1 into purely sonorous, acoustic, figural material. From here, there is nowhere left to go but back to the material of Section A.

90   *'A safe place to go in times of trouble'*

Variation 2 (bars 52–59)

The second variation announces immediately a change in emotional tone. Scored almost exclusively for strings, with delicate reinforcement of chords by the harp and grand piano, it presents a contrast to the expressively cool wind-dominated scoring of the first two variations (Example 4.4). At first the sound is veiled by means of mutes or playing over the fingerboard; gradually, the intensity and warmth increases for a more full-blooded romantic mode of expression. This change is led by the cellos (line (e) in Example 4.4), who have the melody in a sonorous part of their register. Floating an octave-plus-minor-sixth above them, half of the first violin section add a canonic imitation of the cello line (c), albeit with subtle rhythmic distortions.

Vestiges of the harmonic material of bars 44–47 are less immediately obvious. The melodic canons of Variation 2 are initially suspended within four lines that loosely follow on from the descending intervallic cycles of Variation 1. All four of these lines begin as semitonal descents, lines (f) and (b) paired with lines (d) and (a) minor tenth higher (see the analytical reduction). The slow tread of lines (a) and (b), moving in strict rhythmic unison, in particular recalls the chromatic descent of bars 19–25. Midway through the phrase, the semitonal descents of lines (b) and (f) change into whole-tones. Though this recalls the bass of the previous two variations, the harmonic environment differs considerably; just as importantly, the change of bass line combines with the increasingly angular melody to impart greater momentum to the second half of the variation.

Variation 3 (bars 60–67)

The same bass line, transposed to begin on A, can be heard in the third variation. As in Variation 2, it consists of five semitone steps and three whole-tone steps; if the second and fourth pitches are considered as chromatic passing notes, then each variation is underpinned by a complete whole-tone set. (The importance of this becomes clear in the final movement). More saliently, the change of harmonic focus at the start of Variation 3 combines with a dramatic drop in volume and change in texture to tremolando strings. In the upper stratum, there is a chromatic descent from C down to F. In the middle, the melody, shared by second violins and viola with bassoon and muted trumpet, is animated not only by the increasing chromatic insertions, but also through irregular rhythms and phrasing, and surging dynamic shaping. As the melody develops beyond the pattern laid out in Figure 4.1 it becomes impassioned, its upper and lower registers fanning out in contrary motion prior to a climactic recall of the bass oboe melody, a descending <B♭ A E♭ D G F♯> that plunges the material via an enharmonic (F♯/G♭) into E♭ minor. The rapid expansion and proliferation of the melody is supported by an acceleration and crescendo; the emotional temperature heats up considerably, preparing for the full-blooded final variation.

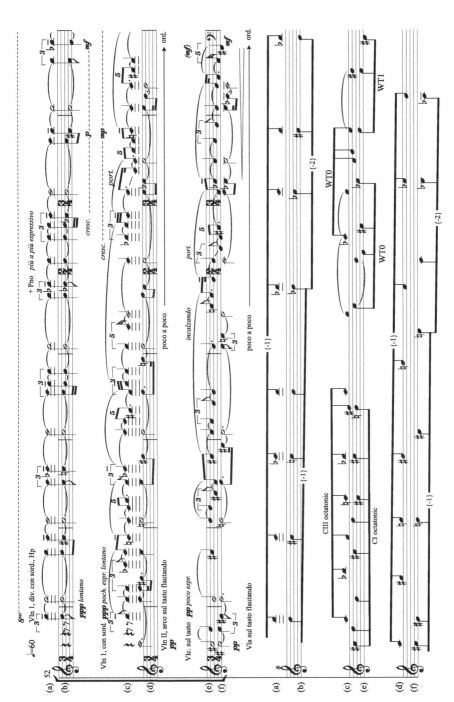

Example 4.4 *Asyla* Op. 17/ii, bars 52–59.

92   '*A safe place to go in times of trouble*'

Variation 4 (bars 68–75)

There are few passages in Adès's early output as expressively direct as this variation. The melody, given to the entire string section (first violins enter after two bars), is dark, sonorous and searching, possessing a late-Romantic intensity.[28] Against this, brooding chords in the wind and brass, punctured by stabs, are built upon the original descending bass of the 'theme', <E♭ D♭ B A>, now stated in its entirety. Upon reaching this harmonic goal in bar 71, the music begins to fragment, spiralling up away from the lower registers (between bars 72 and 75, it rarely dips below middle C). The melody, exaggerated by wide leaps, *portamenti* and extravagant crescendi, begins to take on a hysterical quality at odds with the poise of bars 44–47. The harmonic argument collapses in on itself, centred on a G that acts as a focus for the gestural, figural material that whirls around it.

Initially all but inaudible amidst the maelstrom, a solo horn enters at the end of bar 73 on a high F♭. At odds with the WT1 collection that had oriented the first half of the variation as well as the local focus on G, this pitch eventually moves down to an E♭ in order to present a variation of the bass oboe melody. As this E♭ in turn falls to a D, the harmony beneath it momentarily voices a dominant seventh on G in first inversion, preparing for a sighing cadence into C minor.

Closing section (bars 76–87)

The lowest stratum of the closing section presents one last, slowly unfolding presentation of the $\begin{bmatrix} -1 \\ -2 \\ -2 \end{bmatrix}$ expanded harmonic progression that dominated Section B. Rather than confirm E♭ minor as a tonal centre of gravity, however, the progression, beginning with a C minor chord <C G E♭>, is allowed to run for longer than normal, effecting a transition to E minor (a filling out of the <E B B> that concludes the progression) and the recapitulation.

Despite this, the immediate impression of the closing section is less of motion, but rather a stilled contemplation of the materials of the movement. The glittering figures given to piano, celeste and harp, beginning with yet another iteration of {B♭, C♭} (in the grand piano), dance freely through the semitone pairs and leaps of the bass oboe melody from bars 11–18. These pairs in turn are coloured with spectral echoes in the strings of the *portamenti* from the previous section, drained of their inflated dramatic gestural power.[29] The horn line, as Travers has shown,[30] is based on the original oboe melody but embellished with interlocked intervallic series (in a manner not unlike the variation technique of Section B; see Figure 4.2 for the opening of this process). The superimposition and reworking of ideas in this section helps achieve the 'turning over perspective' described by Adès: a revisiting of materials but stripped of their original emotional connotations.

{-2}			C#					B				
{-3}					F					D		
Oboe	E♭	D	G		F#	B		B♭	D♭	C	E	E♭	G	G♭	(etc.)
melody												

Figure 4.2 Embellishment of phrases 1–2 of the theme, second movement, bars 75–86.

Section A' (bars 88–94)

The horn continues to develop the melody across the boundary from Section B to Section A'. There are good reasons nevertheless for hearing bar 88 as the start of the recapitulation. First, the reworking of the third phrase of the oboe melody results in a prominent appearance of the fetish pitches B/B♭ just prior to the recapitulation. Second, the conclusion of the expanded harmonic progression in bars 76–88 (<F# C# C♮> to <E B B>, to which a minor third is added) presents a re-harmonisation of the <C B> melodic motion originally heard at the outset (compare with *u*, Example 4.1). There is therefore an impression of 'starting again', albeit in a new, transfigured state. From here, the harmonic progression of bars 1–10 returns against the horn melody.

As noted above, the shift of perspective at the end of Section B offers a detached contemplation of the lamentations of Section A. Something of this emotional distance continues into Section A', the emotional tenor of which carries considerably less expressive charge than the equivalent passage in bars 1–18. The change of tone colour (the French horn of the first movement replacing the more plangent bass oboe) contributes to this effect, as does the increase in melodic activity (the embellishments animate the otherwise stately tread of the melody).

Bars 88–94 thus act as the 'meeting point' not for intertextural allusions, but for the expressive and musical trajectories of the movement; in this capacity, it is difficult not to hear them as both recapitulatory and conclusory.

Coda (bars 95–114)

There remains, however, one unresolved musical trajectory. The melodic cadence of the oboe melody, <F B>, is thickened considerably in bars 94–95; the dramatic crescendo on the F undercut by a sudden *pianissimo* on the B, now functioning as a bass. The two 'missing' pitches from the melody, an A and A♭, appear in the upper stratum (CD #2, 5:00–5:05; see also Example 4.5). Significantly, the B drops down to a B♭, reprising the two fetish pitches at the lowest extremity of the orchestral range. This sets up the coda, which can be considered in part as a working-out of the tensions that arose across the movement from the retention of the two fetish pitches amidst more dynamic, directed motion.

The outer strata of the coda present variations of the oboe melody (see the analytical reduction beneath Example 4.5). In the upper stratum, a solo violin pirouettes off to the top of its range with an inverted form of the melody in which each successive statement employs wider leaps. In the lowest, the reverse

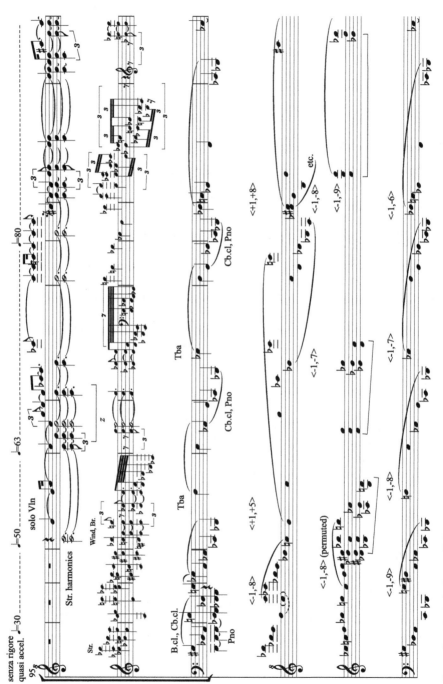

Example 4.5 *Asyla* Op. 17/ii, bars 95–114.

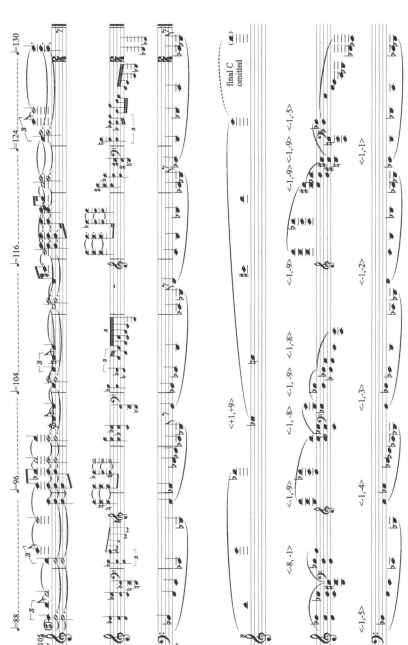

Example 4.5 (Continued)

96   *'A safe place to go in times of trouble'*

happens: successive phrases contract, until they reach the vanishing point of semitone oscillations. Between these strata, the remainder of the orchestra offer harmonised versions of the oboe melody, weaving in and out of synchronisation with the outer voices before finally aligning with the bass in the final bar. From the heaving opening of the coda through to its accelerated close, the interaction of these multiple presentations of the melody has an eerie, almost sickly quality – a final example of the pathological qualities of the movement's lamentation.

Reinforcing this sensation is the organisation of the bass stratum so that each of the contracting phrases end with the fetish notes <C♭ B♭>, a potent musical symbol of the unhealthy obsessional underbelly of the movement. The accelerando to the final oscillation of these pitches in the closing bars, coupled with the alignment with the middle stratum at this point, gives a sense of inevitability to the conclusion.

The solo violin in the upper voice ends with a top B, stopping short of the C that would complete its phrase. This, too, is symbolic (the reworking of the lament in the coda is both unhealthy, but also unresolved). The musical consequences of this dangling thread are picked up at the start of the third movement, as the focus of attention turns from the cathedral to the clubhouse, and from the sacred to the profane.

Notes

1   *Music for the 21st Century*. The narration begins at 23:46.
2   Adès 'thought it was just too specific, it means something specific to many people, which I didn't really intend'. *Performance on 3*, BBC Radio 3 (first broadcast 1 October 1997).
3   Gallon, 'Narrativities', p. 188.
4   Travers, 'Interval Cycles', p. 25. Neither Gallon nor Travers presume any chronological ordering for the composition of the works in question; for the purposes of hermeneutic interpretation, it is the connection between the musical content and expressive atmospheres that matters. It is less clear if this was part of Adès's intention: when comparing shared material in his later music, Adès stressed the separation of musical content over any associative meaning it might accrue in a particular context. *TA:FON*, pp. 30–1.
5   Taruskin, 'A Surrealist Composer', p. 148.
6   Ibid.
7   *TA:FON*, p. 34.
8   Monelle, *The Sense of Music*, p. 155.
9   Cited in Michael Spitzer, 'The Topic of Emotion', in Esti Sheinberg (ed.), *Musical Semiotics: A Network of Significations* (Aldershot: Ashgate, 2012), pp. 211–23, at p. 213.
10 See Michael Spitzer, 'Mapping the Human Heart: A Holistic Analysis of Fear in Schubert', *Music Analysis*, 29/i-ii-iii (2010), pp. 149–213, at pp. 152 and 157.
11 See Ibid., p. 205.
12 Monelle, *The Sense of Music*, pp. 74–5.
13 *Music for the 21st Century*. The narration begins at 26:47.
14 *TA:FON*, p. 33.
15 My account of intervallic cycles overlaps with much of Travers's excellent introduction to the movement ('Interval Cycles', pp. 10–31), though we differ in the interpretative conclusions we draw from the underlying structures.
16 See Gallon, 'Narrativities', pp. 185–6; Roeder, 'Co-operating Continuities', pp. 126–7; Travers, 'Interval Cycles', pp. 10–13; and Edward Venn, '"Asylum Gained"? Aspects

of Meaning in Thomas Adès's *Asyla*', *Music Analysis*, 25/i–ii (2006), pp. 89–120, at pp. 108–9.

17 Roeder, 'Co-operating Continuities', p. 127. This particular hexatonic scale, like the whole-tone and octatonic scales, can only be transposed a limited number of times (in this case, four) before repeating itself. Roeder also notes that the three phrases of the melody are hexatonic, octatonic and chromatic subsets respectively.

18 *TA:FON*, pp. 48–9.

19 This progression would also leave the chromatic, octatonic and hexatonic lines in each of the three registers intact.

20 Adès discusses irrationally functional harmony in *TA:FON*, pp. 144–6.

21 For ease of reading, quarter-tone variations have been normalised to equal tempered pitches in Example 4.1.

22 This is most clearly audible in the quarter-tone flat piano in bars 8–9 (CD #2, 0:28).

23 Travers was the first to make this observation ('Interval Cycles', p. 14).

24 Spitzer, *Metaphor and Musical Thought*, pp. 110–11.

25 Roeder, 'Co-operating Continuities', p. 141.

26 Travers identifies the progression and permutations in bars 36–44 (omitting bars 33–35), but overlooks the A♯ in bar 41 that is a necessary part of the upper cycle. 'Interval Cycles', pp. 19–20.

27 Cao includes 'la partie centrale du deuxième movement d'*Asyla*' as one of a number of works that 'contiennent un movement ou une section sur une basse obstinée' (*Thomas Adès Le Voyageur*, p. 23).

28 Ross has compared it to Wagner ('Roll Over, Beethoven', p. 130) as well as noting elsewhere how 'shades of Wagner and Mahler glide through the orchestration' of the movement as a whole. *The Rest is Noise: Listening to the Twentieth Century* (London: Harper Perennial, 2007), p. 582.

29 Gallon draws a parallel between this passage and, citing Charles Rosen, the use of horn fifths in the Romantic era as 'symbols of distance'. 'Narrativities', p. 190.

30 Travers, 'Interval Cycles', pp. 28–9.

5 'Ecstasio'

A 'freaky, funky rave'?

Having completed the second movement, Adès 'was aware that the third movement needed to be a kind of dance movement. [... S]ome repetition would have to be involved and it was a question of dealing with the repetition without the repetition becoming the point'.[1] Adès solved these problems by turning to contemporary EDM. This provided an extension of the symphonic associations of the emerging work, for there was a 'pun' in that 'the third movement of a Haydnesque symphony would very often [...] be a minuet [...] so I had a dance movement in this as the third movement but it's [... a] popular, modern sort of club music'.[2] It also offered a topical environment for the types of repetition that Adès had been gravitating towards:

> I noticed in dance music today that things are repeated 8, 16, 32, 64 times – it's very powerful indeed. It has an effect over huge crowds of people, it creates a convulsion in a crowd which is a very important discovery in a way, and I wanted to use it in a big movement. It's ecstasy but it's also threatening and vertiginous.[3]

The content of the movement thus addresses polarising contemporary debates, for the effect of such rhythms over large groups, and the threat to law and order that this was deemed to have,[4] had also been noticed by the UK Government. The 'deeply controversial Criminal Justice and Public Order Act 1994, which gave the police enhanced powers to suppress raves [...] famously defined the music it was targeting as "sounds wholly or predominantly characterised by the emission of a succession of repetitive beats"'.[5] The connotations of 'Ecstasio', the movement's title, also freely courts the positive and negative associations of the word.[6] Little wonder Clark describes the movement as a 'freaky, funky rave'.[7]

Adès's emphasis on EDM ought not to obscure the symphonic aspects of 'Ecstasio'. Indeed, 'Ecstasio' stages another 'struggle between [...] topos, [...] and some logic in the material'.[8] Just as the second movement latched on to particular thematic and motivic ideas of the first, 'Ecstasio' takes up and develops different ideas, such as the dance-like implications of the material relating to phrase c in the first movement, in order to explore their symphonic potential. The focus upon repetition can therefore be understood as a large-scale exploration of the repetitive, cyclic qualities found in the first two movements (think of the repeated strophes of the first movement, or the unfolding of intervallic patterns in the theme of the second), raising to a structural principle the propensity of *Asyla*'s material to fold back in on itself.

'Ecstasio' is thus characterised by its precarious balance between the foreground trappings of EDM and certain musical developmental processes associated with the symphonic genre. In the analysis that follows, my focus will be on how the pull of conflicting generic demands gives rise to an exhilarating tension that builds throughout the movement.

'Ecstasio' and EDM

To hear EDM as the guiding stylistic topic of 'Ecstasio' requires at least two conceptual leaps, for 'Ecstasio''s sounds are orchestral rather than electronically generated, and it was not intended for dancing to. The latter is, of course, true of many pieces of concert music that draw on dance topics.[9] It is also true for certain subgenres of EDM in the 1990s, such as 'intelligent techno', which are as much 'head' music as music for the body: functionality is not therefore a prerequisite of EDM.[10] The importance of specifically *electronic* timbre (and manner of production) can similarly be called into question. It is not altogether surprising that musicologists such as Philip Tagg barely touch on it, prioritising other aspects of the musical design,[11] but even practitioners who have written about the composition of EDM tend to privilege parameters such as rhythm, harmony and melody over exclusively electronic aspects.[12] It would be erroneous, of course, to assume that timbre isn't an integral part of the EDM experience, but unusual or unexpected sounds do not preclude us from hearing music as EDM.

In some senses, to hear music 'as' EDM is a metaphorical act, for it maps the listening experience onto the abstract cultural concept of what EDM actually *is*.[13] In this sense, EDM is understood as a collection of musical characteristics, not all of which need be present at any one time, but which are recognised by a competent listening subject as stylistically pertinent. If 'Ecstasio' is to be interpreted in relation to EDM, and not just heard as a crude aping of its gestures, we must therefore look to those musical cues and how they relate to EDM norms and expectations.[14] Doing so once again demands of the listener an active, critical role, one which is informed by stylistic familiarity but which remains receptive to alternative, competing modes of listening – in this case, to the norms of concert orchestral music – in order to discern better its underlying play with convention.

The introduction to 'Ecstasio' exemplifies the dynamic ways in which its foreground material pulls against the expectations generated by the (assumed) topical background of EDM. Example 5.1 presents the principle material used in the opening bars, distinguishing between one- or two-bar melodic/rhythmic ideas (a) and the underlying harmonic structure (b). Table 5.1 shows the distribution of this material in order to highlight the ways in which Adès layers his material. The close

100 *'Ecstasio'*

resemblance between the table and the graphic interfaces of computer-based sequencers highlights certain similarities between the compositional approaches of both EDM artists and, in this movement, Adès.[15] Other similarities between the opening and EDM of the 1990s include the regular oscillation of notes a whole tone apart ($<A\flat\ G\flat>$: see the enharmonically renotated Example 5.1b) that implies a modal harmonic background; the tempo ($\downarrow = 65$); and the use of one- and two-bar patterns in the overlaid percussion and periodic structures that clarify two-, four- and eight-bar units.[16] 'Ecstasio' also employs minimal metrical deletions at the end of every eight-bar phrase that correspond to the slight deviations from EDM norms found in subgenres such as 'intelligent techno'.[17]

However, the tonal language of 'Ecstasio' is more complex than that of most EDM, achieved in part through the use of interlocking intervallic cycles (Example 5.1b; each notated minim represents one bar, though the metric deletions have been reduced out of the example). The upper system of the example moves at a typical EDM pace – every two bars – to generate a four-bar rhythmic cycle. Moving at half this speed, and beginning in bar 4, is a regular oscillation between E♭ and E♮ that outlines an eight-bar rhythmic cycle.[18] Beneath this, and beginning in the second bar, a pedal C♯ is introduced; the varied durations for which this pedal is held establish yet another eight-bar cycle. These interlocking cycles cut across the periodic structure, colouring the harmonic content and creating mild hypermetrical ambiguity.

References to the opening movement are also nestled within these bars. The harmony of Example 5.1a(ii) is built from the third and sixth dyads of *Asyla*'s introduction, {D♭, A♭} and {C, E}. Tenuous, perhaps, but the emergence of a {B, F♯} dyad in bar 5 (see Example 5.1b) strengthens the allusion, and in the light of the first two movements, such connections prove significant.

The opening of 'Ecstasio', therefore, both alludes to and distorts EDM norms. It also presents musical structures that do not derive from EDM and thus problematises how listeners are to understand the EDM norms that they hear. This in turn is characteristic of the movement as a whole. It is for this reason that the importance placed upon EDM in the publicity and reception of 'Ecstasio' is misleading, for it risks steering listeners' expectations of its processes (and wider cultural significations) away from what is actually happening in the music.

Playing with conventions

For Rick Snoman, the governing criteria for formal articulation in EDM lies in the peaks and troughs of energy that trigger collective highs and lows in the crowd; the manipulation of physical affect is paramount (see Figure 5.1).[19] A comparison between Figure 5.1 and Table 5.2, which aligns a formal overview of 'Ecstasio' with a waveform representation of Track 3 of the CD that accompanies this book,[20] suggests that 'Ecstasio' is formally closer to EDM's kinetic model than to traditional symphonic archetypes. Thus, after 'Ecstasio''s introductory Section A, there is an extended passage that falls into two related but distinct halves, labelled B and C, corresponding to the first two peaks in Figure 5.1. The endings of each of

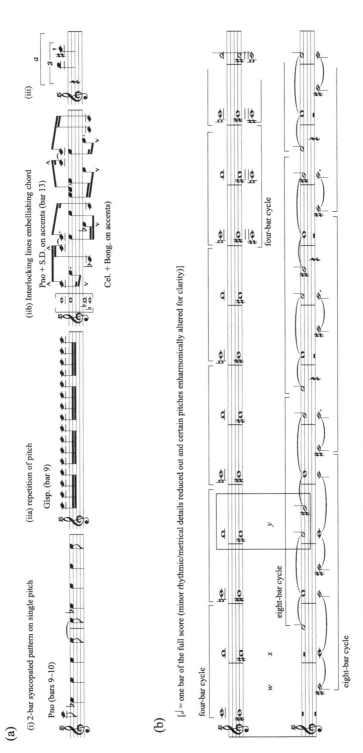

Example 5.1 *Asyla* Op. 17/iii, selected material from bars 1–24.

Table 5.1 Distribution of material in *Asyla*, third movement, bars 1–24

	1	2	3	4	5	6	7	8	9	10	11	12	13	14	15	16	17	18	19	20	21	22	23	24
Sub-section	A1								A2								A3							
Phrasing				8 bars (31 ½ ♩)								8 bars (31 ½ ♩)								8 bars (31 ½ ♩)				
Time signature	$\frac{2}{2}$							$\frac{3}{8}+\frac{2}{4}$	$\frac{4}{4}$							$\frac{3}{8}+\frac{2}{4}$	$\frac{4}{4}$							$\frac{3}{8}+\frac{2}{4}$
Bar no.	1	2	3	4	5	6	7	8	9	10	11	12	13	14	15	16	17	18	19	20	21	22	23	24
Material (see Ex. 5.1)												5.1a(iii)				5.1a(iii)				5.1a(iii)				5.1a(iii)
									5.1a(i)															
									5.1a(ii)				5.1a(ii)				5.1a(ii)							
	5.1(b)																							

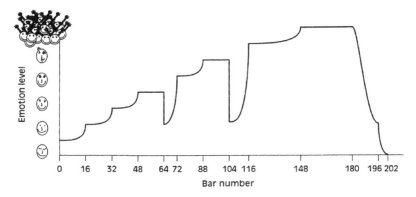

Figure 5.1 Normative rave form (from Rick Snoman, *The Dance Music Manual*).

these sections (bars 83 and 115 respectively; CD#3 2:23 and 3:23) signal progressively larger drops in intensity; the latter is particularly close to the location of the second drop in Figure 5.1 (bar 104). Indeed, the first five sections of 'Ecstasio' all deviate only slightly from 'normative' durations measured in multiples of sixteen crotchets, or four bars of $\frac{4}{4}$. Both Section D and the big trough in Figure 5.1 correspond to the traditional 'break' found in EDM.[21] This precedes a euphoric climax in Section E (which begins with the highest peak on the waveform in Table 5.2). The coda (Section F), conversely, is overly long and complex in comparison to the simple fade-outs of EDM; the presence of two further surges of intensity on the waveform is the most significant deviation from the norms of Figure 5.1. From this synoptic view, the evidence suggests that 'Ecstasio''s formal background is that of EDM, but there are signs that all is not straightforward.

Formal nods to EDM archetypes are accompanied by similar allusions in the material. Example 5.2 presents prominent melodic *paradigms* in Sections B and C. Many of these ideas are repeated in two- or four-bar units; the reliance on this, coupled with the use of syncopations and agglutinative build-ups, are all prototypical EDM devices. Even the chromatic descents that emerge in the harmonic

Section	A (Intro.)	B	C	D ('break')	E	F (coda)
Bars	1–24	25–83	84–115	116–148	149–172	173–221
Length (in crotchets)	94 ½	189 ⅔	124 ⅓	130 ½	93	151 ⅓
'Normative' length (in crotchets)	96	192	128	128	96	—

Table 5.2 Formal overview of *Asyla*, third movement

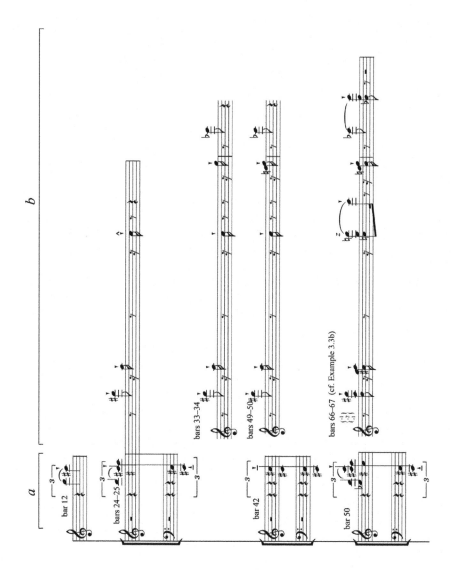

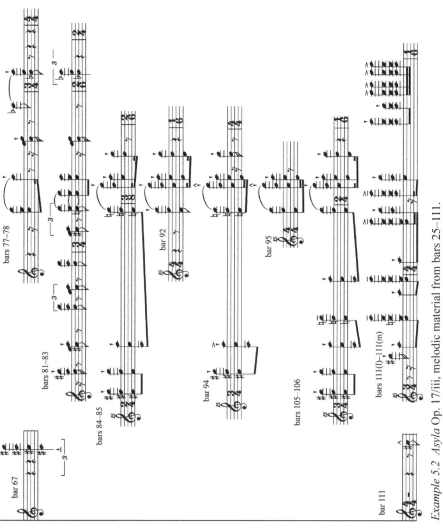

Example 5.2 *Asyla* Op. 17/iii, melodic material from bars 25–111.

106   'Ecstasio'

thickening of the material (as in bars 66–67) might be heard in part as an orchestral analogue to the filtering of harmonics (the 'filter sweep') in EDM.[22] And if the kinetic gestures of Section B resemble those of EDM, so too does the state of being (rather than becoming) that they create.[23]

The material bracketed under *a* in Example 5.2 is based upon a falling semitone, <D C♯>; the latter pitch is always doubled in numerous octaves and sometimes presented on its own as a 'stab' (as in bars 42, 67 and 111 and their repetitions). The idea is frequently but not always conjoined with the material bracketed under *b*. At first (from bar 25; CD#3 0:45), *b* combines with a sustained D in the bass and C in the treble to outline the pitches of a dominant seventh on D. If D^7 is indeed the implied harmony at this point, then it is already stylistically unusual.[24] Whether we hear the melody and bass in combination in this way is questionable, however, given the loose or even non-existent relationships so often found between strata in Adès's music. The argument could even be made that the prominence of the C♯ of paradigm *a* is such that the melodic C♮ of paradigm *b* can be heard as a leading note, with the low D so distant that it too can almost be heard as a C♯. Such a reading would suggest that the material even at this stage strains against the functional clarity typical of its EDM equivalent – the EDM norms are made newly strange even at the point of their first appearance, as part of a distancing, objectifying strategy at odds with the implied community of EDM.

This reading illuminates little, however, of the dynamic nature of the relationship between the material as perceived and the background EDM category. Thus, the process of simultaneously evoking and challenging EDM norms can be considered characteristic of melodic developmental strategies. The thickening out of *b* in bars 66–67, for instance, gradually reveals a $\begin{bmatrix} -1 \\ -2 \\ -1 \end{bmatrix}$ harmonic progression (compare with Examples 2.8 and 3.3b). That the monophonic form of the melody (e.g. bars 33–34) picks out notes from each of the three descending cycles suggests that the progression was conceived first and the melody abstracted from it. The semitonal motion in the outer voices could also be understood as both an extension of the falling semitone of paradigm *a* and a reconfiguring of the lament of the second movement, the mourners in the cathedral finding refuge in a rave.[25] Although the harmonies in bars 66–67 have certain tonal implications that are not alien to EDM, their likely origin in alternative compositional techniques suggests that to hear the chords solely in terms of EDM is to have only a partial understanding of the stylistic sensibilities at play.

The resulting stylistic tension ebbs and flows in the individual sections, acting at times centripetally as characteristic dance material is emphasised, and at other times centrifugally as this material is subsumed or distorted. Moreover, (as in any work) any given section can cause retrospective re-evaluations of earlier sections, indicating that our experience of 'Ecstasio' is far more complex than critical evaluations have so far suggested.[26] For instance, the tension between foreground and background in bars 1–24, described above, might best be construed as relatively neutral. The opening paragraphs of Section B, on the other

'Ecstasio'   107

hand, present formal, rhythmic and harmonic structures that are far more closely related to EDM, allowing for retrospective interpretation of the introduction also in terms of EDM (rather than, say, in terms of the sort of contemporary symphonic music that the first two movements would lead us to expect).

As both Section B and the movement as a whole unfold we find that this state is continually challenged. The harmonic vocabulary of bars 1–24 (Example 5.1b) has numerous correspondences with that of bars 66–67 (the stacked fourths of x are a tritone apart from the stacked fifths of z; the implied suspension found in y can be reheard in the treatment of the expanded harmonic progression, and so on). These connections begin to multiply, becoming figural, and doing so have implications later on in the movement that bring EDM conventions to a breaking point. More locally, matters reach a head at the climaxes of Sections B and C. In the build-up to these moments one finds a manipulation of textural density and timbre that parallels the archetypal developmental strategies of EDM. This allusion is made all the stronger by the introduction of pounding percussion at the climaxes, which simulates the insistent beat of a kick drum (motif s; beginning at bars 66, and more forcefully, with bass drum, at bar 111; CD#3 1:55 and 2:52). However, the melodic material is subjected to transformations that are alien to the style and closer to such traditional concepts as developing variation. The material of bars 66–67, for instance, develops by means of fragmentation (bars 77–78) and internal repetition (bars 81–83); the latter occurs at the peak of intensity in Section B, prior to the 'fall' into Section C.

Section C continues and intensifies the growing disjunction found towards the end of Section B between the developmental (symphonic) foreground and the EDM background. It begins with a version of b that is even more overtly based on a dominant seventh on D (Example 5.2, bars 84–85), but phrasing irregularities from the outset increasingly subvert the implied eight-crotchet norm. Although there are certain weak references to EDM in the phrasing and accompaniment, primarily in the kinaesthetic formal scheme, the material is as reminiscent of composers such as Leonard Bernstein as it is of EDM (consider, for instance, the jazzy horn figures first introduced in bar 86 (CD#3 2:23), versions of which punctuate the melodic material of Example 5.2). Even with the reintroduction at the climax of Section C (bars 111–115) of the archetypal gesture of EDM, the kick drum, the normative close relationship between figure and ground in EDM fails to be reinstated. Typically in EDM, DJs 'drop the beat' (that is, bring back the bass drum) to 'turn the beat around', so that a prior metric 'disorientation [is] followed by a clarification that is surprising in itself'.[27] In 'Ecstasio', however, the bass drum heightens the metric ambiguity by virtue of a lack of metrical coordination between the underlying $\frac{4}{4}$ outlined by the bass, chords and percussion, and the melodic material in the treble (see Example 5.2, bars 111(l)–(m)).[28] It is only at the end of the 32-crotchet phrase that the two metric strata realign, and then only momentarily. Such procedures go far beyond the 'embedded grouping dissonances' that Mark Butler has identified in EDM.[29] Rather, the metrical ambiguity one finds in EDM on the microlevel is re-imagined at the level of the phrase in 'Ecstasio'. Or, to put it another way, the non-repetitive development of material results in more complex stylistic syntheses that threaten to collapse the underlying EDM

108 *'Ecstasio'*

premise entirely, so that the scope for individual expression in EDM is magnified to such an extent that communal ecstasy is overtaken by individual desire.

The 'break' following this tumultuous climax (Section D, bars 116–148) is based on a repeated four-bar phrase that is characterised by a syncopated rhythm reminiscent of early 1990s 'piano anthems'.[30] The use of descending chromatic scales brings to the fore the 'filtering' analogue discussed above; its prominent use here is typical of EDM. Moreover, by virtue of the normative dance phrasing and rhythmic structure, along with the reassertion of formal EDM norms (see again Figure 5.1), the break in 'Ecstasio' suggests that the divergence between the symphonic processes in the foreground and the EDM background that characterised the climax of Section C has seemingly been resolved in favour of the latter. With the concomitant removal of melodic material, traditional forms of musical (individual) subjectivity individuality are temporarily suppressed.

This marks, therefore, a point at which EDM archetypes come once again to the fore and at which individual subjectivity is dampened. Yet it is simultaneously, and characteristically for the movement, the point at which a developmental process (and thus an indication of authorial presence) at odds with the depersonalised character of the material comes to fruition. Example 5.3 charts the various ways between the start of Section B and the end of the break in which the pitch space between D and B♭ is filled in. Initially, D and C provide a frame within which the melodic material of Example 5.2 is suspended (Example 5.3a). The high C is sustained until bar 64; the loss of the low D creates an anticipation of its return (which takes place in bar 66). Beneath this high C are frequent C♯ stabs (Example 5.2, *a*) but also chromatic shifts between C and B♭ (Examples 5.3b and c). The complete chromatic pentachord from D to B♭ is presented in the horns, with its inversion, extended over an additional octave, occurring simultaneously as glissandi in the double basses (Example 5.3d). Alongside the reintroduction of the low D at bar 66 and the chromatic voice-leading that thickens out the melodic material (see again Example 5.2), yet another means of dividing this space, and one that is stylistically typical for EDM, is presented through the means of a rising Aeolian bass line <D F G B♭>. The continuation of this line into what appears to be B or E major (Example 5.3e; note the allusion to Example 5.1b, *y* at the end) has ramifications later on in the movement; in its immediate context, the shift of harmonic perspective contributes to the increasing tension between musical foreground and EDM background. Further reworkings begin in bar 104 (Example 5.3f), and the bass progressions of Example 5.3e return, along with the odd harmonic kink at the end of the progression, at the climax of the section (Example 5.3g).

Through such means, the rising Aeolian bass has become somewhat familiar by the time it returns as the bass of the break (Example 5.3h); it has the paradoxical quality of being a well-established figure at the very point where it becomes a ground. Moreover, the four phrases of Section D (the four lines of Example 5.3h) continue to develop the material further (mirroring the harmonic strategy, though not the content, of the first movement's strophes). At first, the second half of the first phrase retains the D Aeolian modal colouring of bars 116–119, although the final chord picks up on the B major implications of Example 5.3e (here realised as a 4–3 suspension, a transposed version of *y*,

'Ecstasio'   109

over an F♯); the penultimate chord (z) harks back to bars 66–67 as well as the first two movements of *Asyla*. String harmonics provide a gloss to the second phrase, which again ends with a 4–3 suspension. In the third phrase, the harmonics are in (an enharmonically notated) B or F♯ major, thereby combining the two tonal implications of Example 5.3e as well as giving increasing prominence to the referential dyad {B, F♯}.

The increasing focus on B does not at this stage challenge the security of D as a tonic, by virtue of the prominence of the latter pitch in the previous two sections and the frequent return to D in the bass of Section D. Section E reinforces D as a tonal centre by repeating it in the bass and outlining a dominant seventh on D in the melody (from bar 149, CD#3 4:22). Alongside this, the bass drum hammers out motif *s*. Tagg identifies monothematicism as a common feature of EDM, and certainly the melodic material recalls that of earlier sections (see Example 5.2, bars 24–25 and 84–85). At the same time, the presence of the break (Section D) combined with the different textural and timbral strategies of Sections C and E give rise to 'two identifiable sections containing slightly different tonal material and variations in instrumentation'.[31] However it is interpreted, the connection between musical foreground and EDM topical background is reasserted, leading to the climax of the dance. Even when the melodic material of Section E drops a crotchet at the end of every eight bars – a rationalising, perhaps, of the irregular deletions found earlier in the movement (see the later stages of Example 5.2) – the bass drum provides a fill to articulate the earlier-than-expected downbeat.

Previously, passages of relative stylistic stability such as this had been subjected to some measure of disruption, resulting in medium-level metrical ambiguity and necessitating a constantly shifting focus between periodic grounds and aperiodic figures. Because the figure and ground in Section E are as one, disorder is created instead through the superimposition of material in the brass, creating one of the most thrilling passages in all of *Asyla* (see Example 5.4, bars 157–172). Unlike the irregular cross-rhythms at the climaxes of Sections B and C, the added layer here maintains a consistent sense of $\frac{4}{4}$ (in a 3+2+3 additive rhythm), in a metrical relationship of 3:2 to the pulse of the underlying material. Over the prolonged D^7 harmony implied by the rest of the orchestra, the harmonies in the brass project directed motion, assisted by predominantly chromatic voice-leading and a series of 4–3 suspensions (Example 5.4). Along the way, the progression offers echoes of earlier sections with chord *z* (now inverted as stacked fourths) and, at bar 165, the use of chords *x* and *y* (compare with Examples 5.1b and 5.3). This 'collecting up' of material results in yet another complex climactic texture. However, unlike the equivalent passage that closes Section C, there is no reinstatement of the EDM norm afterwards; the accumulated weight of cross-references and reminiscences that has built up across the movement seems to demand an alternative response.

Thus, the coda (Section F) differs significantly from EDM norms. Rather than offer relatively neutral material that enables tracks to be mixed together more easily, the coda presents a continuation of the directed harmonic motion

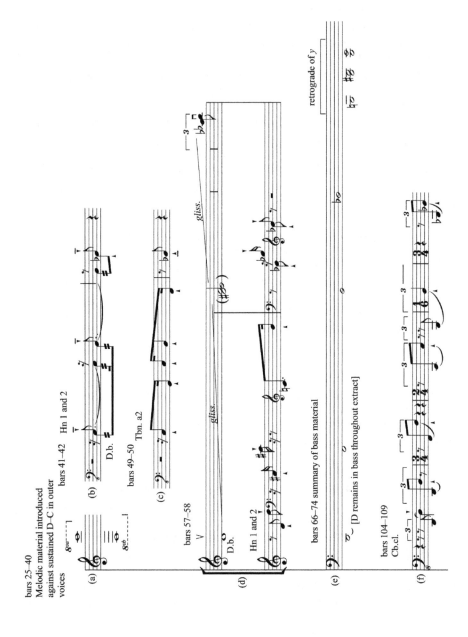

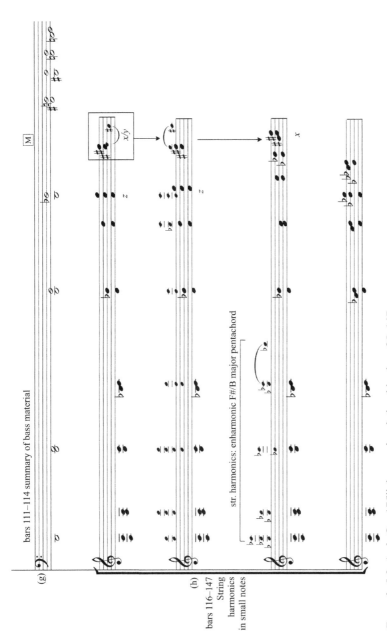

Example 5.3 *Asyla* Op. 17/iii, harmonic relationships bars 25–147.

112   'Ecstasio'

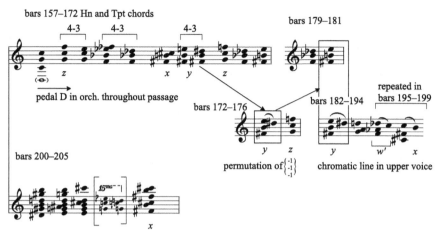

Example 5.4 Asyla Op. 17/iii, harmonic relationships in bars 157–205.

of bars 157–172.[32] As can be seen in Example 5.4, this motion is governed by chromatic lines in the treble and alludes in the final bars to an almost-conventional cadence in B. Rapid juxtapositions of texture and timbre mean, however, that the seemingly smooth lines of the example are in context part of a far more turbulent expressive environment than has hitherto been presented in the movement, and certainly far beyond that which EDM would tolerate in a coda (see the two surges in Table 5.2). The progression from *y* to *z* is repeated from bar 172; in this context, the progression might be heard as a permuted $\begin{Bmatrix} -1 \\ -1 \\ -1 \end{Bmatrix}$. Beginning at bar 182 (CD #3, 5:22), the upper voice presents a series of appoggiatura-like figures that recall similar material from earlier in the work; more significant, the harmonic material is closely related to that of the opening bars (the two chords marked *w'* contain all of the pitches of Example 5.1b's chord *w*). If claims that this amounts to the culmination of a teleological drive across the movement seem implausible, it does not seem to strain credibility to suggest that these bars provide a compact summary and intensification of the network of harmonic relationships that are played out across the movement.

There are two unsuccessful attempts to restart the dance, which has effectively been abolished as a result of the shift in emphasis from melodic and rhythmic arguments (prominent in Sections B–E) to one in which harmony is central. (There is a parallel here with the changes of musical perspective in the first movement.) The first of these (bars 179–181), initially assertive, is frustrated after an uncharacteristic three-bar period; the second is ghostly and resigned (bars 185–186). In the context of the relatively directed motion of the coda, such reminiscences sound alien; the foreground material has become irretrievably and irreversibly distanced from the EDM background.

There is a twist in the tale. Adès has suggested that he used material from 'the end of Act II of *Parsifal* at the end of *Ecstasio*'.[33] There are certainly sufficient tonal, voice-leading and textural parallels between the two (compare Examples 5.4 and 5.5) to invite interpretation. The Act concludes with Parsifal bringing down the walls of Klingsor's *Zauberschloß* [Magic Castle], destroying the vision of a bounteous garden ('Der Garten is schnell zu einer Einöde verdorrt' [the garden quickly withers to a wasteland]). It is tempting, therefore, to hear the coda of 'Ecstasio' as a denouncement of rave culture as an illusory refuge, no more able to provide asylum than the wastelands of the first movement. Paul Griffiths's description of 'Ecstasio' as 'a ferocious assault of mindless repetition and a ferocious outcry against it' would appear to hinge on such a reading.[34] An axiological judgement against EDM of this nature is, however, at odds with Adès's own willingness to embrace popular culture.[35]

Example 5.5 Wagner, *Parsifal*, end of Act II.

114 'Ecstasio'

It is through a cataclysmic effort that the music wrenches itself away from the underlying EDM framework in preparation for the final movement. Its final chord, an ethereally sustained version in string harmonics of chord x (bars 207–215), contains within it the referential dyad {B, F♯}. Perhaps a simulation of the ringing in the ears that often results from listening to high-decibel electronic music, it sounds a disembodied note (in numerous senses) with which to end the movement.

Notes

1 *TA:FON*, p. 166.
2 *Performance on 3* (1 October 1997).
3 *Music for the 21st Century.* The narration begins at 29:45.
4 Ross notes the similarities between 'Ecstasio' and a sequence from Alan Hollinghurst's 1998 novel *The Spell*, in which a 'well-behaved civil servant [...] takes Ecstasy, goes out to a raunchy London club, and finds his bourgeois values in free fall'. 'Roll Over, Beethoven', p. 130.
5 Turner, *A Classless Society*, p. 137.
6 Unlike Adès's concerns over 'Vatican', 'whatever [Ecstasio] suggests to the listener is intended'. Adès, *Performance on 3* (1 October 1997).
7 Clark, 'Adès Delights the Ear'.
8 *TA:FON*, p. 78.
9 Adès has noted that 'Ecstasio' is 'a knight's move away [from EDM] and is related to house music in the way a Haydn minuet might be related to music in a Viennese square'. Wroe, 'Adès on Adès'.
10 '[I]ntelligent techno involved a full-scale retreat from the most radically posthuman and hedonistically funktional [*sic*] aspects of rave music towards more traditional ideas about creativity, namely the auteur theory of the solitary genius who humanizes technology rather than subordinates himself to the drug-tech interface'. Simon Reynolds, *Energy Flash: A Journey through Rave Music and Dance Culture* (London: Picador 1998), p. 157.
11 See Philip Tagg, 'From Refrain to Rave: the Decline of Figure and the Rise of Ground', *Popular Music*, 13/ii (1994), pp. 209–22.
12 An example of this can be found in Rick Snoman's *The Dance Music Manual: Tools, Toys, and Techniques* 2nd edn (Oxford: Taylor and Francis/Focal Press, 2009).
13 See Spitzer, *Metaphor and Musical Thought*, pp. 7 ff.
14 The subsequent discussion focuses on the cues that are most prevalent in discourse about the musical characteristics of EDM. Though such an approach glosses over the many subtleties of this repertoire (as indeed does much of the discourse, for that matter), it nevertheless provides a basis for stylistic norms and expectations against which we can measure 'Ecstasio'.
15 See Snoman, *The Dance Music Manual*, p. 180.
16 For an overview of the characteristics of EDM of the early 1990s, see Tagg, 'From Refrain to Rave', pp. 213–6.
17 Small phrasing irregularities of this nature provide sonic traces of the auteur identified by Reynolds (see note 10). Snoman prizes such details, describing them as the 'human element' in EDM (*Dance Music Manual*, pp. 214–15). Ross likens Adès's use of them to portrayals of 'apparent stumbles and accidents' involving a dancer ('Roll Over, Beethoven', p. 130), which is to suggest that he hears such devices as deviations from a stylistic EDM norm.
18 The E♭ is notated as D♯ in the example to clarify its relationship with material that occurs later in the movement.

'Ecstasio' 115

19 Snoman, *Dance Music Manual*, p. 225. See also Mark Butler, *Unlocking the Groove: Rhythm, Meter, and Musical Design in Electronic Dance Music* (Bloomington and Indianapolis: Indiana University Press, 2006), pp. 221–40.

20 The waveform was created with *Audacity* (http://audacity.sourceforge.net/); as both channels of the stereo mix are to all intents and purposes identical, only the left-hand channel has been reproduced.

21 See Tagg, 'From Refrain to Rave', p. 216.

22 An example of how sweeps sound can be found at http://howtomakeelectronicmusic.com/how-to-create-an-effective-rising-build-up [accessed 12 August 2015].

23 For more on this, see Edward Venn, 'Narrativity in Thomas Adès's *Ecstasio*', *Res Facta Nova*, 11/x (2010), pp. 69–78.

24 Tagg, 'From Refrain to Rave', p. 215.

25 This somewhat incongruous juxtaposition of the sacred and secular is not as forced as one might suspect. A month before Adès premiered *Under Hamelin Hill* in Ely Cathedral (29 July 1992), the cathedral inaugurated its now-annual 'Rave in the Nave' (28 June 1992). Having just completed his studies at Cambridge, less than 20 miles south of Ely, it is likely that Adès would have been aware of the event, and images of the cathedral accompanied the presentation of the second movement of *Asyla* in *Music for the 21st Century*.

26 Examples of this critical reception can be found in Chapter 7.

27 Butler, *Unlocking the Groove*, pp. 246–7.

28 Bars 111 and 112 occupy durations of respectively thirty-two and twenty-four crotchets respectively. Material that is coordinated around the crotchet tread of the kick drum is notated as eight and six bars of ($\frac{4}{4}$ (bars 111–111(vii)) and 112–112(v)). The irrational rhythmic and metric structures of the superimposed melodic material necessitate irregular barring; these are notated as fourteen and twelve bars respectively (bars 111–111n and 112–112k).

29 Butler, *Unlocking the Groove*, p. 158.

30 Numerous online sites offer an introduction to piano anthems. Compare, for instance, CD#3 at 3:23 with www.youtube.com/watch?v=drur9JeMFUk at 7:17 [accessed 12 August 2015].

31 Tagg, 'From Refrain to Rave', p. 215.

32 This is not to imply that there is not some sense of connection between 'Ecstasio' and the fourth movement (see Chapter 6). But there nevertheless remains a signal difference between the ways in which the closing stages of EDM are designed to overlap with the tracks that follow, and the ways in which the movements in *Asyla* follow sequentially in time from one to the next.

33 *TA:FON*, p. 58.

34 Paul Griffiths, 'Everyone Wants a Piece of Adès: This Piece', *New York Times* (6 December 1998).

35 Ross reports how Adès derives pleasure 'from contemporary London and from intellectual company that doesn't cloister itself from popular culture'. 'Roll Over, Beethoven', p. 130. I shall return to the considerable interpretative questions posed by the ending of 'Ecstasio' in Chapter 7.

6   Asylum gained?

Even without the benefit of a programme note, a listener familiar with multi-movement orchestral music would have certain expectations about what might follow 'Ecstasio'. The ordering and content of the first three movements of *Asyla* invite comparison with typical symphonic norms, and with it the anticipation of a finale that incorporates particular summative musical procedures. Such procedures might include the resolution of musical tensions that have been developed over the preceding movements; perhaps a return of certain themes (in the manner of a cyclic symphony); and some sort of culmination and fulfilment of the musical and expressive states that have been played out over the duration of the entire work.

Adès is aware of, and engages with, such expectations. Having struggled initially with 'finding appropriate music to follow the scary hedonism of "Ecstasio"',[1] he settled eventually upon a 'slow sort of passacaglia',[2] which suggests parallels with the finale of Brahms's Symphony No. 4 Op. 98.[3] For Adès, the passacaglia offers the opportunity to create a connecting thread that weaves through the movement, 'a repeating, descending bass that goes through it, although it goes through different keys, so you don't hear it as going round to the start again all the time'.[4] (The first occurrence of the passacaglia theme is given in Example 6.1, below.) There is a parallel here with the treatment of the theme and variations in the middle of the second movement.

Such linear connections offer continuity underneath the surface contrasts of texture, sonority and theme; these in turn articulate the underlying form. As with the first and second movements, the sections that emerge coalesce into a broad ternary form (see Table 6.1). Familiar, too, is the way that the disproportionately long statement of the passacaglia theme, accounting for a full quarter of the movement's duration, leads to compression and acceleration. The harmonic structure of the movement seems initially to pay lip service to traditional tonal organisation in the move to the 'dominant minor' in bars 20–23 in the manner of a second subject. However, the climax occurs at the distance of a tritone from the opening (bars 61–66). If the move to the dominant minor had established expectations of a tonal recapitulation, they are cruelly thwarted both at the point of thematic recapitulation and in the subsequent coda.

Another way of understanding the harmonic argument of the movement is with reference to the intervallic cycles that structure it. The treatment of the passacaglia

Asylum gained? 117

Table 6.1 Formal overview of *Asyla*, fourth movement

Section	Bars/Track Timing (CD #4)	Comments	Tonal Centre/ Bass Pitch Collection	Duration (seconds)
A	1–8 [0:00]	Allusion to Bartók; passacaglia theme	A minor/ WT1	69
	9–12 [1:09]	First statement of 'choral' theme	A minor/WT0	26
	13–19 [1:35]	'Interlude' (tuned percussion and keyboards)	C minor/ ambiguous	35
	20–23 [2:10]	Second statement of 'choral' theme	E minor / WT0→WT1	27
	24–28 [2:37]	Closing section: further allusion to Bartók	F♯ minor/WT1	13
B	29–41 [2:50]	Embellished chromatic descent in woodwind	A♭ major/WT1	15
	42–60 [3:05]	Superimposition of material from movements I–III	E major – G/ D♭ major/ ambiguous	33
A′	61–66 [3:38]	Third statement of 'choral' theme; allusion to Mahler	E♭ minor	35
Coda	67–72 [4:13]	Allusion to first movement	G major/minor	22

Timings taken from CD accompanying this book.

bass in Sections A and A′ gives rise to large-scale alternations of material based on the WT0 and WT1 collections; these in turn establish the foundations for expanded harmonic progressions. In Section B, the emphasis shifts from harmony to melody and counterpoint, and the coda offers a more cryptic survey of the musical issues of the movement (and indeed, work) as a whole. The relationship between these intervallic cycles and fragments of functional progressions contributes to the allusive harmonic character of the movement. In this sense, the motion between the tritone poles of A and E♭ emerges not as a challenge to functional tonality, but as a logical consequence of the nature of the musical material.

The use of intervallic cycles is also one of the primary means by which Adès is able to refer to material from elsewhere in *Asyla* without disturbing the underlying continuity. There are numerous recollections of the tuned percussion interludes from earlier movements, but the centrepiece of the finale is an extraordinary passage in which material from the first three movements is drawn together in a whirling vortex that hints at some mode of resolution (bars 42–60). The grand climax beginning in bar 61 would appear to confirm this reading, but the change of perspective provided in the coda offers an enigmatic close.

All told, the content of the finale aims for

a musical resolution to all the questions and problems that had been set up by the rest of the piece. It has a big choral effect, as an idea which as a chorus keeps coming back during it, often one part of the orchestra in

118 *Asylum gained?*

one speed, and one in another speed and it will flare up, and that suddenly breaks down and you have a passage where everything is rushing in at you, like a black hole. Everything rushes in from the rest of the piece and then it has one huge statement of this idea: it's as though you are released at the end.[5]

Despite such seemingly overt nods to 'the safety of tradition', the finale approaches such expectations obliquely: all of the above procedures can be found within it, but characteristically they are problematised, blurred, as the music explores the play between notions of 'tradition' and 'daunting freedom'.[6] If, as Porter suggests, the 'close brings a sense of asylum gained', then it is a hard-won gain, and one that demands close scrutiny.[7]

Section A (bars 1–28)

The expressive character of the opening section emerges from the contrast between, and combination of, the lugubrious passacaglia theme, first announced by the basses (see Example 6.1), and the idea Adès associated with a 'choral effect' (hereafter, 'choral theme'; Example 6.2). Though the latter shares something of the former's lamenting tone, successive presentations are by turn consoling and, in the peroration of the whole work, sublime. Harmonic contrast between the themes comes from the pronounced use of whole-tone steps in the passacaglia, and the semitonal descent of the *passus duriusculus* in the choral theme. In both melodic contour and propensity towards trochaic rhythmic organisation, both of these thematic ideas recall the horn melody of the first movement, as part of the continued exploration of the fundamental building blocks of the work across all four movements.

As the section progresses, the whole-tone collections that underpin each phrase begin to interact with other, hierarchic modes of organisation. In the presentation of the passacaglia theme in bars 1–8, the relative conformance between linear (whole-tone) and vertical (harmonic) material suggests a degree of tonal stability. With the entry of the choral theme in bar 9, this provisional equilibrium is challenged by the conflicting strategies that govern pitch and rhythmic organisation in the melody, harmony and bass. Given its progressive destabilisation, it is paradoxical that the choral theme should end with a cadence in C minor, in the most direct allusion to functional tonality of the movement, (CD #4, 1:35; compare with the start of the closing section in the second movement). The simultaneous tendencies towards stability and instability within the two themes are thus made to coexist, albeit uneasily.

Passacaglia theme (bars 1–8)

A measured silence of six bars separates 'Ecstasio' from the final movement. Any positive connotations that might have been attached to the conclusion of 'Ecstasio' are soon dispelled by the sombre, elegiac chords that follow it, superimposed over

Asylum gained? 119

a mourning, drawn-out theme (Example 6.1). As with the link between the first and second movements, the third and fourth are connected by intervallic cycles: a $\begin{Bmatrix} -1 \\ -2 \\ -2 \end{Bmatrix}$ expanded progression carries chord x <B F# C#> across the silence to <A E C♮>.[8] After the hyperactive urban nightscape of 'Ecstasio', the slow tread

of one chord per bar, exacerbated by the slow tempo ($\quarternote = 52$) and drawn-out metre (Adès notates it in 7/4), suggests an entirely different nocturnal environment. We might locate this more precisely: the opening woodwind flourishes and embellishing chords in the strings that together constitute the upper stratum mimic figuration to be found in Bartók's *Bluebeard's Castle*.[9] Bartók's music is frozen onto a repeated A minor chord, and similarly Adès's, though slightly more mobile, circles around the same harmony. Of all the material in *Asyla*, this is one of the most musically and expressively direct passages.

Attention is focussed initially upon a lugubrious reminiscence of the first movement's horn melody, scored for solo tuba and double basses. Beneath it, the passacaglia theme slowly descends in the basses, harmonised by perfect fifths in the wind and string accompaniment, only to change course after four bars to return to A minor. Supported by this relatively traditional harmonic vocabulary, the slurred pairs of pitches in the melody suggest an equally traditional interpretation. Thus, the <C D / D C> motion suggests a typical neighbour-note motion, in which the initial ascent creates a melodic tension that is resolved in the complementary descent. Yet the harmonic motion complicates this reading, for the repeated D is heard as consonant above the G in the bass, and the concluding melodic C creates a dissonance.[10] Contextually, this final C can therefore be heard as simultaneously embodying harmonic dissonance as well as melodic resolution. Its continuation maintains this double function. Whilst the implied melodic suspension <C B> in bar 3 behaves in a more traditional manner (the dissonant <G♭ C> relaxes into the enharmonic fourth <G♭ B>), its repetition in bar 4, which results in a stable perfect fifth <F C> 'resolving' onto a tritone, is an intensification of the situation in bar 2. (Note, once again, the recurrence of the referential dyads.)

Three soft drum beats (played by timpani and bass drums), recalling motif *s*, divide the two halves of the passacaglia theme. The articulation of the formal structure is significant: motif *s* returns throughout the movement in increasingly insistent guises, clarifying the form and, most significantly, leading to the climax.

The second half of the passacaglia theme reworks the material of bars 1–4. It begins as though repeating the antecedent, but its final two bars divert the music into new regions. The melodic phrasing above it suggests a similar pattern of tension and release as before, but once again the harmonic environment qualifies such experiences. In bar 7, the descent from D♭ to B♭ (the first leap of the theme) would traditionally suggest that both notes are consonant (hinting at a B♭ minor or perhaps D♭ added-sixth chord); the subsequent E♭-rooted chord in turn would imply a functional fifth-relationship between chords. For this reason, the melodic rise <B♭ C♭> (the fetish pitches of the second movement) in bar 8 is ambiguous.

Example 6.1 Asyla Op. 17/iv, bars 1–12 (reduction, with melodic details of bars 1–8).

Asylum gained? 121

By inverting the semitone fall of bar 4, it implies closure (analogous with similar patterns in the first and second movement), but to hear the C♭ as a melodic goal conflicts with the implied harmonic progression. As with so much in Adès's music, there is a functional ambiguity: listening preferences that prioritise the melody encourage an interpretation of the final bar based upon an A♭ minor chord (in which the B♭ functions as a neighbour to the C♭), whereas focussing on implied harmonic roots encourages a greater sense of directed motion (in which the final C♭ is heard as contextually dissonant).

Less ambiguous is the descending bass of the consequent, which is solely in whole-tone steps drawn from the WT1 collection. This distorts the original harmonic progression, and if bar 8 is heard as an E♭-rooted harmony, the motion across the eight bars from A to E♭ minor presents in miniature the tonal structure of the movement as a whole. The projection of a symmetrical set in this manner weakens the gravitational pull of the initial 'tonic', which is otherwise asserted through contextual factors (for instance, the prominence of A at the beginning of each four-bar phrase) rather than through the attraction of traditional pitch hierarchies. The lack of tonal pull is emphasised further in the continuation of the whole-tone descent to a C♯ in bar 9, a subtle means of creating continuity between sections beneath the ear-catching changes of texture, tempo and instrumentation.

The opening bars, therefore, offer a clearly expressive but gently ambiguous musical environment. The lilting stepwise motion of the melody above the passacaglia theme suggests some sort of songfulness (though displaced into a register that few could sing in); the allusions to Bartók provide intertextual connotations of mourning that give this song a lamenting quality. Yet even here the material is refracted so that the direct qualities of expression are balanced by less certain undercurrents: unlike the Bartók, in which melody and harmony cooperate in a unified tonal space, Adès's material refuses to gel.

First choral theme (bars 9–12)

When Taruskin claims that the horn melody from the first movement returns, inverted, in the finale, it is possible that he is thinking of the choral theme introduced in bar 9 (Example 6.2a) rather than that of the opening eight bars.[11] It is not a literal inversion, of course: although the choral theme traces a descending line, and the pitches of the first oboe line spell out a complete CII octatonic set,[12] the meandering descent, repeatedly turning back on itself, recalls the relative immobility of the passacaglia theme rather than the dynamism of the horn melody. There is an expressive inversion, however: the heroic striving of the horn theme has become a keening lament. The lament is treated heterophonically: as the two oboes and cor anglais circle around one another, the *idea* of a melody is suggested – indeed, as the annotations to Example 6.1 suggest, the twisted skeleton of a *passus duriusculus* can be identified – but a single unambiguous statement is avoided. This is a communal mourning, the heterophonic strands chafing together to create intense, painful semitone dissonances that melt into fleeting, beautiful consonances and temporary emotional release.

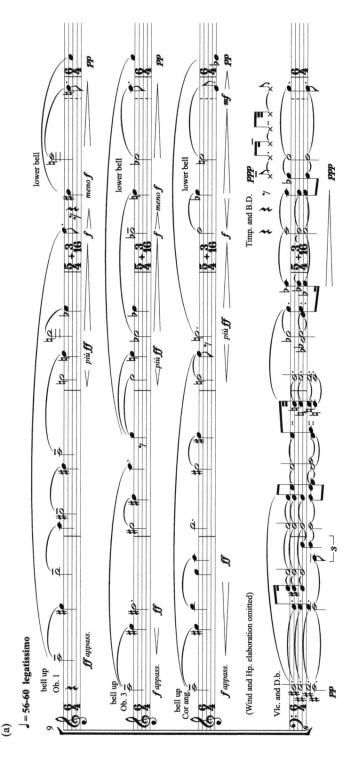

Example 6.2 *Asyla* Op. 17/iv. (a) bars 9–13; (b) bars 20–23; (c) bars 60–63.

Example 6.2 (Continued)

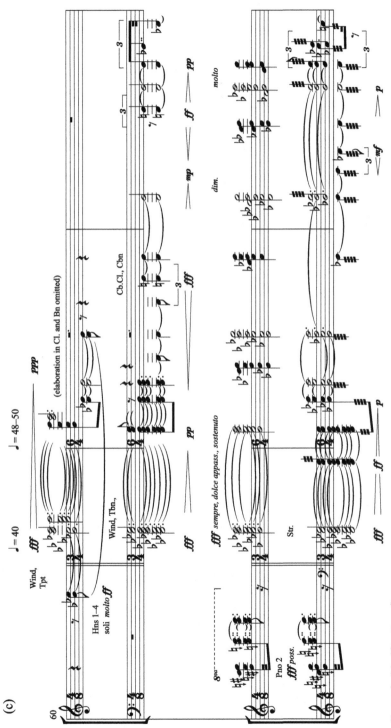

Example 6.2 (Continued)

Asylum gained?   125

Although the tempo is only slightly faster from bar 9 ($\bullet$ = 56–60), the rate of harmonic change is just over twice as fast as in the opening eight bars; this, coupled with the more active melodic layer, heightens the sense of contrast between the two sections. The impression of A as a tonic recedes, despite the choral theme taking it up as a melodic centre of gravity. The sense of centrifugal motion away from this centre can be felt in the passacaglia theme in the bass, transposed to begin on F♯ (initiating a descent through WT0, rather than WT1, to A♭),[13] and in the allusion to a functional, directed cycles of fifths progression in the middle stratum (to which the lower wind add flourishes, providing continuity with bars 1–8). Every other chord in the middle stratum contains a referential dyad from _Asyla_'s introduction (in turn {B, F♯}, {F, C} and {D♭, A♭}). Barely audible is the harp's slow arpeggiation through the material of the lower and middle strata, creating a 5:4 cross rhythm against the crotchet motion in the upper stratum and subtly preparing for more extensive metric canons later in the movement. The section ends with the muffled drum beats of motif _s_.

Once again, explicit topical and expressive references (the keening of the oboes) are situated in a harmonic/melodic environment that is ambiguous. Indeed, these four bars are even less harmonically focussed than the opening eight, for the tonal materials brought into play are more diffuse – octatonic in the upper stratum, diatonic fifth-based progressions in the middle and whole-tone in the bass, with only occasional points of contact between them. The seductive nature of the material might encourage listeners to gloss over such disjunctions, but their presence serves nevertheless to complicate the emotional message.

Bars 13–19

The musical tensions of the choral theme are intensified in bars 13–19. The section begins with an apparent cadence in C minor (see Examples 6.1 and 6.3), and another shivering wind and string flourish, itself sustained by string harmonics which glissando down into silence. From this icy chill emerge the two upright pianos in a distorted echo of the choral theme, shadowed by a gong a triplet quaver behind it. The melodic line begins with the outline of a descending chromatic cycle that echoes the _passus duriusculus_ of bars 9–12 before suddenly accelerating and distorting under pressure from the second piano's quarter-tone tuning. Underneath, there is an even more meandering, unfocussed descent in the bass that retains little of the purpose of the passacaglia theme. The melody and bass barely interact or cohere: there is motion without movement. Despite a further quickening of pulse ($\bullet$=66–69), time is suspended.

Another cowbell and piano flourish (bar 17; CD#4, 1:58) initiates an uncertain version of the choral theme, delivered by both upright pianos. Above it, in a mensuration canon, there is a slow, sickly sweet version of the choral theme, scored for a stratospherically high trio of solo violins and viola. Both of these versions, suspended in their respective strata, have no active bass material to ground them; the result is far removed from the expressive focus of the oboe presentation of the same material. In conjunction with the other-worldly, detached associations of the

126 *Asylum gained?*

Example 6.3 Asyla Op. 17/iv, reduction of bars 13–19.

tuned percussion that have accrued over *Asyla*, the effect is less of thematic development, but of interruption (and a recollection of the drooping lines of the slow movement). The choice of timbres seems calculated to emphasise the structural disjuncture and harmonic instability which results from the floating textures and directionless bass and which begins increasingly to haunt the work.

Second choral theme (bars 20–23)

Tonal bearings are momentarily re-established with the presentation of both the choral and passacaglia themes in the lower strings (see Example 6.4). The former is more clearly based around a *passus duriusculus* (here, between G and D) than in its first statement; the latter begins with an emphasis on whole-tone steps, at first drawing on WT0 before filling out a <B♭ A♭ F♯> WT1 descent (each of these roots on a metrically strong beat) with chromatic passing notes. Homophonic rather than heterophonic, the combination of both themes in the lower strings offers a rich, consolatory expressive environment. Yet this arises only as the result of individually overlapping lines, none of which contain either of the themes in their entirety. What we perceive as melody emerges only in the composite effect of massed string lines, an audible metaphor for groups coming together in an altogether more dignified mourning than the wails of the first presentation.

Nevertheless, the expressive immediacy of this material is set into relief by the continuation of the dissonant version of the choral theme in the solo strings that maintains an almost exact 5:4 mensuration canon with the lower stratum. The increasingly elaborate percussion flourishes of the middle stratum maintain the reference to Bluebeard's lake of tears (or at the very least, if listeners do not recognise the Bartók allusion, the decoration provides a connection to impersonal, hostile, mournful atmosphere of the first eight bars of the movement). The result is an image of disunity that serves to fracture the community forged by the lower strings.

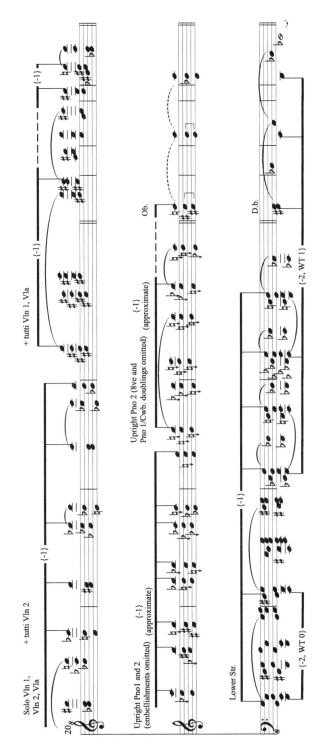

Example 6.4 *Asyla* Op. 17/iv, reduction of bars 20–28.

128   *Asylum gained?*

Closing section (bars 24–28)

Another clearing of the texture, along with a recollection of the material and atmosphere of the opening eight bars, creates a frame that encloses the first two choral themes; bars 24–28 can be heard therefore as a closing section to Section A. In the bass stratum, the passacaglia theme returns in truncated form: two descending whole-tone steps through the WT0 collection from F♯ to D. Above this, the upper double basses oscillate between A and B♭ in what seems to be a failed attempt to recall the melody from bars 1–8. Wind flourishes shadow the passacaglia bass, but do not coincide with its changes exactly.

Such reminiscences bear the traces of the expressive experiences of the previous twenty-four bars. The upper stratum from the previous section remains, now given to tutti violins and violas, an eerie hangover from the collective lament(s). There is also an accelerando through the passage – a move that recreates in a few bars the gradual accelerando heard over the first few minutes, which, in conjunction with a crescendo in the final bar, imparts a sense of urgency to the material. The static contemplation that characterised much of the earlier passacaglia material yields to a growing anxiety; the musical and extramusical whirlwind of *Asyla*'s material is about to hit.

Section B (bars 29–60)

To hear the previous section 'as' a closing section draws on a range of stylistic knowledge: the recollection of material in a brief passage after a climactic theme suggests formal closure, but the motion from A minor and WT0 in bars 1–8 to F♯ minor and WT1 in 24–28 creates a tonal tension that necessitates continuation. Such knowledge arises not only from familiarity with musical precedents from the past centuries ('the canon') but also from formal patterns established with and across *Asyla* (most tangibly in the first movement). But this stylistic knowledge also sets up formal expectations of contrast. Generically, Section B resembles a scherzo by virtue of its light, quicksilver figuration, animated by a predominantly semiquaver surface rate. Set at a dancing tempo of ♩. = 76, it suggests the acceleration through Section A has (temporarily) reached a hiatus. The passacaglia theme moves into the middle of the texture, drifting in and out of focus. At the same time, however, the speed of the bass line slows drastically, resulting in long pedal points. The combination of different rates of motion is reminiscent of Sibelius, though the expressive world is far removed. The giddy, teeming effect instead recalls the close of the first two movements of *Asyla*. 'Everything rushes in', and as reminiscence of earlier movements piles upon reminiscence, the music charges towards its climax.

Bars 29–41

The section begins with chirruping flutes that resemble the stylised birdsong of the first movement, singing out over a static E♭ in the bass (the ostensible tonic of the second movement). Poised between these two extremes, pizzicato strings and cowbell combine with the decorations in the flute to imply two expanded $\left\{\begin{smallmatrix} -1 \\ -2 \\ -2 \end{smallmatrix}\right\}$

harmonic progressions. The first of these progressions (bars 29–33) is concise, the lower voice, deriving from the passacaglia theme, is implied as often as it is present (see Example 6.5). Nevertheless, the notional harmonic roots of the middle stratum belong to the WT0 collection and the bass pedal to the WT1 collection, thereby superimposing the two harmonic areas of Section A.

The second phrase (bars 34–41; CD#4, 2:58) relates to the first in the same way that the two halves of bars 1–8 relate: it begins as if a direct repetition, but the melodic and harmonic motion is contorted so that it ends in unexpected tonal waters. This is achieved through the introduction of a contracting intervallic series <E♭ D C A F C F♯ B D♯ F♯ G♯ A> that rises from the bass to thicken the texture but also to deflect the implied expanded harmonic progression of the inner voices towards {F, C} and {B, F♯}.[14] The stage is thus set tonally (all of these pitches belong to the CII octatonic collection) and referentially (with the opening dyads of the first movement); a further accelerando to ♩= 120–126 ushers in a more comprehensive, climactic review of material from earlier movements.

Bars 42–60

In fact, the reminiscences begin just before the new tempo is reached: in bar 40 (CD#4, 3:04) muted horns and trumpets steal in, *ppp poss.*, with the start of the horn theme from the first movement. The ghostly, virtually inaudible beginning is characteristic: as with the distorted recollections of the *idée fixe* in the concluding opiate dream of a Witches' Sabbath in Berlioz's *Symphonie Fantastique*, Adès's material returns perverted, corrupted, as if the entirety of *Asyla* to date is recalled in a paranoid hallucinogenic flashback. This is the comedown from 'Ecstasio'.

The musical framework in which the reminiscences are suspended follows a similar pattern to bars 29–41. A descending semitone cycle continues to impart direction to the florid upper woodwind line; cycles begin on A in bars 42 and 46, and then on D♭ in bars 50 and 55 (an octave higher than at bar 29; see Example 6.5). The increasingly hyperactive inner voices (scored primarily for frantic pizzicato violins) begin with an assertion of the expanded harmonic progression, but a deflection to {B, F♯} in bar 44 sets the tone for subsequent repetitions of the upper wind phrases; although {B, F♯} keeps returning amidst the tumult as a reference point, there is a loss of harmonic purpose. The bass is characterised by a slow pendulum swing between B and D, recalling the key centres of the third movement. Untuned percussion (three large tins and bass drums) provide a consistent low-level clattering and rumbling.

The distorted reminiscences are threaded through this. No longer strident, the horns present their melody from first movement *pianissimo*, each note choked by handstopping; the trumpets that accompany them stifle their own brassy timbre with whisper mutes. This profound change in colour and emotional tone is matched by an elongation of the first note of each trochee so that they are

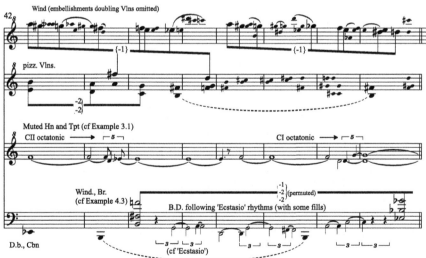

Example 6.5 *Asyla* Op. 17/iv, reduction of bars 29–60.

Asylum gained? 131

Example 6.5 (Continued)

grotesquely disproportionate to the shorter notes: the approximate sense of metrical regularity apparent in Example 3.1 is lost in the haze. There is uncertainty, too, about tonal direction: opening at first with a subset of the CII octatonic collection, the material migrates via a subset of CI to conclude with pitches drawn from CIII. If the opening kink in the melody of the first movement suggested long-range closure, this final recollection of the material resolutely fails to provide it.

The slow movement is represented by the first three chords of *The Fayrfax Carol*, which may in turn account for the degraded treatment of the expanded $\begin{Bmatrix} -1 \\ -2 \\ -2 \end{Bmatrix}$ harmonic progression in the upper strata of the previous section. As with

132   *Asylum gained?*

the horn melody, these are transformed timbrally (now given to lower wind, brass and strings), harmonically (the order of chords is permuted) and rhythmically (the placement of chords is unpredictable). Similarly, the cyclic melody of Section E of 'Ecstasio' is slowed inexorably, lumbering in the double basses and contrabassoon, accompanied by bass drum; the accented *fortepiano* articulating each note exaggerating the articulation of the original theme.

The textural complexity of these bars provides little opportunity for the manner of vertical integration between layers seen in, for instance, the second movement. Rather, the effect is a heightened version of the tensions found in the climaxes of 'Ecstasio': the profusion of materials leads to crisis rather than meaningful coexistence. And thus the proceedings are brought dramatically to a head: a pair of chords (suggesting I–V in D♭ major) is repeated twice, only to grind to a halt on a C♭-rooted chord. From this, two bass drums hammer out motif *s*, its trajectory across *Asyla*, culminating with a bone-shaking *ffff*, its regular pulsations stretched to breaking point by a substantial ritardando that reduces the tempo eventually to ♩ = 40. A cryptic pair of chords on the quarter-tone piano suggest a V–I cadence in E♭ minor, but it is a bar early: the real climax is to follow.

Section A' (bars 61–66)

Asyla's expressive highpoint arrives with the *molto fortissimo* cadence of the horn melody that ran through bars 40–58; the fourth <B♭ E♭> that it reaches at its peak (bar 60) plunges down through an octave, enveloped in a cataclysmic E♭ minor chord (Example 6.2c). Roderic Dunnett's description of this moment as Mahlerian only tells half of the story:[15] the chord has a structural and (possibly) emotional function comparable to the catastrophic appearance of the same harmony in the Scherzo of Mahler's Third Symphony (between Figs. 31 and 32). This is perhaps no coincidence: at its premiere, *Asyla* was followed by the Mahler, and the vital role played by E♭ minor in *Asyla* would make such a connection all the more likely.[16] This similarity is reinforced by the fact that both pieces move from E♭ minor to a tonal centre on D♭, even if the musical logic governing the move differs. There are internal cross-references, too. From this shattering moment emerges the peroration of the choral theme, the melody presented in its entirety by the upper desk of first violins, supported by rich harmony in the upper strings. The centre of gravity of the melody is G♭, as if the multiple harmonisations of F♯ with a B across *Asyla*, beginning in bar 18 of the first movement (if not bar 3) has been finally and irrevocably abandoned in favour of an enharmonic resolution in E♭ minor. It follows the chromatic descent of the *passus duriusculus* heard in the previous two state-ments of the choral theme, but it fails to descend through the full fourth from G♭ to a (metrically strong) D♭, remaining tantalisingly poised on the brink of closure.[17]

Beneath the magnificent melodic apotheosis, lower wind supplies rapid figu-ration that conclude the sequence of Bartókian flourishes that permeate the move-ment. The bass shifts from E♭ to G♭ (the latter decorated with its upper chromatic neighbour G), but the most important harmonic motion occurs with a reprise of the passacaglia theme in an inner voice, outlining a descending WT1 scale from

Asylum gained? 133

E♭ to F. This is harmonised by chords based first on E♭ minor to D♭ minor and then the bare fifth of {C♭, G♭} (enharmonic {B, F♯}); the continuation leads to chord *z* <F C G>, and within it, the opening dyad of *Asyla* (see Example 6.6).

Example 6.6 *Asyla* Op. 17/iv, reduction of bars 61–74.

The passage would thus appear to fulfil certain functions required of a symphonic climax: after the fractured textures of Section B, it presents an image of thematic, tonal, textural and rhythmic synthesis, along with relative stability. Harmonically, the layers are unified somewhat in the restoration of the bass as the root of the chord at bar 61. If the WT1 collection functions as an extended tonic within the movement, then the 'return' to it (albeit centred on E♭ rather than A) can be construed as a tonal return and with it the moment of maximum stability within the movement.

134 *Asylum gained?*

Coda (bars 67–72)

The precarious state of stability achieved with this climax is dismantled and critiqued over the course of the final twenty seconds of the movement. The conclusion presents another of Adès's 'aerial overviews' as the camera zooms out from this human drama to something altogether more dispassionate and objective. Such a view encourages us to make connections between the material and its precedents earlier in *Asyla*. Emma Gallon points out how the expanded $\begin{Bmatrix} -1 \\ -2 \\ -2 \end{Bmatrix}$ harmonic progression at the end of the work would link up, if continued, to the start of the work, as well as the way in which the upper woodwind in the final bars of *Asyla* mirror the upright piano figuration in its opening bars.[18] We might also note that the chromatic lines in the upper register that outline one final *passus duriusculus* recall the texture of the stylised birdsong of the first movement and fourth movements, as well as the prominent use of tuned percussion (most notably the cowbells). For Gallon, '[w]e are thus encouraged to rehear the "peripheral" timbres that open and close the work [...] in newly stable terms'.[19]

Yet just how stable is this material? The smooth voice-leading implied by the expanded harmonic progression (shown in the box in the second system of Example 6.6) is in fact fractured; the stepwise motion typically heard elsewhere in *Asyla* is blasted across multiple octaves (compare with the treatment of motifs in Example 2.6c). The chords are thus heard in multiple registers, the connection between them strained. The unshackling once more of the harmonic material from the bass (such as it exists) presents a floating texture once more in need of grounding; the music concludes 'not with an apotheosis but as conflict resolution left with a question mark'.[20] The return to the musical and expressive state just prior to the opening of the symphony suggests that the whole cycle of violence, refuge, madness and ecstasy is to begin once again, repeating infinitely.

* * *

The three statements of the choral theme, in which the first two are characterised by increasing rhythmic dislocation, and the third by a 'coming together' of primary material and tonal perspectives offers a simple progression towards some form of musical and extramusical resolution that would in turn suggest an underlying narrative purpose – a 'quest for safety', to adapt Griffiths's characterisation of *Asyla*.[21] Equally, it is highly tempting to equate passages manifesting a sense of acoustic order with the dual implications of shelter and repression afforded by the notion of 'asylum'. Yet to smooth over the myriad structural dislocations and disjunctures would be to distort the musical experience; the closing bars of *Asyla* in particular are responsible for engendering a lasting impression of structural and semantic equivocation. The contrast effected between such localised indeterminacy and the arguably more focussed tonal regions found elsewhere in the finale is further heightened by the prominence given to the use of tuned percussion.

Rather, the mutual existence of stability and instability, of tradition and uncertainty, suggests that Adès is unwilling to choose between the options he sets himself of 'whether to be safe, or mad'.[22] Far from being a case of 'asylum gained', the ending of the work leaves us pausing at the asylum gate. It is for the individual listener to decide whether to enter, to turn away, or to remain on the threshold, balanced precariously between the constraints of self-certainty and self-abandon.

Notes

1 Ross, 'Roll Over, Beethoven', p. 130.
2 *Performance on 3* (1 October 1997).
3 Adès finds Brahms's finale to be 'a terrible waste of space'. *TA:FON*, p. 174.
4 *Performance on 3* (1 October 1997).
5 *Music for the 21st Century*. The narration begins at 44:43. More specifically, there are 'a couple of endings, some in a row and then some on top of each other'. *TA:FON*, p. 5.
6 Tarnopolsky, Programme note to *Asyla*.
7 Andrew Porter, CD notes for *Asyla*, EMI 5 56818 2 (1999); reused as notes for EMI DVD 7243 4 90325 9 0 (2003).
8 Travers, 'Intervallic Cycles', pp. 33–4.
9 Béla Bartók, *Duke Bluebeard's Castle* (1911, rev. 1917), Fig. 91, bars 1–3. The emotive content of the allusion – a lake of *tears* – has broader implications for some of the emotional connotations of the work, and in particular the plight of political refugees. (That Adès singled out Hungarian refugees in his commentary on the first movement provides us with a compelling cultural link to Bartók himself.) See also Chapter 7.
10 Recall, though, that Adès hears the fourth as stable. See Chapter 2, n.16.
11 Taruskin, 'A Surrealist Composer', p. 149. A more prominent reminiscence of the horn melody occurs later in the movement.
12 The heterophonic additions of the third oboe and cor anglais predominantly draw on the same octatonic set, but with some chromatic additions.
13 There is a voice-exchange of sorts between the outer strata of the first two sections, in which the A-centeredness of the passacaglia bass is transferred to the choral theme, and the <C B♭> in the upper stratum of bars 1–8 flowers into the WT0 bass of bars 9–12.
14 Note, too, how the series provides a reversal (and alternative route) between the pitches of A and E♭ that framed the bass motion of bars 1–8.
15 Roderic Dunnett, 'How to Give Mahler a Run for His Money', *Independent* (3 October 1997).
16 The links to the Mahler throw into relief another quality of *Asyla* too: its compression. In the same broad span of time that it takes for the Scherzo of Mahler's Third Symphony, *Asyla* encompasses an entire gamut of emotional and expressive states; accordingly, its E♭ minor climax (which, proportionally, occurs at roughly the same point in *Asyla* and Mahler's Scherzo) is made to bear a greater burden.
17 The whole-tone descent at the end of third choral theme divides it into two, recalling the similarly chromatic and whole-tone qualities of the two halves of the passacaglia theme in bars 1–8.
18 Gallon, 'Narrativities', p. 203. This reading places considerable emphasis on the decorative quarter-tone flat D♭ in the piano at the outset of *Asyla* as a surrogate for an equally tempered, and harmonically significant, C♯: compare Example 6.6 with Example 3.2a.
19 Ibid., p. 204.
20 Thomas Schulz, Programme note to *Asyla* for 7–9 September 2002, Berlin Philharmoniker, trans. Richard Evidon (2002).
21 Griffiths, 'Everyone Wants a Piece of Adès'.
22 Anon., 'Not Yet 30'.

7 Interpreting *Asyla*

Critics recognised *Asyla* as a major work in its own right as well as an important landmark in Adès's development. For Clark, *Asyla* 'more than justifies the hope and hyperbole surrounding [Adès ...] *Asyla* represents a quantum leap [...] of breathtaking confidence and scale'.[1] Writing after the premiere, Clements also suggested that Adès 'had taken a leap forward';[2] two months later, he confirmed this opinion by describing *Asyla* as Adès's 'most ambitious score and his finest achievement so far'.[3] Previewing the US premiere in Minnesota, Michael Anthony described *Asyla* as 'a remarkable and exciting four-movement work that suggests why people are talking about Ades [sic] [...] "Asyla" is music with an eerie, compelling beauty by a composer we will surely be hearing much from'.[4] Not quite a year after its premiere, Morrison confidently claimed that *Asyla* is 'a cracker [, ...] a little masterpiece'.[5]

Sir Simon Rattle's inaugural concert with the Berlin Philharmoniker brought *Asyla* back into the public eye. Five years had not dimmed its impact: for Rob Cowan, '[t]he audience was transfixed, and the orchestra not exactly of a single mind. Some players seemed disconcerted, even confused, while others – the boys on the big drums, for example, who between them would soon raise merry hell – were plainly having a ball'.[6] Alan Rusbridger found *Asyla* to be 'an unflinching and profound work',[7] and for Morrison, *Asyla* is (or remains) 'a thrilling, highly original work [...] like a hurricane blowing through the hallowed Philharmonie hall'.[8] Later that year, Holland, reviewing a performance by the Boston Symphony Orchestra under Christoph von Dohnyani, was left agog: '[i]ts four movements evoke an astonishment that deepens with every hearing. Where did this wholly original orchestra sound come from?'[9]

Nearly twenty years since its premiere, *Asyla*'s ability to shock and inspire remains undimmed. To take a handful of examples from the first half of 2015, we find Georgina Rowe describing *Asyla* as 'a mesmerizing four-movement orchestral piece by one of Great Britain's greatest living composers [...] it registers with striking depth [...] nothing quite prepares you for the third movement, titled "Ecstasio" – here, Ades [sic] bears down with spectacular intensity'.[10] Something of this intensity led Ivan Hewett to place 'Ecstasio' in a list of ten pieces to interest teenagers in classical music, citing its 'fascinating combination of dance-floor energy and delicate aural imagination'.[11] Writing for *The New York Times*, David Allen describes the same movement as 'influential', and *Asyla* as one of Adès's

Interpreting Asyla   137

'finest earlier scores'.[12] William Robin describes *Asyla* as 'a singular fount of inspiration' for young American composers:

> A compressed symphonic masterwork, 'Asyla' was the culmination of Mr. Adès's omnivorous early style, and its 1999 recording entranced [the composer Andrew] Norman and his college classmates. 'We would just listen to that thing over and over again and discuss it – a lot of us stole quite liberally from it,' he said. Others attested to the persuasive grip of 'Asyla'. 'There was this moment where the third movement of "Asyla" circulated in the new-music community almost like a hit single,' the composer Gabriel Kahane said. [...] The composer Ted Hearne recalled a debate among friends over the best new orchestral music: 'I remember them being like: It's "Asyla," Ted! It's "Asyla".'[13]

The prevalence of such comments in sources belonging to the (public) sphere that might loosely be described as 'music appreciation' is unsurprising, for it is generally in this domain that issues of (extra)musical meaning are paramount. These sources include programme notes, reviews of concerts and recordings, and CD and DVD sleeve notes. More generally, these comments contribute to the ways in which *Asyla*'s meanings are constructed not within its musical text, but through the interplay between its structures and the discursive practices with which it is associated in the media. (Recall the discussion in Chapter 1 about the role of the media in the distribution of artistic messages.) Publically, at least, Adès is equivocal about such matters. On the one hand he has contributed actively to the dissemination of *Asyla*'s programme, in interviews and through approved programme notes. On the other, he used his Grawmeyer Award acceptance lecture to situate the work critically 'in the context of communication and the role it plays in how music is experienced'.[14] For Adès, '[d]ay-to-day life now saturates us with information. We're more accessible as individuals to personal and social outside influences than our forebears ever were'. To this end, Adès suggests music – and by implication, *Asyla* – can access 'a level of feeling' that is 'beyond words and it's not communication that's taking place at these moments. It's at a level beyond that which we can put in a communicable order'.[15] Nevertheless, *Asyla*'s location within a communicative network *does* mean that our responses cannot ever be unmediated, even if there remains some excess, some aspect of the music that cannot be expressed verbally.

The correspondence in content between statements made by Adès in interviews, Tarnopolsky's programme notes and critical response is neither unusual and nor is it a product solely of the 1990s. More representative of this media-saturated and mediated decade, however, is the way in which such channels are *exploited* in order to communicate not just what the piece is 'about', but what the piece (notionally) is *not* about (even if this message is lost in translation). One way of understanding the function of this paratextual communication is to consider its relationship to the notion of writing *sous rature* (often translated as 'under erasure').

138   *Interpreting* Asyla

Sous rature refers to the retention of a crossed-out word or concept so that it may still be read. For Jacques Derrida, it is 'a strategy of using the only available language while not subscribing to its premises';[16] a move that recognises the usefulness of concepts as a tool, but that at once highlights the problems and limitations inherent in relying on such tools as authoritative or as some sort of guarantor of truth value. This becomes 'a question of explicitly and systematically posing the problem of the status of a discourse which borrows from a heritage the resources necessary for the deconstruction of that heritage itself'.[17]

Writing *sous rature* might explain Adès's otherwise disingenuous withdrawal of the second movement's title (ostensibly due to its connotations), only to then widely publicise the name and the fact of its deletion. It would not have been difficult to keep the notion of cavernous interiors in the public imagination should he have wished to do so, via programme notes or less connotatively freighted titles than 'Vatican'. Whether intentional or not, the strategy suggests a playful courting of the media, of courting controversy whilst simultaneously distancing *Asyla* from it.[18]

A more discursive role can be found in the evocation and treatment of the symphonic genre as 'heritage', which offers the potential to critique the genre from within. Doing so presents on the grandest scale the opportunity to make the familiar unfamiliar. Just as Adès's use of expanded harmonic progressions cause the contextual, culturally determined value of functional tonality to be re-thought and reheard, *Asyla* challenges and questions the inherited musical and cultural certainties of the symphony as genre.[19] In this sense, *Asyla* stands in contrast to the coterminous heritage movement described in Chapter 1; rather than preserve in aspic an illusory and uncritical image of the past, *Asyla* seeks to probe and lay bare the issues and contradictions within that heritage. Whether or not it achieves this aim is another matter, of course. The rather uncritical discussions of the symphonic genre in reviews of *Asyla* (cited in Chapter 2) would suggest that, aside from expanding the instrumental resources of the symphony orchestra, *Asyla* is too squarely situated within the heritage it is attempting to critique.

Or perhaps not. As noted in Chapters 3–6, those framing passages that bring unusual instrumental timbres to the fore set the symphonic logic into relief, questioning the musical and thematic certainties that characterise *Asyla* as symphonic. A parallel could be made with the process of *sous rature*, but realised temporally rather than visually. The sonic, narrative and discursive shifts that the percussive passages engender highlight the conventionality of the material that they frame, as if placing it under erasure. To hear such passages in these terms is not to deny the power and persuasiveness of the symphonic development that they interrupt, but rather to reflect upon the nature and function of this development.

Adès's symphonic practice offers one example of how musical text and verbal paratexts (in this case, the media's contribution to communicating ideas *sous rature*) come together dynamically, and with critical function. The purpose of this chapter is to extend my interpretation of *Asyla* to take into account the broader discursive practices in which it is situated, and its active participation in meaning

Interpreting *Asyla*   139

construction. Though it is not my intention to provide a comprehensive reception history of *Asyla*, the themes that I survey – asylum, moral panics and surrealism – are those that recur frequently in critical responses to the work.

Asylum

Persistent references to the multiple connotations of its title abound in the reception of *Asyla*. Tarnopolsky's original programme note set the tone for subsequent commentary, noting that '[t]he title, the plural of "asylum" is deliberately ambiguous. It refers both to madhouses and their duplicitous functions, and to sanctuaries (for example "political asylum")'. Explicit here, and implicit in later commentaries, is the notion of the 'duplicitous asylum', a notion given prominence in Michel Foucault's *Madness and Civilisation*.[20] Foucault's well-known thesis is that the modern conception of insanity descends from the classical model, in which madness was treated as a subcategory of unreason, and for which internment functioned as a means of keeping such elements away from the reasoned main body of society. This results in a concept of the asylum not as a *haven* for the mad, but as a means by which society might *exclude* those who, for whatever reason, do not conform to social norms.

Specialised discourse about mental health care, be it in institutions or the community, similarly problematises the concept of asylum. As one example amongst many, Dylan Tomlinson and John Carrier, writing in the mid-1990s, state that 'true asylum as retreat or refuge is a concept that is surprisingly ill-defined'.[21] Such hazy notions of what asylum means to different social groups make it impossible to advance any single interpretation.

The practices of social conformity and exclusion are also integral to the notion of asylum as sanctuary, a concept normally treated by commentators on Adès's music as transparent. Although Adès's depiction image of masses fleeing across a landscape was not mentioned explicitly in Tarnopolsky's programme note, the concepts of political asylum and political refugees were associated with the work from the start.[22] As with madness, the status of 'asylum seeker' is conferred not by the individuals themselves, but by the nation from whom they are seeking asylum. As Robert Barsky has argued, refugees need to use the asylum process as a means of identifying themselves as the eponymous 'productive other': aliens who nevertheless would be able to integrate with the prevailing social orthodoxy.[23] Failure to construct this image results in exclusion from the host society. The first responses of society are to exclude, rather than to embrace, elements that resist easy integration.[24] In this light, the notion of 'bogus' asylum seekers prevalent in political discourse of the 1990s seeks exclusion on two counts: first, by denying haven, and second, by denying the rights of the individual to seek asylum in the first place.

Commentators tend to underemphasise the extent to which *Asyla* can contribute to such a discourse. For Clark, the title 'is relevant only as a clue to the alternately open and confined atmosphere of the music'.[25] Tarnopolsky also restricts his comments on asylum to location.[26] Others offer more precise mappings between

140   *Interpreting* Asyla

location and asylum: for Driver, 'Ecstasio' offers a 'lurid, deafening re-creation of this new-fangled place of asylum',[27] and Rusbridger suggests that there is 'more madhouse than refuge' within the music.[28] Thomas Schulz deserves special mention for moving beyond simple pictorialism to suggest genuine metaphoric correspondences between musical and extramusical imagery:

> *Asyla* is an example of Adès's juxtaposition of two conflicting levels of sonority, corresponding to the double meaning of the title: the plural of 'asylum' alludes both to a save haven – a refuge from political persecution – and to a madhouse. Stability and insecurity criss-cross one another from the very first bar of the score.[29]

The examination of the relationship between musical process and imagery in Chapters 3–6 is a large-scale response to the issues Schulz identifies. Nevertheless, given the more superficial treatment of asylum by other commentators, it would have been equally possible to have focussed on purely internal musical logic, in full agreement with Dunnett's assertion that *Asyla* 'stands well on its own, without [need of] any specified programme'.[30] Yet I would argue that the pervasiveness of 'asylum' in the reception of the work is a symptom of more than just critical parroting of Tarnopolsky's programme note, or a tip of the hat to *Asyla*'s evocative title and suggestive musical atmosphere. Rather, it reflects a sense of the ways that *Asyla*'s music, when brought into conjunction with notions of asylum,[31] invites and confronts the issues and hegemonic assumptions bound up in its discourse.

It is significant that – for all of Rusbridger's assertions – there is no conventional depiction of the asylum as 'madhouse' amongst the multiple locations presented in *Asyla*.[32] In keeping with the notions that mental and political asyla are social constructions, it is fitting that the locations portrayed musically are concerned with *attitudes* towards sites and acts of refuge (or incarceration) rather than *representations* of them. The shift of emphasis towards attitudes and processes throws into relief the socially constructed nature of asylum, and with it the groups that determine, respond to and are affected by such constructions.

This is, perhaps, one reason why the second movement's subtitle 'Vatican' proved superfluous, for the music is less about specific places of worship (or denominations as such) than a psychological exploration of civic need for sanctuary in response to external threat. But asylum as a social construct requires a sense of self – the 'us' that accepts, excludes or labels as deemed appropriate – and the 'other' that is welcomed, excluded or (re)defined. The lack of definition of an external agent in the second movement is telling: unable to project negative motions onto an 'other', the lamenting subject(s) turns in on themselves in waves of increasing intensity and hysteria. As the lamenting melody multiples and proliferates, it finds itself unable to cohere into a single statement (consider the thematic and textural polarisation of the close of the movement), bearing witness, perhaps, to the impossibility of discourse about asylum to offer coherent solutions amidst the competing and conflicting voices.

The first movement, on the other hand, casts 'us' as observers of 'others' fleeing across a landscape. In Chapter 3, I highlighted the ways in which the melodic material of the movement continuously altered its pitch identity in order to 'fit' with the perceived underlying (harmonic) order. This is clearly analogous to Barsky's notion of the 'productive other', and the sense of a refugee projecting themselves as able to integrate. The percussion interlude at the end of Section A acts in the manner of a filmic dissolve, changing scenes for Section B's presentation of the emotional consequences of flight. But this overt narrative act, made from the perspective of 'Elsewhere',[33] serves to emphasise the fact that Section A is itself presented from a (different) perspective: in short, it is mediated. Out of this arises a narrative twist in the tale. At first listeners are encouraged to identify with the horn theme as protagonist (the a- and b-phrases) and its struggles against an un-named antagonist (the c-phrases). An obvious interpretation in the light of the publicised programme would be to read this as a conflict between refugees and their oppressors. Yet the conclusion of the work problematises such identification, insofar as the a-phrase material disperses to become 'background', whilst the harmonic focus of the c-material becomes thematised, and thus 'foreground'. Are listeners, after all, to identify with the oppressors? Have *we* been the oppressors all along? And if so, who is this 'we', and why do we exclude? Can, indeed, we *ever* be inclusive, and what might this mean musically? Or socially? A return of the tuned percussion at the end leaves the critical (and musical) questions hanging.

Masses of a different nature form an undercurrent to 'Ecstasio': here, they are implied less in polyphonic textures (though the material receives heterophonic treatment), but in the topical references to 'us' and 'them' that informed the discourse around club culture in the 1990s and the moral panic that ensued (more on which below).

In the final movement, the repeated presentations of the choral theme highlight the masses once again. This constitutes, perhaps, the first positive affirmation of human presence in *Asyla*. From the inhospitable landscapes of the first movement, through the awe-inspiring voids of the second, to the collective rite of the third, *Asyla* has hitherto offered an environment that precludes human individuality. Adès provides further support for an interpretation of the piece as a hymn of emancipation, suggesting that after all 'the questions and problems that had been set up by the rest of the piece' have been resolved (or at least aired again), the choir is free to 'sing' for one last time; it is only then that one can experience release. The suggestion, no matter how fleeting, of an eventual redemption indicates that the 'asylum gained' is ultimately benign. The human journey encapsulated in the fourth movement (which can be read in this light as a commentary on the whole of *Asyla*) is thus one from pain to purification.

There are problems with this reading, however. It remains unclear who 'sings', who they are singing for, and who – if anyone – is excluded by means of the asylum that has been won. Nor does the balance struck between musical stability and instability (see Chapter 6) lend itself to unambiguously positive depictions of asylum. Above all, however, the critical content of the final movement emerges through its allusions to Bartók and Mahler. The reference to *Bluebeard's*

142   *Interpreting* Asyla

Castle makes possible a number of semantic references to ideas both within and external to *Asyla*. First, we might associate the lake with the outdoor imagery that sprang from, and maybe influenced, the musical content of the first movement. The location of Bluebeard's lake as a fixture perversely integral to his castle may relate to the confined programmatic setting of the second movement of *Asyla*, and possibly that of the third also. Second, its mournful expressive tone connects with the laments that permeate the work, and looks ahead to the incomplete *passus duriusculus* of the final 'resolution'.

The second quotation is more overtly critical in function. According to Mahler, the Scherzo of his Third Symphony was 'really a sort of face-pulling and tongue-poking on the part of all Nature' whose 'Panic humour' meant that one was 'more likely to be overcome by horror than laughter'.[34] Thus, as with the reference to the lake of tears, there is a deliberate association formed not just with Nature, but a Nature, as in the first movement of *Asyla*, far removed from the idyllic pastoral tradition:

> Only at the end of the [movement] does there fall once more the heavy shadow of lifeless Nature, of still uncrystallized, inorganic matter, that is thrown over the conclusion of the introduction. But here it represents a relapse into lower forms of animal creation before the mighty leap towards consciousness in the highest earthly creature, Man.[35]

However interesting it may be to speculate on a link between Adès's image of frozen wastelands in the first movement, the desolation revealed via *Parsifal* at the end of 'Ecstasio', and Mahler's description of a 'lifeless Nature', the connection may well be coincidental. Nevertheless, despite the Nietzschian character of Mahler's observations, we can observe a parallel between what makes the appearance of Man possible in the Third Symphony, and the peroration of the choral idea in *Asyla*. The undertone of horror that Mahler describes leads Peter Franklin to state that 'this scherzo does not seek to destroy itself, but rather, having won its own stability, rounds to threaten *us*'.[36] Stability, then, but at what cost? The allusion to Mahler must force us to ask the same question about the conclusion of *Asyla*. Perhaps, the music seems to be saying, the gaining of asylum carries with it a burden too great to bear.

Moral panics and 'Ecstasio'

Even though (or perhaps because) it is one of Adès's least typical works, 'Ecstasio' dominates the reception of *Asyla*. The *Süddeutsche Zeitung*'s description of the movement's conclusion as a 'splendidly calculated, in-no-way chaotic, compositional piling-up of wild *Sacre*-esque pounding rhythms and noxious Techo twitchings' is typical.[37] Clark has depicted it as 'smoky, claustrophobic and viscerally exciting, like a wild communal dance which is constantly threatening to run out of control'.[38] Clements wrote that the movement 'works itself up into an almost sexual frenzy';[39] for Driver, the 'mind-blowing, unforgiving beat' contributes to

Interpreting Asyla   143

the 'lurid, deafening re-creation' of EDM.[40] Put bluntly, whilst club music is perceived to evoke heady and hedonistic pleasures, it is also the site of threatening and destructive impulses.

The tensions between the symphonic logic manifest in 'Ecstasio' and the topical background of EDM discussed in Chapter 5 are clearly not so great that the secondary associations of EDM – the social, historical and cultural signifieds that animate our responses to it – are rendered neutral. In fact, I would argue that it is precisely because of these tensions that these secondary associations are so forcibly called into play and into question. In the process, easy interpretations of the movement that equate it solely with EDM are problematised: 'Ecstasio' is not *just* a 'freaky, funky rave'. Nevertheless, these easy interpretations, as the reviews of *Asyla* and 'Ecstasio' have shown, proliferate: it is very difficult to divorce the musical gestures of EDM, no matter how unfocussed they are defined in 'Ecstasio', from their cultural connotations.

Broadly speaking, two strongly contrasting cultural discourses are relevant here. In the decade leading up to the composition of 'Ecstasio', the relationship between the drug Ecstasy and EDM (in particular, rave) was a crucial feature of both of these discourses; Steve Redhead has argued that 'to de-contextualise Ecstasy use in Britain from its predominant setting within what has loosely been called rave culture is both unrewarding and misleading. It is clear that Ecstasy and rave culture go hand in glove'.[41] The first of these discourses, located primarily in the mainstream media, can be equated with moral panic.[42] The coverage in the late 1980s in the British tabloid *The Sun* of the emerging dance scene demonstrates the confusion over and fear of what the potent combination of EDM and Ecstasy represented. Faced in autumn 1988 with the emergence of rave culture into the public eye, *The Sun* at first threw its lot in with clubbers, offering on 12 October to each of its readers a 'groovy and cool [...] Acid House T-shirt', whilst warning nevertheless of 'Evil LSD'. Within a month editorial policy changed to adopt a stern authoritarian position intended, no doubt, to capture the hearts of the perceived moral majority. On 7 November 1988 the newspaper reported that

> [p]olice raided a huge Acid House disco yesterday – then fled to let 3000 teenagers carry on raving it up at the sex and drugs orgy [...] *Sun* reporters saw PUSHERS openly selling Ecstasy, a drug which heightens sexual awareness, but can lead to hallucinations and heart attacks [...] OUTRAGEOUS sex romps taking place on a special stage in front of the dance floor.[43]

Despite, or more likely because of, such sensationalist reporting and further knee-jerk reactions such as BBC Radio 1's banning of rave music from its playlists,[44] 1989 and the early 1990s saw an increased popularity and commercialisation of acid house music and its culture. Similarly, Ecstasy, once considered an 'expensive and short lived fad', became 'a major part of certain drug using circles in Britain'.[45]

Whilst the levels of the British mainstream media interest in EDM never returned to the high-water mark of late 1988, high-profile deaths attributed to

144 *Interpreting* Asyla

Ecstasy such as that of sixteen-year-old Claire Leighton in July 1989 continued to generate ghoulish interest and moral opprobrium in equal measure. Even more firmly in the public eye, some seven years after Ecstasy first hit the headlines, the death of Leah Betts on her eighteenth birthday (16 December 1995) provided a focal point for anti-drug campaigners and for continued outrage and fear for the nation's youth. Ecstasy and EDM remain intertwined in the public consciousness, infusing the latter with lasting associations of illegality, risk and loss of safety.[46]

The harsh glare of the media contrasts with the experiences of those within the rave culture, in which the subculture, music and drugs all combine to create an environment within which one is rendered anonymous and de-personalised. For writers such as Simon Reynolds, 'there was a liberating joy in surrendering to the radical anonymity of the music, in not caring about the names of tracks or artists. The "meaning" of the music pertained to the macro level of the entire culture, and it was so much huger than the sum of its parts'.[47] Thus, for rave's participants, this culture was liberating: a chance perhaps to throw off the pressures of the working week in an environment that, by virtue of its anonymity, freed the dancers from the gaze of others and from the need to assert a particular identity. The rave became a place of sanctuary, cut off from the outside world. And, if the moral panic over which the tabloids anguished portrays the same site as one of bacchanalian degradation, a madhouse if you will, then we find that these discourses can map onto the same ambiguities conjured up by the musical and titular ambiguities of *Asyla*.

A handful of the press responses to 'Ecstasio' belong to this second discourse, as in Clark's invocation of a 'communal' dance.[48] The majority, however, as cited in the introduction to this section and doubtless spurred on by the movement's title, draw primarily from the moral-panic discourse – witness the prominence of sexual, 'primeval' and 'thrashing' content. Even if one senses that the reviewers are (covertly or otherwise) rather enjoying themselves, they are tapping into, and thus proliferating, cultural associations of EDM with danger, with the body's carnal desires running wild over rational thought.

'Ecstasio' embodies many of the characteristics of 1990s art, in the (relative) accessibility of its materials which draw into its orbit both high culture (Wagner) and low (rave); in the portrayal of rave culture as an alternative experience to that of the mainstream; and in the channelling of prominent social topics. The press reception of *Asyla* is complicit in the promotion of such characteristics. Were this to be all that 'Ecstasio' had to offer, then it would also risk attracting the accusations of superficiality that cling to so much art of the period. However, the way in which 'Ecstasio' plays with listeners' (presumed) expectations challenges both musical and listening subjectivities: those familiar with the symphonic repertoire would be likely to take references to EDM as a style topic on trust, having been presented with the minimum amount of information required to identify EDM as a broad guiding topic. On the other hand, some listeners will be only too conscious that artistic license has been taken with the musical material. Thus the question must be asked: what might be a likely reason for the distance between 'Ecstasio's' appropriated gestures and their musical origin, and what does this have to say about the meaning of the movement?

Interpreting Asyla   145

To begin to answer this, I will first return to the metrical ambiguities inherent in EDM. Butler has suggested that, for listeners, such ambiguities can result in a constant shifting of focus in which there can be no privileged position.[49] Examining such processes from the standpoint of musical subjectivity, Rebecca Leydon argues that implied hierarchies give rise to what she calls a 'kinetic trope' – one in which the musical subject demonstrates kinaesthetic competence and volitional confidence.[50] Conversely, Eero Tarasti describes such processes in terms that suggest a far more passive role for the subject, remarking that the act of listening to minimalism is 'an emancipatory, impersonal ritual [...] permitting the object to influence oneself'.[51] For Tagg, this sense of individuals giving themselves over to the collective whole mirrors the breakdown of the distinction between figure and ground that is characteristic of the style and offers an alternative to traditional Western subjectivities.[52] The same loss of the traditional subject characterises writing about the cultural significance of EDM, such as in Antonio Melechi's 'ecstasy of disappearance',[53] or in the way that 'social marginality, when musically encoded, translate[s] into an enduring, radical, and intense de-centring of the traditionally core melodic and harmonic components of popular music. Rhythm and timbre has [sic] shifted to the fore'.[54] More strongly, Peter Jowers claims that 'music facilitates new identities'.[55] In short, these interpretations of EDM relate its inherent perceptual ambiguities to new representations of the role of the subject.

In 'Ecstasio', one finds perceptual ambiguities with regard to harmony, rhythm, form and topicality on both the micro- and macro-level that go far beyond the norms of EDM. In particular, the coda abandons the kinetic gestures of EDM for a relatively directed linear–harmonic syntax. More broadly, 'Ecstasio' moves from a state of being, in which the object is permitted to influence the subject (Tarasti's 'impersonal ritual'), to a state of becoming, in which the individual is able to assert him- or herself. One might conclude, in this light, that the progression in 'Ecstasio' from one state to another reflects Adès's own irrepressible artistic desire to impose his musical sensibilities on his material.[56]

Such a reading, in which the subject emerges gasping from the onslaught of dehumanising repetitions, might appeal to the audience member more familiar with the subjectivities of symphonic music than with those of EDM, particularly if they associate the latter with moral panic. Conversely, the extent to which the developmental processes ape those found in more conventional works, and to which coherence between form and motivic material is lacking, suggests that from a 'symphonic' perspective the movement is unsatisfactory. For listeners more sympathetic to the 'ecstasy of disappearance', the uneasy relationship between symphonic argument and dance gestures prevents a fusion of all the component parts of the music. As a result, the 'forcefield of pulsating, undulating euphoria' that Reynolds identifies with EDM fails to materialise.[57] Coupled with the emergence of a distinct subject, this might be taken as evidence of reactionary moral values and a failure to grasp the full potential of the EDM style.

But, as I have already suggested, the distortions of materials, topical references and cultural values in 'Ecstasio' are probably both deliberate and provocative. The music remains forever poised, sometimes delicately, sometimes violently,

146 *Interpreting* Asyla

between numerous conflicting impulses: between symphonic development and the repetitions of dance; between directed motion and kinetic impulses; between the evocation of the concert hall and the club; and between madness and sanctuary. To hear the music in this way, as neither on the one hand a perverted symphonic scherzo nor on the other as an over-intellectualised dance, is to avoid deciding between perceptual ambiguities, and instead embracing their coexistence. The tensions that arise from these opposing forces contribute to the overwhelming intensity of the movement; favouring one or the other can lead all too readily to disappointment. Like the dance-music culture that 'Ecstasio' implicates in its network of associations, the musical material 'generally guarantees a stance of [...] intransigence, a refusal to be co-opted or cop out'.[58]

There is a parallel with the 'context-dependent adaptability' which Reynolds identifies with the effects of Ecstasy, drawing attention to its 'profound but curiously "meaningless" experience. You have to supply the meaning. The overpowering feelings, sensations and idealism generated by the drug demand some kind of articulation'.[59] What is true for the musical and cultural forces which come together in various states of conflict and cooperation in 'Ecstasio', and which in turn encourage the listener to challenge received listening habits, to confront expectations of genre and to think anew on the nature of the listening subject, is true for *Asyla* as a whole.

The (sur)real

In recent years, Tom Service has begun to describe *Asyla* as 'a surrealist symphony'.[60] In doing so, he connects to a critical tradition that stems from Taruskin's review of the EMI recording of *Asyla*, in which Taruskin highlighted the surreal quality of Adès's of painterly, spatial effects, as well as commonalities with Poulenc's work.[61] With the precedent established, the subsequent reception of Adès often fell back on surrealism as an explanatory or evocative term.[62] For Hamilton, a surreal lineage ties Adès to Ligeti, and surrealism is pressed in the service of presenting states of altered consciousness (as in *Living Toys*).[63] The capacity for surrealism to allow the late-twentieth century music of Adès to rub shoulders with both Poulenc and Ligeti suggests it has limited value as a stylistic or historical marker.[64] Nevertheless, the fact that Christopher Fox and Taruskin liken Adès's vivid musical details to analogous techniques in the paintings of Dalì and Magritte serves to situate Adès's so-called surrealism within the context of the 'Golden Age' of the movement, collapsing the considerable chronological distance between the composer and the early 1930s.[65] Notwithstanding the communicative expediency for the reader who may only have a passing awareness of surrealism, such comparisons are clearly ripe for critique: there is much to be done to explore the ways in which surrealism developed, and how Adès's music relates to this.[66]

The value of surrealism to an interpretation of Adès's music lies in its capacity to function as a metaphor, even if it would appear to run counter to André Breton's dictate that, in Taruskin's words, the true surrealist 'strove for [...] irreducible and uninterpretable images that could not serve as metaphors'.[67] By drawing analogies between Adès's compositional technique and painting techniques, Taruskin and Fox encourage us to hear Adès's music metaphorically. Fox likens Adès's use of intervallic cycles to the way in which surrealist paintings preserve

> the integrity of the picture plane; what is depicted may be fantastic nonsense but there is a logic within the depiction itself which is reassuringly reminiscent of codes of visual representation familiar from earlier schools of narrative painting. A similar process takes place within Adès's music: he presents us with an extraordinarily inventive wealth of melodic and harmonic detail but virtually all of it can be related to a few intervallic relationships, usually introduced at the beginning of the work.[68]

The 'but' is significant, for it establishes a binary between surface inventiveness and underlying musical logic. Fox is encouraging us to hear the relationship between the two as tensional, coloured (if not conditioned) by the metaphor of surrealism.

A similar interpretative stance characterises Taruskin's earlier portrait of Adès's music, which

> achieves its special atmosphere, and projects its special meanings, through improbable sonic collages and mobiles: outlandish juxtapositions of evocative sound-objects that hover, shimmering, or dreamily resolve, in a seemingly motionless sonic emulsion. I know of no other music quite like it in these defining respects, but many paintings, by Dalì, de Chirico, Magritte. Mr. Adès himself seems to 'see' his music rather than hear it […] Indeed, great heights – and depths – of pitch are among the elements Mr. Adès musters to produce his uncanny effects of 'spatial form'.[69]

Elsewhere, Taruskin has likened spatial form to collage technique;[70] a connection implicit but pivotal in Taruskin's manoeuvring of Adès alongside Poulenc. When we compare Adès's admiration of Poulenc's ability to use popular music 'convincingly in concert music'[71] to Taruskin's admiration for Adès's 'success at toeing the line […] between the arcane and the banal'[72] we get the sense of just how much of Poulenc's spiritual heir Adès might be.

But if the injunction to hear Adès's music 'as' surreal is to have any critical and metaphorical purchase, it needs to do more than stipulate historical and artistic connections. And this is what Fox and Taruskin do when they compare, with varying degrees of explicitness, the ways in which Adès's music generates meaning, inviting (and making) comparison with the semantics of the Golden Age of Surrealism. As Daniel Albright observes, surrealism

> is a phenomenon of semantic dislocation and fissure. It is impossible to disorient unless some principle of orientation has been established in the first place […] In other words, you can't provide music that means wrong unless

148   *Interpreting* Asyla

> you provide music that means something. [...] [T]he surrealism of Poulenc and his fellows didn't try to create a new language of music – it simply tilted the semantic planes of the old language of music. Just as surrealist paintings often have a horizon line and a highly developed sense of perspective, in order that the falseness of the space and the errors of scale among the painted entities can register their various outrages to normal decorum, so surrealist music provides an intelligible context of familiar sounds in order to develop a system of meanings that can assault or discredit other systems of meanings.[73]

For Taruskin, such devices mean that '[t]he recognizable world was subverted by decontextualization – or recontextualization in incongruous juxtapositions – and became a dream world'.[74] And this in turn became 'the essential surrealist *musical* device, as Poulenc (following Satie) demonstrated again and again, was to surround the extravagant dream-imagery with a music that sounded insistently "normal" and commonplace in its evocation of the familiar music of one's surrounding "lifestyle"'.[75]

It is easy to see how this maps onto an interpretation of *Asyla*. Consider the opening of the work. In Chapter 3 I noted how the late-Romantic (Brucknerian) symphony provides a frame of reference – a principal of orientation, to use Albright's term – against which we can register surreal distortions. Accordingly, there are multiple musical cues that might therefore encourage a hearing of the opening as 'surreal', including its ambiguous tonal function, the blurring of the orchestral sound, and the ruptures caused by the shifts of harmonic organisation in bars 7 and 10. The tension between the expectations afforded by the late-Romantic background and the foreground discontinuities and non-sequiturs contributes to the dream-like logic of the material.

Nevertheless we might ask how apt the metaphor of surrealism is here. As noted earlier, the conceptual ground upon which Fox, Taruskin, and others use surrealism to explain Adès's music is that of the music (and art) of the 1920s and 1930s. The latter can be understood with reference to Albright's reading of 'Ma blessure, ma blessure', the cry of pain from a wounded tree at Fig. 103 of Ravel's *L'enfant et les sortileges* (1919–25) and an allusion to it found in Poulenc's 'Bois meurtri bois perdu' (*Un soir de neige*/iii, 1944). In both cases, the harmonic motion consists of pairs of tritonally related chords (in the Ravel, bare fifths on <D G♯ C F♯>, and minor chords on <F♯ C E B♭> in the Poulenc). For Albright, the comedy of the wounded tree is transformed in Poulenc's depiction of a ruined forest. He concludes that, in Poulenc's version, '[t]he *bois meurtri* theme has a strong semantic content – it straightforwardly means *sadness* – but this content hovers over the text without adhering intimately to it, *since it inhabits two contexts at the same time*'.[76] The simultaneity of these two contexts – the comedy of Ravel and the sadness of the Poulenc – contributes to the surreal quality of the passage in the latter.

The comedy of the Ravel derives in part from exaggerated portandi that connect the pitches of the melody, not dissimilar to the blurring of objects found in Adès. But it also stems, I would argue, from the oddness of this passage within the

Interpreting Asyla   149

context of the harmonic language of the opera as a whole, which carries sufficient traces of functional tonality for the harmonic progression to register as semantically freighted. Ravel employs the frame of reference of traditional tonality, but the syntactical plane, like the semantic, is tilted. Poulenc's music similarly trades on the fact that deviations register as such because of the traditional norms that underpin them.

The opening four dyads of *Asyla* are a transposed permutation of the progression found in Ravel and Poulenc, and share something of the semantic dislocations found in these earlier works. But the crucial distinction is that Adès's music, though operating with recognisable pitch centres, is unable to tilt the syntax in the manner found in the music of the French composers. Rather, Adès establishes his own compositional logic that happens to trigger associations with functional tonality, but which is nevertheless divorced from it. In other words, one of the primary means by which the music of the 1920s and 1930s is able to register as surreal is denied to Adès. Thus, when critics focus on the jarring or dream-like effect that emerges from Adès's material, as when Taruskin talks about 'ordinary events, like common chords or particles of diatonic melody [...] [which] seem [like] objects bizarrely suspended and, in consequence, made newly strange',[77] they do so because they seize upon the cultural memory of what a common chord does in functional tonality, rather than attending to the unfolding compositional logic that has resulted in such a chord being unearthed in the first place. They are, in other words, hearing the music 'as' surreal.

However, when Adès talks about 'irrationally functional harmony' – at least with respect to his own music – he may well be referring to the ways in which a harmony can embody such a dual perspective: on the one hand, common chords emerge from his own compositional logic, belonging intimately to, and deriving meaning from, this framework, but on the other, they irrationally trigger associations with functional tonality.[78] In this light, Taruskin's comment, cited earlier, that in the surrealist music of the 1930s '[t]he recognizable world was subverted by decontextualization – or recontextualization in incongruous juxtapositions – and became a dream world' is turned on its head by Adès. Adès supplants the familiar world of functional tonality with his own musical logic, presenting from the very outset a dream world that is subverted by the recontextualisation and incongruous juxtapositions of recognisable elements. It is for this reason that Adès is less a surrealist in the mould of Poulenc *et al.*, and more a *second-order* surrealist, whose semantic innovations arise not from a tilting of the musical logic of functional tonality, but rather from a tilting of the musical logic of the surrealists themselves.

Adès might, however, owe a deeper debt to the surrealists than might have been realised to date. For sure, the dual quality of Adès's musical language recalls the ways in which Poulenc's appropriation of Ravel retains something of the meaning of the original even as the new context strives to be heard. But tellingly, Adès's aesthetic attempt to re-describe the world has remarkably similar goals to that of Guillaume Apollinaire, who, long before Breton and his dismissal of metaphor, charted a new course for surrealism. As has already been noted, for Adès, 'I think what happens [when composing] is that you try to create *a simulacrum of the real world,*

150   *Interpreting* Asyla

a reflection. The piece is *a way of trying to make the real world real again*, in a sense'.[79] Compare this to Apollinaire, who argues for 'a kind of super-realism *[sur-réalisme]*', which counters, according to Albright, the way in which art traditionally suppresses the 'dissonances of our commonplace sensory experience'.[80] In this light, Albright argues, Apollinaire's vision of surrealism was 'a natural evolution of realism' and profoundly metaphorical, 'in which the principle of equivalence is switched from the level of structure to the level of function – likeness pertains to what things do, not to how things look'.[81] And back to Adès: 'It doesn't seem real to me, the style of a piece. [...] I can see the difference between Italianate ornamentation and, I don't know, Germanic counterpoint. But I can also see that the reality of the music is behind that, it's not in these surfaces.'[82] It is for this reason, Adès maintains, that his music is so overtly polystylistic, not (necessarily) to induce dream-like states through incongruous juxtapositions, but 'by making it honestly unignorable that the surface is just that – transparent, evanescent – and moving though the available material in such a way that the real form becomes clearer'.[83]

And this, perhaps, is why even a rigorously logical scheme such as that found in the opening theme of *Asyla*'s second movement so readily gives up its sources in Bach and Franck's music. Yes, there's a whiff of surreal collage about it all, and a tangible expressive charge about the topical references to the lament, but if we take Adès at his word, then the play of allusions only serves to reinforce the super-reality of the musical argument itself. It becomes corporeal, figurative, metaphorical. By over-determining, if not overloading, the musical content – a semantic simultanism that challenges conventional, habitual responses to music, it forces us to confront the real anew.

This is the paradox. To hear *Asyla*, and indeed any of Adès's music, 'as' surreal means to attend to the disjunctions, the non-sequiturs and the challenges to received listening habits. Yet, at the same time, motivations such as these are precisely those qualities that Adès intends as a means to offset, and thus bring to the fore, his presentation not of a dream world, but a reflection of the real world. Or, to put all of this another way, Adès's music can be thought of as donning the mask of the Golden Age of surrealism, just as the examples just considered are wearing the masks of Bruckner, Poulenc, Bach and Faure. Such an attempt, to make the real world real again, is less a claim to some sort of representational quality of music, but rather an appeal for us to reclaim something of the sensory overload of existence, to engage with reality in as unmediated a form as possible. This is one of the ways in which *Asyla* can access 'a level of feeling [...] beyond that which we can put in a communicable order' and it is, I believe, one of the most significant aspects of Adès's sur-real aesthetic project.

Notes

1 Clark, 'Adès Delights the Ear'.
2 Andrew Clements, 'From the Banal to the Sublime', *Guardian* (4 October 1997).
3 Clements, 'Thomas Adès Takes Over the Asylum'.
4 Michael Anthony, 'Wild, Eerie "Asyla" Gets a Fine US Debut', *Star Tribune* (21 November 1997).

5 Richard Morrison, 'A Glorious Goodbye', *The Times* (31 August 1998).
6 Rob Cowan, 'Lightening Conductor', *Independent* (13 September 2002).
7 Rusbridger, 'Rattle's Glorious Berlin Debut'.
8 Richard Morrison, 'Rattle's Hurricane Debut Shakes Artistic Berlin', *The Times* (9 September 2002).
9 Holland, 'Burying the Hatchet'.
10 Georgina Rowe, 'Berkeley Symphony Delivers Stunning "Asyla"', *San Jose Mercury News* (16 January 2015).
11 Ivan Hewett, 'Don't Dumb Down Classical Music for Teenagers', *Telegraph* (20 May 2015).
12 David Allen, 'Death Dances to Its Own Tune, Sparing Not a Soul', *New York Times* (14 March 2015).
13 William Robin, 'They're Always Taking His Stuff; For American Composers, Thomas Adès Offers a Wealth of Inspiration', *New York Times* (8 February 2015).
14 Marvin Young and John Drees, 'Grawemeyer Winners Return to Share Ideas', *Inside Uof L online* (7 April 2000) www.louisville.edu/ur/onpi/inside/4-7-00/grawemeyer.html [accessed 26 February 2003].
15 Cited in Ibid.
16 Gayatri Chakravorty Spivak, translator's preface to Jacques Derrida, *Of Grammatology* (Baltimore and London: The Johns Hopkins University Press, 1976), pp. ix–lxxxvii, at p. xviii.
17 Jacques Derrida, *Writing and Difference*, trans. Alan Bass (London and New York: Routledge, 1978), pp. 356–7.
18 At the time of *Asyla*'s composition, the Catholic church was beset by numerous scandals, most prominently with child abuse cases in Ireland and the USA.
19 Adès is by no means the first to do this, of course.
20 Michel Foucault, *Madness and Civilisation: A History of Insanity in the Age of Reason*, trans. Richard Howard (London: Routledge, 1967).
21 Dylan Tomlinson and John Carrier (eds), *Asylum in the Community* (London: Routledge, 1996), p. 1.
22 Adès was candid about this imagery in interviews around the time of the premiere, as in *Performance on 3* (1 October 1997).
23 Robert Barsky, *Constructing a Productive Other: Discourse Theory and the Convention Refugee Hearing* (Amsterdam: John Benjamins Publishing Company, 1994).
24 In May 2002, a British MORI poll found that 64% of respondents felt the most commonly used phrase used in media descriptions of asylum seekers was 'illegal immigrant'; 22% said 'bogus'. There is thus an extensive lexicon surrounding the concept of asylum that is used for exclusionary purposes, spanning political discourse (see Chapter 1) and popular usage, www.refugeecouncil.org.uk/assets/0001/5594/mori_report.pdf [accessed 11 June 2015].
25 Clark, 'Adès Delights the Ear'.
26 Tarnopolsky, Programme note to *Asyla*.
27 Driver, 'New Spin on the Cycle'.
28 Rusbridger, 'Rattle's Glorious Debut'.
29 Schulz, Programme note to *Asyla*.
30 Dunnett, 'How to Give Mahler a Run for His Money'.
31 It should be stressed that 'asylum' provides just one possible, if incredibly rich, framework to orient an interpretation of *Asyla*: I am not claiming this is the only interpretative avenue available. See Venn, 'Asylum Gained?', pp. 93–8.
32 The allusion to *Bluebeard's Castle* trades, perhaps, on readings of the opera as a psychological exploration of the titular Duke, but this remains nevertheless an internal asylum. See Elliott Antokoletz, *Musical Symbolism in the Operas of Debussy and Bartók: Trauma, Gender, and the Unfolding of the Unconscious* (Oxford and New York: Oxford University Press, 2004).

152   *Interpreting* Asyla

33 Of the tuned percussion that dominates this section (and others), Adès has noted: that '[t]hey've been a symbol of "elsewhere" in symphonic music. [...] The cowbells in *Asyla* become a metaphor for Elsewhere, as in Mahler or Webern, although there the cowbells are not tuned'. *TA:FON*, p. 71.

34 Cited in Peter Franklin, *Mahler: Symphony No. 3* (Cambridge: Cambridge University Press, 1991), p. 59.

35 Ibid., p. 65.

36 Ibid.

37 Anon., 'Symphonische Manöverkritik', *Süddeutsche Zeitung* (9 September 2002). The original text reads: 'Im dritten Satz ("Ecstasio") kulminiert alles in einer kompositorisch glänzend kalkulierten, keineswegs chaotischen Auftürmung von wilden "Sacre"-Stampfrhythmen und giftigem Techo-Zucken.'

38 Clark, 'Adès Delights the Ear'.

39 Clements, 'From the Banal to the Sublime'.

40 Driver, 'New Spin on the Cycle'.

41 Steve Redhead, 'The Politics of Ecstasy', in Steve Redhead (ed.), *Rave Off: Politics and Deviance in Contemporary Youth Culture* (Aldershot: Avebury, 1993), pp. 7–28, at pp. 12–13.

42 Ibid., p. 12.

43 Antonio Melechi, 'The Ecstasy of Disappearance', in Steve Redhead (ed.), *Rave Off: Politics and Deviance in Contemporary Youth Culture* (Aldershot: Avebury, 1993), pp. 29–40, at p. 35.

44 Ibid.

45 Redhead 'The Politics of Ecstasy', pp. 9–10.

46 The frequently reported tale of Adès going to hospital after hyperventilating after completing the composition of 'Ecstasio' relate to this topic.

47 Reynolds, *Energy Flash*, p. xv. See also Melechi, 'The Ecstasy of Disappearance', p. 34.

48 Clark, 'Adès Delights the Ear'.

49 Butler, *Unlocking the Groove*, p. 137.

50 Rebecca Leydon, 'Towards a Typology of Minimalist Tropes', *Music Theory Online*, 8/iv (2002) www.mtosmt.org/issues/mto.02.8.4/mto.02.8.4.leydon.html [accessed 14 June 2016].

51 Eero Tarasti, *A Theory of Musical Semiotics* (Bloomington and Indianapolios: Indiana University Press, 1994), p. 279.

52 Tagg, 'From Refrain to Rave', p. 219.

53 Melechi, 'The Ecstasy of Disappearance', p. 32.

54 Peter Jowers, 'Timeshards: Repetition, Timbre, and Identity in Dance Music', *Time and Society*, 8/iii (1999), pp. 381–96, at p. 385.

55 Ibid., p. 386.

56 Reynolds draws a distinction between 'happy hardcore', characterised by a wilful submission to what he calls the 'drug-tech interface', and 'intelligent techno', in which issues of subjectivity and traditional musicality rise to the fore. *Energy Flash*, p. 157.

57 Ibid., p. xvi.

58 Ibid., p. xvii.

59 Ibid., p. 416.

60 See, for instance, Tom Service, *Music as Alchemy: Journeys with Great Conductors and Their Orchestras* (London: Faber and Faber, 2012), p. 139.

61 Taruskin, 'A Surrealist Composer'.

62 Echoes of Taruskin's influential interpretation of Adès informs, for instance, Ivan Hewett, 'He's Brilliant – but Can He Deliver?', *Daily Telegraph* (2 February 2004); Vivien Schweitzer, 'Great Expectations, and Versatility to Match', *New York Times* (23 March 2008); and Tom Service, 'A Guide to Thomas Adès's Music', *Guardian* (1 October 2012) www.theguardian.com/music/tomserviceblog/2012/oct/01/thomas-ades-contemporary-music-guide [accessed 12 August 2015].

Interpreting Asyla 153

63 Hamilton, 'Introduction to the Music of Thomas Adès'.
64 An exception can found in Christopher Fox's parallel between *America: A Prophecy* and the 1929 Surrealist map of the world, which firmly locates Surrealism within its historical context of the 1920s and 1930s. 'Tempestuous Times: The Recent Music of Thomas Adès', *Musical Times*, 145 (Autumn, 2004), pp. 41–56, at p. 41.
65 Fox, 'Tempestuous Times', p. 43; Taruskin, 'A Surrealist Composer', p. 147.
66 Adès has described surrealism as 'the only "ism" that I feel at all comfortable with'. Schweitzer, 'Great Expectations'.
67 Richard Taruskin, *The Oxford History of Western Music: Vol. 4 The Early Twentieth Century* (Oxford and New York: Oxford University Press, 2005), p. 590.
68 Fox, 'Tempestuous Times', p. 45.
69 Taruskin, 'A Surrealist Composer', p. 147.
70 Taruskin, *Oxford History of Western Music*, p. 595.
71 *TA:FON*, p. 22.
72 Taruskin, 'A Surrealist Composer', p. 149.
73 Daniel Albright, *Untwisting the Serpent: Modernism in Music, Literature and Other Arts* (Chicago and London: University of Chicago Press, 2000), pp. 289–90.
74 Taruskin, *Oxford History of Western Music*, p. 567.
75 Ibid., p. 576.
76 Albright, *Untwisting the Serpent*, p. 297. Emphasis added.
77 Taruskin, 'A Surrealist Composer', p. 147.
78 *TA:FON*, p. 141.
79 Ibid., p. 54.
80 Albright, *Untwisting the Serpent*, pp. 245, 248.
81 Ibid., pp. 248, 250.
82 *TA:FON*, p. 78.
83 Ibid., p. 80.

Epilogue
After *Asyla*

At the time of writing, those compositions by Adès that pre-date *Asyla* (1989–97) are roughly equal in number to those that follow it (1997–2015), depending on how one counts arrangements and selections from his operas. Inevitably, the growing demand for Adès as a pianist, conductor and music director has encroached upon his compositional work. The declining rate at which new scores are produced can also be attributed to the fact that the post-*Asyla* works intensify a trend towards large-scale, intricate and compositionally demanding musical structures. The most significant of these is undoubtedly Adès's second opera, *The Tempest* Op. 22 (2003–04), which opened up not just new textural possibilities, but also a new vein of emotional directness. In this light, the works composed between *Asyla* and *The Tempest* group more naturally with the former than the latter. Although those pieces that follow *The Tempest* are aesthetically closer to the opera, many of *Asyla*'s musical and extramusical and concerns continue to emerge within them, finding new forms and new modes of expression.

Between *Asyla* and *The Tempest* (1997–2004)

Premiered just under four weeks after *Asyla* (28 October 1997) by BCMG, and directed by Adès from the piano, the *Concerto Conciso* provided an immediate reminder of Adès's more playful, spiky, neo-classical impulses. Scored for solo piano and chamber ensemble, the timbral palette of the work is necessarily more restricted than in *Asyla*, and accordingly an even greater burden is placed on the working-out of material. The outer sections in particular explore respectively the interaction of material presented in different metres and of overlaid ostinati; the central panel of the piece is a weighty chaccone.

The virtuosic demands of the *Concerto Conciso* pale against those of the Piano Quintet Op. 20 (2000). Its opening expanded $\left\{ \begin{smallmatrix} +2 \\ +3 \\ +4 \end{smallmatrix} \right\}$ harmonic progression on solo violin (inverting the distorted horn calls of the Chamber Symphony) highlights the distance between the work and tonal models through its logical extension of the intervallic patterns of a clichéd cadential signal. The progression develops,

Epilogue 155

along with other associated intervallic cycles, by means of the superimposition and juxtaposition of material, leading to extraordinarily intricate polyrhythms, many of which make frequent use of irrational metres.[1] Although this emphasis on 'purely musical matters' might seem to distance the Piano Quintet from the more explicit extramusical concerns of *Asyla*, its capacity to suggest gendered or narrative readings has not gone unnoticed. [2]

The generic title of the work brings to mind nineteenth-century precedents, and commentators have been quick to make connections between Adès's Piano Quintet and those of Schubert, Schumann and Brahms.[3] Fox in particular has stressed the Brahmsian connection in Adès's somewhat startling use of sonata form (complete with a repeat of the exposition),[4] though Beethoven's Op. 28 piano sonata also lurks in the formal background.[5] As with three of the four movements of *Asyla*, the Piano Quintet's recapitulation is a highly compressed, continuous accelerando that balances the far longer exposition by virtue of its increased energy.

But here, sonata form is used as a vehicle to articulate Adès's ingenious manipulations of time. By frequently requiring the performers to feel the pulse in ever-changing and often irregular subdivisions of the crotchet, Adès gives the music an elastic, improvisatory feel. Nevertheless, rhythmic precision is paramount, for lines frequently converge, articulating certain points of arrival, only to shift out of temporal focus once again. As one might expect, the development serves to intensify the temporal processes of the exposition, touching on the two logical extremes that these processes imply. At first the individual lines reach a state of maximum dislocation, a violently dissonant climax, before fading dramatically into a series of gentle chords played in rhythmic unison. As with so much of the exposition, the actual rhythm of these chords is irregular, and though terrifyingly complex on the page, the aural effect is one of continual ebb and flow, rather like breathing. To repeat in the recapitulation the localised warping of time that characterised the exposition would seem forced after the development. Thus the floating temporalities of the exposition are re-imagined, positioned within the lengthy accelerando which sweeps all in its path. The use of sonata form is thus no mere crutch or affectation: it is central to the organisation of the unfolding temporal drama.

The implicit Brahmsian qualities of the Piano Quintet are made explicit in *Brahms* Op. 21 (2001), a setting for baritone and orchestra of a poem by Alfred Brendel in which the ghost of Brahms haunts the music room of a house. As with so much of his music, Adès takes familiar material and reworks it, extending the chains of thirds found in Brahms's late compositions and subjecting them to a series of rhythmic, metric and expressive transformations. En route, numerous allusions to works by Brahms tantalise our ears, but, like the ghost depicted in the poem, they drift by insubstantially. *Brahms* is a clever, witty work, and despite the irreverent 'anti-homage' to its subject, it raises vital critical questions about our relationship to the past.[6]

The somewhat oblique critical content of the Piano Quintet and *Brahms* is more explicit in *America*, even if Adès continues to avoid making unequivocal extramusical statements on the matter. The cyclic image of time central to the Mayan texts

156 *Epilogue*

that Adès sets means that they can act as both histories and prophecies.[7] Through it, *America* reminds the contemporary USA that previous civilisations have risen, fallen and become lost.[8] *America*'s transition from musical ebullience to numbed elegy, interspersed with triumphantly joyful passages derived from sixteenth-century Spanish music, is clear. Against and alongside this directed expressive trajectory, the music eddies back and forth, rotating through small pitch cells that gradually expand and contract, but always turning back on themselves, offering a vivid image of the cyclical time. Though the technique recalls those found in, amongst other works, *Origin of the Harp* and *Asyla*, it is explored here on a much larger scale.

The period between *Brahms* and *The Tempest* was bookended by critical recognition – Adès won the Hindemith Prize in 2001, and was celebrated at the 2004 Salzburg Easter Festival – but no new scores appeared.[9] The original operatic commission for Covent Garden, intended for 2001, never materialised. It was intended to be about cults, based on a libretto by the poet James Fenton that was subsequently rejected.[10] As with *America*, the plot had millennialist overtones of change: '[w]e're coming to the end of an era, but we just can't see what's to be the next era. People seem to need to follow behind someone'.[11] There were echoes, too, of the masses implicit in *Asyla*: 'I thought if I could get the pacing right, it could be a kind of crowd opera, like *Boris Gudounov*, where the crowd is like a single organism'.[12] In the end, it was a different aspect of *Asyla* that saw operatic light of day, when the confinement of the mental asylum (or Duke Bluebeard's castle) became that of Prospero trapped upon his island.

The Tempest

It was only relatively late in the day that the librettist (Meredith Oakes) and subject (*The Tempest*) were chosen for Adès's second opera; the composition of the work famously did not get completed until five days before the premiere, requiring a number of composers to be brought in to finish the orchestration.[13] The mildly controversial decision to write a libretto *after* Shakespeare may have irritated purists, but Oakes's paraphrase of the play has much to commend it. Extracting from the original a traditional narrative highlighting the power of redemptive love, Oakes simplified the plot, rendering it more suitable for the opera house, and reworking the characters: Prospero, for instance, begins the opera far more hell-bent on revenge than his Shakespearian counterpart, and Caliban, written for tenor, assumes a far nobler role. The verbal idiom has similarly been updated, with pervasive use of short rhyming couplets replacing Shakespearean iambic pentameter, offering on occasion highly poetic transformations of the original. This literary conceit, mirroring the artifice of Prospero's island, does not inhibit rich poetic statements.

What is most convincing about Adès's score is the fact that its musico-dramatic structures are satisfying intellectually and emotionally.[14] The narrative demands of the plot and the nature of the libretto requires that the music inhibits (perhaps 'constrict' is the better word) the expression in the first act, with the exception of

Epilogue   157

Ariel's beautiful 'Five fathoms deep' (Act 1 Scene 5, Fig. 90) and the subsequent entrance of Ferdinand. With the second and third acts, however, the expressive range of the music begins to open up. Ariel's music, written for high soprano, provides a concise example of such planning. The vocal writing in the first act is stratospheric, circling around top E. Recognising both the physical demands on the singer and Ariel's growing empathy for the humans he torments, the general tessitura descends throughout the opera: Ariel's lowest note tellingly and hauntingly coincides with the words 'if I were human' (Act 3 Scene 3, Fig. 305^{-3}).

Working alongside long-term designs such as these are short, vivid and characterful scenes teeming with invention. The handling of the orchestra offers a considerable advance on earlier works: whilst maintaining the contrapuntal ingenuity and exploitation of registral extremes, Adès adds to it a fuller-blooded mode of expression and more vivid colours. In doing so, it opened up artistic avenues that Adès has explored in his most recent music.

Thus in the second act, which concentrates at first on the delegation from Naples, Adès's aria for Caliban reveals a new-found lyricism in a largely diatonic A major, offering at the same time a reading of Caliban not as a savage, but as a fey dispossessed prince (Act 2 Scene 2, Fig. 170). But it is in the final scene, in which Miranda and Ferdinand duet with a Mahlerian intensity, that the lyricism reaches new heights, dissipating suspicions that the romantic sensibilities lurking under the music of the first act were but another mask for Adès to hide behind. In the final act, Adès's music finally unleashes the magic of Prospero's island. Emphasising the unambiguous romanticism of Adès's language, one finds an abundance of familiar musical and dramatic gestures, not least in the use of a passacaglia (recalling Ligeti's *Le Grand Macabre*) to underscore the reconciliation quintet (Act 3 Scene 4, Fig. 311).

The distance between Adès's treatment of expression in *The Tempest* and *Asyla* is best demonstrated by material first sung by Prospero that follows the contours of the main melody of the slow movement of *Asyla* (hereafter, '*Asyla* theme'). The pervasiveness of this motif in the first act recalls the pathological lamentation of *Asyla*, but in *The Tempest* it is anger, rather than fear, that counterpoints sadness. Unlike the expanding intervals of the original *Asyla* theme, the majority of Prospero's music is restricted to alternations of descending semitones and perfect fifths, suggesting, perhaps, an emotionally crippled state.

Prospero's intensity is set into sharp relief by the psychologically and dramatically necessary conventional use of the *pianto*. For instance, observing the titular tempest from afar, Prospero's daughter Miranda 'woe[s] the day' to a chromatically descending line, harmonised in a sort of D minor that invests the descent with quasi-tonal significations (Act 1 Scene 2, Fig. 17^{-3}).[15] Shortly afterwards, to a torrent of furious versions of the *Asyla* theme, expressive of anger by virtue of volume, timbre, tempo and articulation, Prospero tells Miranda of the treachery that led them to be cast away on the island. Blessed, as we shall see, with a 'natural' innocence (and thus according to dramatic convention a degree of psychological insight), Miranda sees Prospero's anger for what it really is. 'Such grief', she sings (Act 1 Scene 2, Fig. 35), whilst in the orchestra the *Asyla* theme

158   *Epilogue*

continues hesitantly, subcutaneously reinstating sadness as the dominant emotion. Over on another part of the island, the King of Naples laments what he believes to be the loss of his son Ferdinand's life to an accompaniment of melting chromaticism (Act 2 Scene 2, Fig. 194), corroborating – as if it were not already clear enough – that in musico-dramatic terms, those characters able to access genuine emotions do so by means of conventional musical codes.

But what of Prospero and the *Asyla* theme? The theme's network of significations include the grieving associated with the *pianto* – this is perhaps the dominant twentieth-century interpretation of it – but Prospero's grief is twisted, problematised. As depicted by the music, Prospero is fixated in the anger stage of grieving, psychologically unable to move on. To choose but two examples from a host of possibilities, we find the same obsessional usage of the *Asyla* theme early on in the opera when he sings of his brother (Act 1 Scene 2, Fig. 33) as well as in the final act when he gloats of his eventual revenge (Act 3 Scene 2, Fig. 281). Some kind of dysphoric state, most likely grieving, is connoted topically. Musically, however, the acoustic cues point to anger as a basic emotion. The two combine to imply an anger that results from grief, but this is troped further by the dysphoric state that arises from the mechanical alternation of intervals, the Escher-like tumbling sequences that characterise the *Asyla* theme, and the multiple imitations in both voice and accompaniment. The result is both asphyxiating and splenetic, and supremely appropriate for the dramatic situation.

This mention of the mechanical, systematic nature of the *Asyla* theme is timely. Not all semitones, as Raymond Monelle rightly reminded us, need be expressions of sighing or weeping.[16] Indeed, just as healthy grief is conveyed by conventional means within *The Tempest*, so too are other dramatic states. Magic and sensuousness are both central themes in the opera, and Adès, drawing on the same conventions that Monelle finds in Wagner's music, clothes these in semitones. Examples of both can be found in Caliban's first scene: consider, for instance, the discussion of Prospero's art (Act 1 Scene 4, Fig. 61) and Caliban's lust for Miranda (Act 1 Scene 4, Fig. 72). Prospero's own music is distinguished from passages such as these by virtue of its mechanical systems of extension. (One might also note the dramatic and intertextual contexts in which these systems appear, and how their obsessional properties reflect the particular emotional worlds that Adès seeks to depict.)

Yet *The Tempest* concludes with forgiveness, and thus Prospero's material has to reflect this change. The impetus comes from Miranda's love for Ferdinand. Within Act 1, Miranda had already come to be associated with perfect fifths and *major* seconds, as when she sings of the island ('headlands for climbing', Act 1 Scene 2, Fig. 38) or as she wakes from a magical slumber (Act 1 Scene 6, Fig. 97^{+2}). Both of these examples invoke nature (and imply Miranda's close connection to it), either in its physical form, or in its opposition to the artificial, the magical. Strengthening such associations are the pentatonic leanings generated by the combination of perfect fifths and major seconds. These intervals (or their inversions) return in Miranda and Ferdinand's love duet (Act 2 Scene 4, Fig. 218), and Prospero's ultimate redemption is prefigured in the mutation of his characteristic semitones into tones at the end of Act 2 (Act 2 Scene 4, Fig. 227). In the third act, the 'major second' version of the formula becomes increasingly prominent, beginning with the orchestral introduction, in which it appears in an ascending form, and again at the end of the opera once all but Ariel and Caliban have departed (Act 3 Scene 4, Fig. 329).

The process thus described characterises, in Robert Hatten's terms, an expressive trajectory from a furious pathological lament (governed by the *Asyla* theme) to the pastoral.[17] Nevertheless, I would argue that even this pastoral conclusion is ultimately governed by the lament by virtue of the motivic relationship between the material that suggests the two topics. What emerges is mediation of the pastoral by the lament, in a return to the melancholic Arcady of 'O Albion' or the mournful landscapes of *Asyla*.[18] Why else would Prospero's aria to the impermanence of the physical world ('with my art I've dimmed the sun') climax with a restatement of the *Asyla* theme (Act 3 Scene 2, Fig. 282)? This in turn undercuts the otherwise tender (if not happy) close of the opera, as if true grieving has finally become possible – indeed, could *only* become possible – amidst the reconciliations.

After the storm

The first post-*Tempest* work is series of scenes drawn from the opera for concert performance (Op. 22a, 2004). So too is *Court Studies* (2005), a series of brief character portraits from the second and third acts arranged for the same forces as *Catch*. More-or-less direct transcriptions from the opera, with no linking material, the studies are somewhat monochromatic compared to the original version, but the re-scoring intensifies the Renaissance-like atmosphere of the music written for the members of the court. (*Powder Her Face*, too, has provided two further works, first for full orchestra in Dances from *Powder Her Face* (2007) and second in a Concert Paraphrase for piano (2010) in the Lisztian tradition.) Adès also revisited his admiration of Couperin in his arrangement of three pieces for chamber orchestra in *Studies from Couperin* (2006).

The main works that followed *The Tempest* were orchestral. The Violin Concerto Op. 23 (2005), explores in the first movement ('Rings') intricate *moto perpetuo* figures and in the third ('Rounds'), irregular, enigmatic dance rhythms. The concerto's subtitle, 'Concentric Paths', gives an indication of the nature of the harmonic procedures at play: like the repeated strophes of the first movement of *Asyla*, or the rotations through pitch cells in *America*, the Violin Concerto balances forward motion with circular procedures. Much of the material of the first movement is based on expanded harmonic progressions, generally in three or four distinct layers, so arranged as to give emphasis to stacked fifths (and thereby echo the open strings of the solo violin). Unlike the more varied intervallic content of *Asyla*, each of the intervallic cycles within these progressions is based on semitones alone; although the rate of change within each cycle is unpredicatable, the motion produced feels inexorable and potentially infinite.

The heart of the Violin Concerto can be found in its moving central slow movement, 'Paths'. As in the *Concerto Conciso*, it is a chaconne, based in this instance upon a sequence of fourteen chords, which Alexi Vellianitis has shown consists

160 *Epilogue*

of two interlocking types of harmonic material.[19] The second variation introduces another version of the *Asyla* theme; as in the second movement of *Asyla* and the first act of *The Tempest*, the idea is taken up in increasingly dense contrapuntal textures. But here there is an expressive release, for the seventh variation yields to a thinner, chorale-like texture, with warmer harmonies and gracefully descending melodic lines that are embellished with gently rocking upper neighbour notes. Like the 'Arietta' from *Under Hamelin Hill*, the line ends not through the resolution of its musical tensions, but through the physical limitations of the instrument: upon reaching its bottom string, the violin is compelled to stop. The closure is therefore provisional.

Adès's description of the 'Concentric Paths' in terms of 'harmonic orbits',[20] along with his depiction of the entire first movement offering 'an ariel view',[21] suggests a more 'cosmic' perspective than that offered by *Asyla*'s landscapes and interiors.[22] A similar metaphor, albeit with added theological resonances, informs *Tevot* Op. 24 (2007), an extended single-movement work for large orchestra, commissioned by Stiftung Berlin Philharmoniker and The Carnegie Hall Corporation. Like *Asyla*, the title has multiple meanings. In Hebrew, Tevot means 'bars of music'; in addition, the Bible contains two uses of the singular tevah to represent specific containers that carry humans through a landscape (Noah's ark, and the cradle that carried the baby Moses along the river). Adès relocates the biblical associations into the space age:

> I liked the idea that the bars of the music were carrying the notes as a sort of family through the piece [...] But I was thinking about the ark, the vessel, in the piece as the earth. The earth would be a spaceship, a ship that carries us – and several other species – through the chaos of space in safety. It sounds a bit colossal, but it's the idea of the ship of the world.[23]

In some respects, *Tevot* continues where *Asyla* left off: there is the sense of a journey, and of some sort of refuge. Yet the ambiguities and ambivalences of *Asyla* are abandoned for a more direct mode of expression. The work opens with echoes of *The Tempest* and the Violin Concerto, not least in the use of multiple descending chromatic intervallic cycles that maintain a distance of roughly a perfect fifth from each other at all times. Out of this emerges a chorale for brass, beginning on a C major chord (a composer friend of Adès's found it 'shocking' and 'beyond taste').[24] There follow a number of episodes characterised by a level of rhythmic and textural complexity that Adès had hitherto restricted to chamber music or soloist roles,[25] concluding with many minutes of rapt orchestral outpourings of warmly lyrical lines and a triumphant final cadence that take up and extend the close of 'Paths' in order to achieve genuine resolution. Not even *The Tempest* dares Romanticism as overt as this, and *Tevot*'s conclusion even caught Adès off-guard. In comments that surely apply to *Asyla*, he stated that he was 'shocked by the resolution, how wide open it is. In my twenties, I would have botched the end, hidden it a bit, made it ironic'.[26] Critics did not seem to find the emotionalism concerning: later in 2007, *Tevot* followed *Asyla* by receiving a Royal Philharmonic Society Prize for large-scale composition.[27]

Epilogue 161

The incipient cinematic elements of *Asyla*, partially realised in *Music for the 21st Century*, come to the fore in *In Seven Days* for piano and orchestra with moving image Op. 25 (2008), and *Polaris* Op. 29 (2010), a 'voyage for orchestra'. Both works were composed in collaboration with Adès's civil partner, the video artist Tal Rosner, who created video installations that combine with the music (though the music stands on its own). In *In Seven Days*, the visuals, like so much of Adès's output, take familiar images (from the two concert halls that commissioned the work) and transform them into something new and beautiful. For *Polaris*, Rosner develops the notion of journeying and navigation by following 'two mysterious characters who roam a desolate shore [...] they are on the outlook, constantly searching the coastline while stars flicker and shadows of the sailors appear as ghostlike presences';[28] the immersive experience is extended still further by locating brass groups around the hall, literally creating the distance effects sought by the orchestration of *Asyla*.

In Seven Days retains *Tevot*'s cosmic, theological perspective. The title is a reference to the Creation. Accordingly, the music consists of seven interlinked movements, the first and second group of three movements providing a large-scale complement to one another, and the final movement presents anew the somewhat austere and neo-classical theme that begins the work. More specifically, the work is a set of double variations; the second theme develops a chord sequence from *The Tempest*.[29] The music teems with invention, continuously revisiting ideas and exploring new facets of them, and in doing so, offering a potent musical metaphor for Creation as a 'meeting-point between science and religion', or between rational thought and unfathomable mysteries.[30]

Polaris is altogether more straightforward, befitting its smaller dimensions and function (it was commissioned for the opening of the New World Symphony concert hall, Miami; in this respect, it is the descendent of *These Premises are Alarmed*). At first, a shimmering orchestral background, dominant by wind, harps and piano, gradually accumulates a seven-note idea, continually cycling back to its opening pitches. The texture teeters between heterophonic melody and harmonic field. The arrival of brass instruments, performing the same material in inversion, polarises the texture into melody (the brass) and accompaniment. Gradually the space fills out and the dynamics build, leading to a dramatic climax as the centre of gravity shifts from C♯ to G (bar 149). The process begins over, albeit less transparently: there is another large-scale motion, this time to A (bar 255), which remains the focus until the end. As with *Tevot*, the ending is emphatic.

Alongside these grand public statements exist four more intimate scores. Returning to solo piano music for the first time since *Traced Overhead*, Adès composed Three Mazurkas Op. 27 (2009) and the afore-mentioned *Concert Paraphrase on Powder Her Face*. Just as Adès drew on specific nineteenth-century models to frame the generic play of *Asyla* and the Piano Quintet, he 'is not so much playing with the Mazurka as a dance form, but with Chopin's Mazurka'.[31] *Lieux retrouvés* Op. 26 for cello and piano (2009) offers four virtuosic depictions of landscapes (the title roughly translates, with Proustian overtones, as 'places revisited'; there is therefore a genetic resemblance to *Arcadiana*). It is not

162   *Epilogue*

just places that are returned to: the second movement, 'La Montagne' revisits and reworks the expanded harmonic progressions of the Piano Quintet, and the third, 'Les Champs', finds new possibilities from material also examined in the third of the Mazurkas.[32] Framed by a depiction of water, 'Les Eaux', and the concluding 'cancan macabre' of 'La Ville', *Lieux retrouvés* returns to the four-movement quasi-symphonic design last essayed in *Asyla*. The major chamber work of recent years is *The Four Quarters* for string quartet Op. 28 (2010). Here, again, is a four-movement design (as with *Lieux retrouvés*, the middle movements are respectively fast and slow). The central metaphor here, the diurnal cycle, invokes another blend of directed motion and cyclical procedures.

The traditions that nurtured Adès's dramatic thirty-five-minute *Totentanz* (2013), for mezzo-soprano, baritone and orchestra, are both ancient and modern. It belongs to a line of dances that thread their way through Adès's output, from the central tango mortale of *Arcadiana* via 'Ecstasio' to 'La Ville', as well as revisiting the theme of death that haunted much of his pre-*Tempest* work. *Totentanz* sets the text that accompanied a now destroyed fifteenth-century frieze housed in the Marienkirche, Lübeck that depicts Death's summoning of all of mankind (from the Pope down to a child). Adès follows the structure of the text closely. *Totentanz* begins with a short prologue, based around expanding intervallic series that move outwards in wedge-like shapes. Death is sung by the baritone soloist: his call to dance is also structured by means of expanding intervallic series; later there is greater use of interlocking intervallic cycles as he summons the deceased. These calls are interspersed with the responses of his addressees (all sung by the mezzo-soprano).

Adès takes risks here: in conjunction with the prevalence of the expanding intervallic series with which the work opens, such a mechanical alteration between voices invites sterility. This is avoided by a number of means. On the largest scale, the work falls into two broad sections, divided by a raucous climax, replete with controlled aleatoric elements;[33] the contrast between these sections gives both dramatic and musical shape. Thus, the first half places Death to the fore, symbolised in the prominence given to the off-kilter rhythms and melodic contortions of his dance, announced initially by the folk-like piccolos and joined later by (amongst the many percussion instruments, requiring eight players) animal bones, played like spoons. The second half places greater emphasis on the various roles inhabited by the mezzo-soprano, and with it greater musical variety, although Death's musical signatures are never far from the surface. By varying the speed of the individual episodes (those with the Mayor, Doctor, Usurer and Merchant pass by at a dizzying rate) and at times overlapping lines in order to create duets (although there is little genuine dialogue between Death and his victims, but rather position statements), Adès generates considerable musical and dramatic momentum.

Totentanz is frequently atmospheric – the passage after the mid-point climax is especially eerie – but it is also brutal and at times even funny, as in the waltz used to signify Death's 'seduction' of the Monk. Riskiest of all, when Death turns to the child, the music blossoms into something resembling Strauss or Mahler (shades of *Kindertotenlieder*, perhaps). Whilst undoubtedly being glorious, beautiful music,

Epilogue 163

this sudden identification with a victim, and the suggestion of transcendence, sits awkwardly with the objectivity adopted elsewhere. Yet the moment proves to be fleeting, elusive. As with the equivalent summoning of Mahler at the climax of *Asyla*, there is an abrupt switch in mood, returning here to a short, dark coda that re-establishes the dominant, macabre atmosphere, casting a shadow back over the preceding heart-on-sleeve emotions, the final dramatic gesture of a strangely unsettling work.

* * *

For all of the undoubted significance *Asyla* has within Adès's career, this brief survey demonstrates how little it directly shaped the music that followed it. This is in keeping with the observations made in Chapter 2: a useful way to understand Adès's output is to imagine a continuous shuffling and reconfiguration of ideas, with the occasional addition of new techniques or modes of expression added to the melting pot. Sometimes certain ideas get brought to the fore; in other works they recede into the background in order to allow other material to breathe. In other cases still, the same material is revisited in order to see what other musical potentialities exist within it. At times, Adès portrays such activity in quasi-scientific terms, whether as a physicist pushing and pulling magnets around, or as a chemist mixing elements or pharmaceuticals.[34] But there is also an alchemy, as when the various components come together in mysterious, unexpected, and profoundly moving ways. For me, this describes *Asyla*, a work that reveals something new on every hearing, and which continually poses challenging and rewarding musical and critical questions.

Notes

1 See Stoecker, 'Aligned Cycles'.
2 See, for instance, Kenneth Gloag, 'Thomas Adès and the "Narrative Agendas" of "Absolute Music"', in Beate Neumeier (ed.) *Dichotonies: Gender and Music* (Universitätsverlag, Heidelberg, 2009), pp. 97–110; and Emma Gallon, 'Narrativities in the Music of Thomas Adès: The Piano Quintet and *Brahms*', in Michael L. Klein and Nicholas Reyland (eds), *Music and Narrative since 1900* (Bloomington: Indianapolis University Press, 2013), pp. 251–63 [to avoid confusion, subsequent references to 'Narrativities' will continue to cite Gallon's 2011 PhD thesis].
3 Gloag, 'The "Narrative Agendas" of "Absolute Music"', p. 100.
4 Fox, 'Tempestuous Times', p. 47.
5 *TA:FON*, p. 50.
6 See Edward Venn, 'Thomas Adès and the Spectres of *Brahms*', *Journal of the Royal Musical Association*, 140/i (2015), pp. 163–212.
7 Tom Service, 'Altered States', *Guardian* (29 August 2002).
8 For an account of *America* that explores the overlaying of 'different Americas with different narratives to tell', see Gallon, 'Narrativities', pp. 127–45.
9 Recognition of a different sort came in 2002 when his portrait was commissioned for the British National Gallery.
10 See Hewett, 'He's Brilliant – But Can He Deliver?'
11 Anthony, 'The Astonishing Thomas Adès', p. 24.
12 Ibid.

164 *Epilogue*

13 Hewett, 'He's Brilliant – But Can He Deliver?'
14 The opera received – and continues to receive – mostly positive reviews; in 2005 it won for Adès his second Royal Philharmonic Society Prize for large-scale composition.
15 The textures of this scene were influenced by the music of Gerald Barry, whose music Adès greatly admires. *TA:FON*, p. 148.
16 Monelle, *The Sense of Music*, p. 76.
17 Robert Hatten, *Interpreting Musical Gestures, Topics, and Tropes: Mozart, Beethoven, Schubert* (Bloomington: Indiana University Press, 2004), pp. 53 ff.
18 For an alternative interpretation of *The Tempest*, see Gallon, 'Narrativities', pp. 254–302.
19 Alexi Vellianitis, 'Kuusisto's Joke: Reconstructing the Rubble of Tonality in Thomas Adès's Violin Concerto' (MMus diss., University of Oxford, 2012), p. 43.
20 Thomas Adès, Composer's Note to Violin Concerto Op. 23 (2005). For a detailed exploration of this celestial metaphor and its usefulness in understanding the first movement of the Violin Concerto, see Daniel Fox, 'Multiple Time-Scales in Adès's *Rings*', *Perspectives of New Music*, 52/i (Winter 2014), pp. 28–56.
21 *TA:FON*, p. 45.
22 It is Service who suggests a cosmic approach to space in Adès's later music; Adès's reply is non-committal. *TA:FON*, p. 171.
23 Cited in Tom Service, 'Writing Music? It's Like Flying a Plane', *Guardian* (26 February 2007).
24 *TA:FON*, p. 39.
25 Belling, 'Thinking Irrational'.
26 Culshaw, 'Don't Call me a Messiah'.
27 Adès was the first person to receive the award three times.
28 www.talrosner.com/projects/polaris [accessed 12 August 2015].
29 *TA:FON*, p. 30.
30 Ibid., p. 31.
31 Samuel John Wilson, 'An Aesthetics of Past-Present Relations in the Experience of Late 20th- and Early 21st-Century Art Music' (PhD diss., Royal Holloway, University of London, 2013), p. 251.
32 For an analysis of 'Les Champs', see John Roeder, 'Transformation in Post-Tonal Music', in Alexander Rehding (ed.), *Oxford Handbooks Online in Music* (New York: Oxford University Press, 2014).
33 The work was commissioned in memory of Witold Lutosławski and his wife Danuta, which may explain some of the more Lutosławskian textures within *Totentanz*.
34 *TA:FON*, pp. 3, 56.

References

An up-to-date list of Adès's compositions and recordings can be found at:
http://thomasades.com/.
Many of Adès's scores can be perused online at:
www.fabermusic.com/composers/thomas-adès/works.

Bibliography

Adès, Thomas, Composer's Note to Score of *Arcadiana* Op. 12 (Faber Music, 1995).
———, Composer's Note to Score of *Chamber Symphony* Op. 2 (Faber Music, 1995).
———, Composer's Note to Score of *Darknesse Visible* (Faber Music, 1998).
———, '"Nothing but Pranks and Puns": Janáček's Solo Piano Music', in Paul Wingfield (ed.), *Janáček Studies* (Cambridge: Cambridge University Press, 1999), pp. 18–35.
———, Composer's Note to Violin Concerto Op. 23 (2005).
Adès, Thomas and Tom Service, *Thomas Adès: Full of Noises* (New York: Farrar, Straus and Giroux, 2012).
Albright, Daniel, *Untwisting the Serpent: Modernism in Music, Literature and Other Arts* (Chicago and London: University of Chicago Press, 2000).
Allen, David, 'Death Dances to Its Own Tune, Sparing Not a Soul', *New York Times* (14 March 2015).
Anon., 'Not Yet 30, Britain's Leading New Composer Goes From Strength to Strength', *Economist* (12 June 1999).
Anon., 'Symphonische Manöverkritik', *Süddeutsche Zeitung* (9 September 2002).
Anthony, Michael, 'Wild, Eerie "Asyla" Gets a Fine US Debut', *Star Tribune* (21 November 1997).
———, 'The Astonishing Thomas Adès', *American Record Guide* (March/April 1999), pp. 23–6.
Antokoletz, Elliott, *Musical Symbolism in the Operas of Debussy and Bartók: Trauma, Gender, and the Unfolding of the Unconscious* (Oxford and New York: Oxford University Press, 2004).
Aragay, Mireia, Hildegard Klein, Enric Monforte and Pilar Zozaya (eds), *British Theatre of the 1990s: Interviews with Directors, Playwrights, Critics and Academics* (Basingstoke: Palgrave Macmillan, 2007).
Barsky, Robert, *Constructing a Productive Other: Discourse Theory and the Convention Refugee Hearing* (Amsterdam: John Benjamins Publishing Company, 1994).
Bauer, Amy, *Ligeti's Laments: Nostalgia, Exoticism, and the Absolute* (Aldershot: Ashgate, 2011).

166   *References*

Belling, Huw, 'Thinking Irrational, Thomas Adès and New Rhythms' (MA diss., Royal College of Music, 2010).

Bentley, Nick, 'Introduction: Mapping the Millennium. Themes and Trends in Contemporary British Fiction', in Nick Bentley (ed.), *British Fiction of the 1990s* (London and New York: Routledge, 2005), pp. 1–18.

Bracewell, Michael, *The Nineties: When Surface Was Depth* (London: Flamingo, 2002).

Butler, Mark, *Unlocking the Groove: Rhythm, Meter, and Musical Design in Electronic Dance Music* (Bloomington and Indianapolis: Indiana University Press, 2006).

Cao, Hélène, *Thomas Adès Le Voyageur: Devenir compositeur. Être musician* (Paris: Éditions M.F., 2007).

Christiansen, Rupert, 'Blissfully Calm after the Storm Opera', *Daily Telegraph* (11 February 2004).

Clark, Andrew, 'Adès Delights the Ear', *Financial Times* (31 October 1997).

Clarke, Peter, *Hope and Glory: Britain 1900–2000* (London: Penguin, 2004).

Clements, Andrew, 'Crocodile Tears Before Bedtime', *Guardian* (3 July 1995).

———, 'From the Banal to the Sublime', *Guardian* (4 October 1997).

———, 'Thomas Adès Takes over the Asylum', *BBC Music Magazine* (December 1997).

Collin, Matthew, *Altered State: The Story of Ecstasy Culture and Acid House* (London: Serpent's Tail, 1997).

Cork, Richard, *Breaking Down the Barriers: Art in the 1990s* (New Haven and London: Yale University Press, 2003).

Cowan, Rob, 'Lightening Conductor', *Independent* (13 September 2002).

Cross, Jonathan, *Harrison Birtwistle: The Mask of Orpheus* (Aldershot: Ashgate, 2009).

Culshaw, Peter, 'Don't Call me a Messiah', *Daily Telegraph* (1 March 2007).

Derrida, Jacques, *Writing and Difference,* trans. Alan Bass (London and New York: Routledge, 1978).

Driver, Paul, 'A New Spin on the Cycle', *Sunday Times* (12 October 1997).

Dunnett, Roderic, 'How to Give Mahler a Run for His Money', *Independent* (3 October 1997).

Dyja, Eddie, *Studying British Cinema: The 1990s* (Leighton Buzzard: Auteur, 2010).

Farkas, Zoltán, 'The Path of a Hölderlin Topos: Wandering Ideas in Kurtág's Compositions', *Studia Musicologica Academiae Scientiarum Hungaricae*, T. 43, Fasc. 3/4 (2002), pp. 289–310.

Finch, Hilary, 'Thomas Adès', *The Times* (19 March 1994).

Foucault, Michel, *Madness and Civilisation: A History of Insanity in the Age of Reason*, trans. Richard Howard (London: Routledge, 1967).

Fox, Christopher, 'Tempestuous Times: The Recent Music of Thomas Adès', *Musical Times*, 145 (Autumn 2004), pp. 41–56.

Fox, Daniel, 'Multiple Time-Scales in Adès's *Rings*', *Perspectives of New Music*, 52/i (Winter 2014), pp. 28–56.

Franklin, Peter, *Mahler: Symphony No. 3* (Cambridge: Cambridge University Press, 1991).

Gallon, Emma, 'Narrativities in the Music of Thomas Adès' (PhD diss., Lancaster University, 2011).

———, 'Narrativities in the Music of Thomas Adès: The Piano Quintet and *Brahms*', in Michael L. Klein and Nicholas Reyland (eds), *Music and Narrative since 1900* (Bloomington: Indianapolis University Press, 2013), pp. 251–63.

Gąsiorek, Andrzej, '"Refugees From Time": History, Death and the Flight from Reality in Contemporary Writing', in Nick Bentley (ed.), *British Fiction of the 1990s* (London and New York: Routledge, 2005), pp. 42–56.

References 167

Gloag, Kenneth, 'Thomas Adès and the "Narrative Agendas" of "Absolute Music"', in Beate Neumeier (ed.) *Dichotonies: Gender and Music* (Universitätsverlag, Heidelberg, 2009), pp. 97–110.

Greenwood, Jaqueline Susan, 'Selected Vocal and Chamber Music of Thomas Adès: Stylistic and Contextual Issues' (PhD. diss., Kingston University, 2013).

Griffiths, Paul, 'Everyone Wants a Piece of Adès: This Piece', *New York Times* (6 December 1998).

Hadley, Roger and Roger Clough, *Care in Chaos: Frustration and Challenge in Community Care* (London: Cassell, 1996).

Hamilton, Andy, 'Introduction to the Music of Thomas Adès', in *Thomas Adès: List of Works* (Faber Music, 2005).

Hatten, Robert, *Interpreting Musical Gestures, Topics, and Tropes: Mozart, Beethoven, Schubert* (Bloomington: Indiana University Press, 2004).

Hensher, Philip, 'How to Write an Opera', *New Statesman & Society*, 8 (6 June 1995), p. 31.

Hewett, Ivan, 'He's Brilliant – But Can He Deliver?', *Daily Telegraph* (2 February 2004).

———, 'Don't Dumb Down Classical Music for Teenagers', *Daily Telegraph* (20 May 2015).

Hewison, Robert, 'Rebirth of a Nation', *The Times* (19 May 1996).

Hicken, Stephen, Review of Adès, *Living Toys*, EMI CD 72271, *American Record Guide* (March/April 1999), pp. 71–2.

Holland, Bernard 'Burying the Hatchet, Sounding Fine', *New York Times* (23 November 2002).

Jowers, Peter, 'Timeshards: Repetition, Timbre, and Identity in Dance Music', *Time and Society*, 8/iii (1999), pp. 381–96.

Kallberg, Jeffrey, 'The Rhetoric of Genre: Chopin's Nocturne in G Minor', *19th-Century Music*, 11/iii (1988), pp. 238–61.

Kübler-Ross, Elizabet, *On Death and Dying* (New York: Macmillan, 1969).

Lambert, Philip, 'Interval Cycles as Compositional Resources in the Music of Charles Ives', *Music Theory Spectrum*, 12/i (1990), pp. 43–82.

Leydon, Rebecca, 'Towards a Typology of Minimalist Tropes', *Music Theory Online*, 8/iv (2002) www.mtosmt.org/issues/mto.02.8.4/mto.02.8.4.leydon.html [accessed 12 June 2016].

Massey, Drew, 'Thomas Adès at 40', *Salmagundi*, 174–175 (2012), pp. 194–202.

McManus, Andrew, 'Nancarrow's Rhythmic Structures in Thomas Adès's *Asyla*' (MA diss., Eastman School of Music, 2009).

Melechi, Antonio, 'The Ecstasy of Disappearance', in Steve Redhead (ed.), *Rave Off: Politics and Deviance in Contemporary Youth Culture* (Aldershot: Avebury, 1993), pp. 29–40.

Mermelstein, David, 'The Meanspirited Wunderkind', *New Criterion*, 17/vii (1999), p. 51.

Metzer, David, *Musical Modernism at the Turn of the Twenty-First Century* (Cambridge: Cambridge University Press, 2009).

Monelle, Raymond, *The Sense of Music: Semiotic Essays* (Princeton: Princeton University Press, 2000).

———, *The Musical Topic: Hunt, Military and Pastoral* (Bloomington and Indianapolis: Indiana University Press, 2006).

Morgan, Kenneth O., *Twentieth-Century Britain: A Very Short Introduction* (Oxford and New York: Oxford University Press, 2000).

Morrison, Richard, 'Prodigy with a Notable Talent for Sounding Off', *The Times* (9 June 1995).

168   References

————, 'A Glorious Goodbye', *The Times* (31 August 1998).

————, 'Rattle's Hurricane Debut Shakes Artistic Berlin', *The Times* (9 September 2002).

O'Hagan, Peter, 'Introduction', in Peter O'Hagan (ed.), *Aspects of British Music of the 1990s* (Aldershot: Ashgate, 2003), pp. xv–xviii.

Porter, Andrew, Sleeve notes to Adès, *Living Toys*, EMI CD 72271 (1998).

————, Sleeve notes to Adès, *Powder Her Face*, EMI CD 56649 (1998).

————, CD notes for *Asyla*, EMI 5 56818 2 (1999); re-used as notes for EMI DVD 7243 4 90325 9 0 (2003).

Ravenhill, Mark, 'A Touch of Evil', *Guardian* (22 March 2003).

Redhead, Steve, 'The Politics of Ecstasy', in Steve Redhead (ed.), *Rave Off: Politics and Deviance in Contemporary Youth Culture* (Aldershot: Avebury, 1993), pp. 7–28.

Reynolds, Simon, *Energy Flash: A Journey through Rave Music and Dance Culture* (London: Picador 1998).

Robin, William, 'They're Always Taking His Stuff; For American Composers, Thomas Adès Offers a Wealth of Inspiration', *New York Times* (8 February 2015).

Roeder, John, 'Co-operating Continuities in the Music of Thomas Adès', *Music Analysis*, 25/i–ii (2006), pp. 121–54.

————, 'A Transformational Space Structuring the Counterpoint in Adès's "Auf dem Wasser zu singen"', *Music Theory Online*, 15/i (March 2009) www.mtosmt.org/issues/mto.09.15.1/mto.09.15.1.roeder_space.html [accessed 12 June 2016].

————, 'Transformation in Post-Tonal Music', in Alexander Rehding (ed.), *Oxford Handbooks Online in Music* (New York: Oxford University Press, 2014).

Ross, Alex, 'Roll Over, Beethoven: Thomas Adès', *New Yorker* (26 October 1998), pp. 111–41.

————, *The Rest is Noise: Listening to the Twentieth Century* (London: Harper Perennial, 2007).

Rowe, Georgina, 'Berkeley Symphony Delivers Stunning "Asyla"', *San Jose Mercury News* (16 January 2015).

Rusbridger, Alan, 'Rattle's Glorious Berlin Debut', *Guardian* (9 September 2002).

Schulz, Thomas, Programme note to *Asyla* for 7–9 September 2002, Berlin Philharmoniker, trans. Richard Evidon (2002).

Schweitzer, Vivien, 'Great Expectations, and Versatility to Match', *New York Times* (23 March 2008).

Service, Tom, 'Altered States', *Guardian* (29 August 2002).

————, 'Writing Music? It's Like Flying a Plane', *Guardian* (26 February 2007).

————, *Music as Alchemy: Journeys with Great Conductors and Their Orchestras* (London: Faber and Faber, 2012).

————, 'A Guide to Thomas Adès's Music', *Guardian* (1 October 2012) www.theguardian.com/music/tomserviceblog/2012/oct/01/thomas-ades-contemporary-music-guide [accessed 12 August 2015].

Sierz, Aleks, *In-Yer-Face Theatre: British Drama Today* (London: Faber and Faber, 2001).

Snoman, Rick, *The Dance Music Manual: Tools, Toys, and Techniques* 2nd edn (Oxford: Taylor and Francis/Focal Press, 2009).

Spitzer, Michael, *Metaphor and Musical Thought* (Chicago and London: University of Chicago Press, 2004).

————, 'Mapping the Human Heart: A Holistic Analysis of Fear in Schubert', *Music Analysis*, 29/i-ii-iii (2010), pp. 149–213.

————, 'The Topic of Emotion', in Esti Sheinberg (ed.), *Musical Semiotics: A Network of Significations* (Aldershot: Ashgate, 2012), pp. 211–23.

References 169

Spivak, Gayatri Chakravorty, translator's preface to Jacques Derrida, *Of Grammatology* (Baltimore and London: The Johns Hopkins University Press, 1976), pp. ix –lxxxvii.

Stallabrass, Julian, *High Art Lite: British Art in the 1990s* (London: Verson, 1999).

Stearn, David Patrick, 'Adès' Unique Sound Bows to Nobody', *USA Today* (24 July 1997).

Stoecker, Philip, 'Aligned Cycles in Thomas Adès's Piano Quintet', *Music Analysis*, 33/i (2014), pp. 32–64.

Tagg, Philip, 'From Refrain to Rave: the Decline of Figure and the Rise of Ground', *Popular Music*, 13/ii (1994), pp. 209–22.

Tarasti, Eero, *Myth and Music: A Semiotic Approach to the Aesthetics of Myth in Music, especially that of Wagner, Sibelius and Stravinsky* (The Hague, Paris and New York: Mouton Publishers, 1979).

———, *A Theory of Musical Semiotics* (Bloomington and Indianapolios: Indiana University Press, 1994).

Tarnopolsky, Mathias, Programme Note to Thomas Adès, *Asyla* (1997).

Taruskin, Richard, 'A Surrealist Composer Comes to the Rescue of Modernism', *New York Times* (5 December 1999), reprinted with a postscript in *The Danger of Music and Other Anti-Utopian Essays* (Berkeley, Los Angeles and London: University of California Press, 2010), pp. 144–52.

———, *The Oxford History of Western Music: Vol. 4 The Early Twentieth Century* (Oxford and New York: Oxford University Press, 2005).

Teeman, Tim, 'Thomas Adès: Why I Have to Compose', *The Times* (16 February 2011).

Tomlinson, Dylan, and John Carrier (eds), *Asylum in the Community* (London: Routledge, 1996).

Tommasini, Anthony, 'Young, but with Enough Experience to Look Back', *New York Times* (31 March 2008).

Travers, Aaron, 'Interval Cycles, Their Permutations and Generative Properties in Thomas Adès's *Asyla*' (PhD diss., University of Rochester, 2004).

Turner, Alwyn W., *A Classless Society: British Culture in the 1990s* (London: Aurum Press, 2013).

Urban, Ken, 'Cruel Britannia', in Rebecca D'Monté and Graham Saunders (eds), *Cool Britannia? British Political Drama in the 1990s* (Basingstoke: Palgrave MacMillan, 2008), pp. 38–55.

Vellianitis, Alexi, 'Kuusisto's Joke: Reconstructing the Rubble of Tonality in Thomas Adès's Violin Concerto' (MMus diss., University of Oxford, 2012).

Venn, Edward, 'London, Royal Opera House: *The Tempest*', *Tempo*, 58 (July 2004), pp. 72–3.

———, 'Thomas Adès's Piano Quintet', *Tempo*, 59 (October 2005), pp. 73–4.

———, '"Asylum Gained"? Aspects of Meaning in Thomas Adès's *Asyla*', *Music Analysis*, 25/i–ii (2006), pp. 89–120.

———, 'Narrativity in Thomas Adès's *Ecstasio*', *Res Facta Nova*, 11/x (2010), pp. 69–78.

———, 'Thomas Adès', trans. Agnieszka Kotarba, in *Nowa Muzyka Brytyjska* (Kraków: Ha!Art, 2010), pp. 182–200.

———, 'Thomas Adès and the *pianto*', in Nearchos Panos, Vangelis Lympourdis, George Athanasopoulos and Peter Nelson (eds), *Proceedings of the International Conference on Musical Semiotics in Memory of Raymond Monelle* (Edinburgh: ECA – The University of Edinburgh and IPMDS, 2013), pp. 309–17.

———, 'BBC Proms 2013: David Matthews and Thomas Adès', *Tempo*, 68 (January 2014), pp. 59–61.

———, 'Thomas Adès's "Freaky Funky Rave"', *Music Analysis*, 33/i (2014), pp. 65–98.

170 *References*

————, 'Thomas Adès and the Spectres of *Brahms*', *Journal of the Royal Musical Association*, 140/i (2015), pp. 163–212.

Vojcic, Aleksandra, 'Rhythm as Form: Rhythmic Hierarchy in Later Twentieth-Century Piano Music' (PhD diss., City University of New York, 2007).

Wells, Dominic, 'Plural Styles, Personal Style: The Music of Thomas Adès', *Tempo*, 66 (April 2012), pp. 2–14.

Whittall, Arnold, 'Thomas Adès', in Stanley Sadie and John Tyrell (eds), *The New Grove Dictionary of Music and Musicians* (London: Macmillan, 2001), vol. 1, p. 156.

————, 'Dillon, Adès, and the Pleasures of Allusion', in Peter O'Hagan (ed.), *Aspects of British Music of the 1990s* (Aldershot: Ashgate, 2003), pp. 3–27.

————, *Exploring Twentieth-Century Music: Tradition and Innovation* (Cambridge: Cambridge University Press, 2003).

Wilson, Charles, 'György Ligeti and the Rhetoric of Autonomy', *Twentieth-Century Music*, 1/i (2004), pp. 5–28.

Wilson, Samuel John, 'An Aesthetics of Past-Present Relations in the Experience of Late 20th- and Early 21st-Century Art Music' (PhD diss., Royal Holloway, University of London, 2013).

Wroe, Nicholas, 'Adès on Adès', *Guardian* (5 July 2008).

Young, Marvin, and John Drees, 'Grawemeyer Winners Return to Share Ideas', *Inside U of L online* (7 April 2000) www.louisville.edu/ur/onpi/inside/4-7-00/grawemeyer. html [accessed 26 February 2003].

Websites

http://audacity.sourceforge.net/.
http://grawemeyer.org/music-composition/.
http://howtomakeelectronicmusic.com/how-to-create-an-effective-rising-build-up.
www.refugeecouncil.org.uk/assets/0001/5594/mori_report.pdf.
www.talrosner.com.
www.youtube.com/watch?v=drur9JeMFUk.

Discography

Living Toys (EMI CD 72271,1998).

Asyla: Chamber and Orchestral Works (EMI 5 56818 2, 1999).

Mahler: Symphony No. 5/Adès: *Asyla* (EMI DVD 7243 4 90325 9 0, 2003).

Thomas Adès: Music for the 21st Century, produced and directed by Gerald Fox (LWT 1999); included on DVD release of Adès's *Powder Her Face* (Digital Classicals DC 10002, 2005).

Radio broadcasts

Interview with Thomas Adès, *Music Matters*, BBC Radio 3 (first broadcast 15 May 15 2010).

Interview with Thomas Adès, *Performance on 3*, BBC Radio 3 (first broadcast 1 October 1997).

Index

Adès, Dawn 2
Adès, Thomas: and the Aldeburgh Festival
4, 5, 29; and the BBC Young Musician
of the Year Competition 2, 12 n. 13, 16;
as composer-in-residence for the Hallé
orchestra 4; and death 11, 162–3; early
development as composer 2, 16, 18–19;
education 2; and genre 3, 29–30, 155;
influences upon 18, 39 n. 7; interest
in sonority 2, 28; and lament (grief,
mourning etc.) 23, 31–4, 156, 157–9;
and metaphor 7, 25, 34–6, 160, 162; on
Modernism, 7–8; music as landscape
2, 35; as performer 2, 3, 5, 154; and
the press 5, 12 n. 23; prizes 1, 2, 3, 5,
156, 160, 164 n. 14, 164 n. 27; and
theatricality 3, 35; use of titles 1, 30
Compositional techniques (*see also*
entries under *Asyla*):
additive rhythms 28
canon 16
chaconne 23, 154, 159
expanded harmonic progression 16,
17, 18, 22, 33, 154, 159
expressive topics 31, 157–9; *see also*
separate entries for *pianto* and
passus duriusculus
instrumental colour 28–9
interlocking intervallic cycles 22,
60, 162
intervallic cycle 16, 18, 22, 33, 147,
154, 159, 160
intervallic series 16, 17, 18, 19, 162
irrational rhythms 28, 155
line 23, 25, 160
metrical complexity 25, 154–5
musical strata 16, 19, 22, 23, 25
ostinato 23, 25
passacaglia 23, 157
pattern disruption 19, 22, 45

permutation/cycling of pitch
collections 22–3, 156, 159, 161
prominence of perfect fifths/fourths
22, 23, 159
quarter tones 29
quotation and allusion 30, 41 n. 39,
155
rhythmic cycles 25
stylistic allusions 30–1, 33–4, 150
topical references 30–1, 158–9
Individual works
America: A Prophecy (Op. 19) 1, 5, 9,
11, 155–6, 163 n. 8
Arcadiana (Op. 12) 4, 5, 7, 11, 22, 23,
29, 33, 35, 52, 156, 159, 161, 162
Asyla (Op. 17) *see* separate entry
Audabe 12 n. 14
Brahms (Op. 21) 155
... but all shall be well (Op. 10) 3, 23,
30, 38
Cardiac Arrest 11, 12 n. 18
Catch (Op. 4) 3, 29, 35, 159
Chamber Symphony (Op 2) 3, 23, 25,
27, 28, 29, 30, 31, 35, 154
Concerto Conciso (Op. 18) 4,
154, 159
Concert Paraphrase on *Powder Her
Face* 159, 161
Court Studies 159
Dances from *Powder Her Face* 159
Darknesse Visible 3, 11, 31, 32, 33
Fayrfax Carol, The 5, 11, 33, 34, 73,
76, 77, 88, 131
Five Eliot Landscapes (Op. 1) 2, 3,
11, 12 n. 2, 16, 17, 18, 31, 35
Fool's Rhymes (Op. 5) 2, 25
Four Quarters, The (Op. 28) 161
Gefriolsae Me (Op. 3b) 2
In Seven Days (Op. 25) 35, 161
January Writ 5

172 *Index*

Les baricades mistérieuses 12 n. 15
Lieux retrouvés (Op. 26) 161–2
Life Story (Op. 8) 2, 3, 11, 30, 35
Living Toys (Op. 9) 1, 3, 11, 22, 25, 28, 29, 30–1, 35; programme 3, 30, 65, 146
Lover in Winter, The 2, 35, 39 n. 5
Mazurkas (Op. 27) 161, 162
Origin of the Harp, The (Op. 11) 3–4, 22, 41 n. 34, 156
O thou who didst with pitfall and with gin (Op. 3a) 2
Piano Quintet (Op. 20) 154–5, 161, 162
Polaris (Op. 29) 161
Powder Her Face (Op. 14) 3, 4, 9, 10, 11, 14 n. 71, 19, 20–21, 22, 23, 30, 35, 40 n. 9, 41 n. 32, 159
Scenes from *The Tempest* (Op. 22a) 159
Sonata da Caccia (Op. 11) 3
Still Sorrowing (Op. 7) 3, 11, 23, 24, 25, 29, 79
Studies from Couperin 159
Tempest, The (Op. 22) 154, 156–9, 160, 161, 162
Tevot (Op. 24) 35, 160, 161
These Premises are Alarmed (Op. 16) 4, 23, 29, 35, 38, 161
Totentanz 70 n. 20, 162–3, 164 n. 33
Traced Overhead (Op. 15) 4, 15, 16, 161
Under Hamelin Hill (Op. 6) 3, 11, 23, 25, 29, 35, 41 n. 35, 115 n. 25, 160
Vioin Concerto (Op. 23) 159–60
Adès, Timothy 2
Albright, Daniel 147, 148, 150
Anderson, Julian 15 n. 79, 40 n. 15
Asyla (Op. 17): cinematic metaphors 35, 66, 76, 134, 141, 161; commission 1; composition 36–37, 43, 71, 98; discursive shifts 69, 138; influence on other composers 137; instrumentation 37–8; and landscape 139–42; metaphor of asylum 39, 46–7, 65, 71, 118, 134–5, 139–42; and moral panics 142–6; musical logic 38–9, 45, 48, 77–8; premiere 1, 132; press response 38–9, 100, 136–7, 142, 144; programme note 38–9, 137, 139; relationship to discursive practices xv–xvi, 2, 7, 47, 135 n. 9, 137–9; relationship to symphonic genre 38–9, 138; and surrealism 65, 148–50; title 1, 9, 139

Individual movements:
first movement 141: additive rhythms 63; dance of death 63, 65–6; EDM references 54; enharmonicism 49, 54, 70 n. 13; expanded harmonic progressions 57, 58, 62, 66, 68, 69, 131; extramusical inspiration 46–7, 65; figural metaphors 45, 65, 69; form 47–8, 52–3, 62; interlocking intervallic cycles 60; lament 47, 60, 62, 63, 66; musical inspiration 45; pastoral topic 52, 59, 60, 61, 66; pattern disruption 45, 49, 58, 59, 69 n. 3; *pianto* 60; ostinato 63; referential dyads 49, 50–1, 52, 54, 57, 58, 60, 61, 65–6, 149; strata 54, 57, 59, 61, 63, 66; stylised birdsong 59, 66; symphonic logic 45, 48; timbre 48, 54, 59, 68, 152 n. 33
second movement 70 n. 17, 140, 157, 160: canon 80, 86, 87, 90; enharmonicism 90; expanded harmonic progressions 71, 76, 87, 88, 92; fetish pitches 78, 88, 92, 93, 96; figural metaphors 78, 80, 86, 89; form 78–9, 87, 93; harmonic counterpoint 77, 87; inspiration 71, 73, 76; interlocking intervallic cycle 88–9, 92–3; intervallic cycles 77–8, 79–80, 87, 90; lament 73–7, 80, 93, 96; ostinato 79; *passus duriusculus* 73, 78, 80; pattern disruption 78, 80, 86, 96; permutation of pitch collection 89; *pianto* 76; referential dyads 71, 87; suppressed title 71, 73, 96 n. 2, 138, 140; textural density 77, 80, 86, 89, 93; timbre 71, 79, 86, 87–8, 90, 92; transformation of ideas from first movement 71, 77, 78, 79, 93
'Ecstasio' 1, 7, 9, 65, 96, 116, 118, 119, 129, 136, 141, 162: additive rhythms 109; and Ecstasy/rave culture 113, 142–6; EDM as topic 98, 99–100, 106, 107, 114 n. 14, 114 n. 17; enharmonicism 109; expanded harmonic progression 106; form 100. 103; interlocking intervallic cycles 100; inspiration 98; lament 106; melodic material 103, 104–5, 106; metaphor 99, 140; metric ambiguity 107, 109; modal implications 100, 108; and *Parsifal* 113, 142; referential dyads 100,

Index

109, 114; relationship to previous movements 97–8, 108–9, 112; repetition 97–8; rhythmic cycles 100; strata 106; and subjectivity 108, 145–6; symphonic logic 98–9, 107, 112; tension between style topics 98–100, 106–9, 112, 143, 145–6; timbre 99, 112
    fourth movement 115 n. 32, 141–2: enharmonicism 132; expanded harmonic progression 119, 129, 134; form 116–7, 128; generic expectations 116, 128, 132; intervallic cycles 116–7, 119, 121, 125, 126, 128, 129; intervallic series 129; lament 118, 121, 126, 128; metaphor 126, 134–5; metric canons 125, 126; *passus duriusculus* 118, 121, 125, 132, 134, 142; referential dyads 125, 129, 132–3; relationship to previous movements 116, 117–8, 119, 121, 126, 128–32, 134; resolution(s) 118, 128, 134–5, 142; stylised birdsong 128, 134; timbre 129, 131, 134; tonal structure 116–7, 119, 121, 132; use of quotation and allusion 119, 121, 126, 132, 141–2
Allen, David 136
Anthony, Michael 136
Apollinaire, Guillaume 149–50
asylum: discourse about immigration 6–7, 135 n. 9, 139–40, 151 n. 24; discourse about mental health 7, 139–40

Bach, Johann Sebastian 39 n. 7, 77, 150: Passacaglia and Fugue in C minor 69 n. 2; *Weinen, Klagen, Sorgen, Zagen* 73, 75, 76
Bacon, Francis 6
Barry, Gerald 39 n. 7, 164 n. 15
Barsky, Robert 139, 141
Bartók, Béla 117, 135 n. 9: *Bluebeard's Castle* 119, 121, 126, 132, 141–2, 151 n. 32, 156
Beethoven, Ludwig van 39 n. 7: Piano Sonata in D (Op. 28) 155; Symphony No. 9 (Op. 125) 48, 49, 66
Belling, Huw 25
Benjamin, George 12 n. 19, 40 n. 15
Bentley, Nick 36
Berg, Alban 4, 18, 22, 39 n. 7, 40 n. 9, 41 n. 41: *Lulu* 4; *Lyric Suite* 40 n. 11

Berkowitz, Paul 2
Berlin Philharmoniker 1, 12 n. 5, 136
Berlioz, Hector 39 n. 7: *Symphonie Fantastique* 129
Bernstein, Leonard 107
Betts, Leah 144
Billington, Michael 11
Birmingham Contemporary Music Group (BCMG) 5, 154
Blackmore, Michael 2
Boston Symphony Orchestra 136
Brahms, Johannes 39 n. 7, 155: Symphony No. 4 116
Brendel, Alfred 155
Breton, André 146–7
Britpop 11
Britten, Benjamin 5, 10, 39 n. 7: *Serenade for Tenor, Horn and Strings* 29; *The Turn of the Screw* 40 n. 21
Brown, James: 'I feel good' 30
Bruckner, Anton 48, 148, 150
Busoni, Ferruccio 5
Butler, Mark 107, 145

Cao, Hélène 12 n. 13, 19, 30, 35, 41 n. 35, 87
Carrier, John 139
Carter, Elliott 18, 40 n. 11
City of Birmingham Symphony Orchestra (CBSO) xv, 1, 12 n. 4, 12 n. 7
Chopin, Frédéric 18, 46, 161
Christiansen, Rupert 5
Clark, Andrew 38, 98, 136, 139, 142, 144
Clements, Andrew 38, 40 n. 9, 136, 142
Couperin, François 3, 39 n. 7, 159
Cowan, Rob 136
Cowell, Henry 28

Dalí, Salvador 146
Debussy, Claude 3, 18
Derrida, Jacques 138
Dohnyáni, Christoph von 136
Dowland, John: 'In Darknesse Let Mee Dwell' 3, 33, 34
Driver, Paul 28, 140, 142
Dunnett, Roderic 132, 140

'Ecstasio': *see Asyla*
Ecstasy 1: Ecstasy culture 7, 113, 143–6
Electronic Dance Music (EDM) 1, 98–103, 107, 114 n. 14: 'intelligent techno' 99, 100, 114 n. 10, 152 n. 56; and moral panics 141, 142–6; piano anthems 108
Elgar, Edward 4, 7: *Enigma Variations* 33

174 *Index*

Eliot, T. S. 2, 3: *Four Quartets* 3
Ely Cathedral 115 n. 25
EMI 5, 146

Faber Music xv, 2
Farkas, Zoltán 41 n. 34
Fenton, James 156
Ferneyhough, Brian 28
figural metaphors (musical) 35–6, 45
Fitzgerald, Edward 3
Foucault, Michel 139
Fox, Christopher 146, 147, 148, 155
Fox, Erica 2
Frank, César 150: Symphony in D minor
     73, 75, 79

Gallon, Emma 97 n. 29, 134
Goehr, Alexander 2, 40 n. 15
Grawemeyer Award 1, 137
Griffiths, Paul 113
Guinness, Sir Alec 2

Hamilton, Andy 12 n. 13, 146
Hatten, Robert 159
Haydn, Franz Joseph 98, 114 n. 9
Hensher, Phillip 4, 6
heritage 6, 7, 138
Hewett, Ivan 136
Hewison, Robert 11
Hirst, Damien 5, 9
Holland, Bernard 18
Hollinghurst, Alan 6: *The Spell* 114 n. 4
Holloway, Robin 2
Hume, Gary 9

immigration: *see* asylum
intelligent techno: *see* Electronic Dance
     Music
'In-yer-face' theatre 5, 9
Ives, Charles 18, 22, 25, 39 n. 7, 40 n. 9

Janáček, Leoš 5, 39 n. 7
Jowers, Peter 145
Juslin, Patrik 73

Kallberg, Jeffrey 29
Khayyam, Omar 3
Knussen, Oliver 12 n. 19, 40 n. 15
Kubrick, Stanley: *2001: A Space
     Odyssey* 30
Kurtág, György 2, 5, 28, 39 n. 7: *Eletút* 29,
     41 n. 34

Lambert, Philip 40 n. 9
Larkin, Philip 12 n. 14
Leighton, Claire 144
Leydon, Rebecca 145
Ligeti, György 4, 28, 29, 39 n. 7, 41 n. 30,
     146: Horn Trio 40 n. 15; *Le Grand
     Macabre* 157; Violin Concerto 40 n. 17
Liszt, Franz, 159: *Romance oubliée* 3
Lutosławski, Danuta 164 n. 33
Lutosławski, Witold 164 n. 33

madness: *see* asylum
Madness [band] 12 n. 18
Magritte, René 146
Mahler, Gustav 39 n. 7, 97 n. 28, 117,
     158, 162, 163: *Kindertotenlieder* 162;
     Symphony No. 3 132, 135 n. 16, 141–2
Massey, Drew 14 n. 52, 41 n. 3
Masur, Kurt 1
McCawley, Leon 12 n. 13
McQueen, Alexander 11
Melechi, Antonio 145
mental health: *see* asylum
Mermelstein, David 10
Messiaen, Olivier 28: *Quatuor pour
     la fin du temps* 39 n. 2
Minnesota Orchestra 12 n. 4
Monelle, Raymond 158
moral panic: *see* Electronic
     Dance Music
Morrison, Richard 5, 6, 9, 18, 19, 136
Mozart, Wolfgang Amadeus 4
Mussorgsky, Modest 4: *Boris
     Gudounov* 156

Nancarrow, Conlan 3, 5, 25, 28,
     39 n. 7: *Two Canons for Ursula* 41 n. 34
New York Philharmonic 1, 5
Nono, Luigi 18: *Il canto sospeso*
     40 n. 11

Oakes, Meredith 156
octatonic collection: definition 40 n. 14
O'Hagan, Peter 8

passus duriusculus 31, 32: *see also Asyla*
pianto 31, 33–4, 157–8: *see also Asyla*
Porter, Andrew 10, 118
Poulenc, Francis 41 n. 41, 146, 147, 148,
     150: *Un soir de neige* 148. 149
Proust, Marcel 161
Purcell, Henry 10: *Dido and Aeneas* 31

Rattle, Sir Simon xv, 1, 12 n. 4, 12 n. 5,
    12 n. 7, 73, 136
rave culture: *see* Ecstasy, Ecstasy culture
Ravel, Maurice: *L'enfant et les sortileges*
    148, 149
Ravenhill, Mark 7: *Shopping and Fucking*
    13 n. 44, 15 n. 84
Redhead, Steve 143
Reynolds, Simon 144, 145, 146
Ricoeur, Paul 35
Robin, William 137
Roeder, John 49
Rosen, Charles 97 n. 29
Rosner, Tal 6, 161
Ross, Alex 12 n. 13, 12 n. 19, 40 n. 15,
    97 n. 28
Rowe, Georgina 136
Rusbridger, Alan 136, 140

Satie, Eric 148
Saxton, Robert 2
Schubert, Franz 4, 5, 39 n. 7, 155:
    Lebenstürme 41 n. 34
Schulz, Thomas 140
Schumann, Robert 155
Service, Tom 39 n. 7, 146
Shakespeare, William 156
Sibelius, Jean 39 n. 7, 46, 128
Sierz, Alex 7
Snoman, Rick 100
Spice Girls 11
Spitzer, Michael 35, 36, 86
Stearn, David Patrick 12 n. 13
Stockhausen, Karlheinz 7–8

Stoecker, Philip 40 n. 9
Strauss, Richard 4, 162
Stravinsky, Igor 4, 5, 28, 39 n. 7, 87:
    Fireworks 4; *The Rake's
    Progress* 4
surrealism 2, 146–50

Tagg, Philip 99, 109, 145
Tarasti, Eero 145
Tarnopolsky, Mathias 38, 137, 139
Taruskin, Richard 5, 9, 10, 25, 28, 73, 121,
    146, 147, 148, 149
Tate, Jeffrey 12 n. 4
Tomlinson, Dylan 139
Travers, Aaron 49, 92
Turnage, Mark-Anthony 15 n. 79,
    40 n. 15

'Vatican': *see Asyla*, second movement
Vellianitis, Alexi 159
Verdi, Giuseppe 4

Wagner, Richard 39 n. 7, 46, 97 n. 28, 158:
    Parsifal 73, 76, 113, 142, 144
Watteau, Jean-Antoine: *The Embarkation
    from the Island of Cythera* 4
Wells, Dominic 40 n. 17
Whittall, Arnold 1, 30
whole-tone collections: definition
    42 n. 74
Williams, Tennessee 2, 3
Wilson, Charles xvi

Young British Artists 5, 9

CD details

"Asyla: I"
Performed by Sir Simon Rattle and City of Birmingham Symphony Orchestra
(P) 1999 Warner Classics, Warner Music UK Ltd.
Produced Under License From Warner Music UK Ltd.

"Asyla: II"
Performed by Sir Simon Rattle and City of Birmingham Symphony Orchestra
(P) 1999 Warner Classics, Warner Music UK Ltd.
Produced Under License From Warner Music UK Ltd.

"Asyla: III Ecstasio"
Performed by Sir Simon Rattle and City of Birmingham Symphony Orchestra
(P) 1999 Warner Classics, Warner Music UK Ltd.
Produced Under License From Warner Music UK Ltd.

"Asyla: IV"
Performed by Sir Simon Rattle and City of Birmingham Symphony Orchestra
(P) 1999 Warner Classics, Warner Music UK Ltd.
Produced Under License From Warner Music UK Ltd.
All rights reserved. Unauthorized copying, reproduction, public performance,
broadcasting, hiring or lending prohibited.